FIGHTING WORDS

How George W. Bush's Leadership and Speaking Countered Opposition and Confronted Terrorism

by

LeRoy L. Lane, Ph.D.

Resource Publications
An imprint of Wipf and Stock Publishers
Eugene, Oregon

Resource Publications
An imprint of Wipf and Stock Publishers
199 West 8th Avenue, Suite 3
Eugene, OR 97401

Fighting Words
How George W. Bush's Leadership and Speaking Countered Opposition and Confronted Terrorism

ISBN: 1-59752-230-9
Publication Date: August 2005

10 9 8 7 6 5 4 3 2 1

To Janis K. Lane –
my wife and my friend

Table of Contents

Chapter 1
George W. Bush at Ground Zero

Victory at all costs, victory in spite of all terror,
victory however long and hard the road may be;
for without victory, there is no survival.
— Winston Churchill, Speech, May 13, 1940

We all remember the picture of President George W. Bush at Ground Zero standing on the hulk of a demolished fire truck, speaking through a bullhorn to a crowd of cheering hardhats. He would have gone sooner to the mountain of twisted steel and unrecognizable debris that was once the towering World Trade Center, but he didn't want to interfere with the initial search for survivors and victims. However, three days after the unprecedented attack on America's homeland, Bush decided that he had waited long enough to visit Ground Zero and see for himself the terrorists' declaration of war, which they had written in death and destruction. He also wanted to thank personally the men and women who had come to help in any way they could—the firefighters, police officers, pipe fitters, engineers, paramedics, volunteers from across the nation—with the arduous task of locating the dead and digging out the streets.

Leaving Secret Service personnel behind, Bush impulsively moved among the hundreds of hardhats, shaking hands, patting shoulders, expressing appreciation in behalf of the country. The image he and the hardhats presented created a symbol of unity and hope against a backdrop of devastation. Desiring to talk to the whole crowd and not just to the few he could reach, he made an overturned truck a platform, sharing it with an elderly firefighter, whom he put his arm around. Someone gave him a bullhorn, which, at first, failed to work properly. Unable to hear the President, some of the men began to heckle him, and chide him good naturedly to speak louder. One hardhat hollered, "George! We can't hear you!" In response, Bush yelled loudly into the bullhorn so that the crowd heard, "I can hear *you*!" His fast rejoinder produced approving laughter from the crowd and silenced the hecklers. The laughter led to supportive cheers, claps, whistles, and hand waves, all of which brought a smile to Bush's face. He repeated, "I can hear you." Then he added, "The rest of the world hears you. And the people who knocked these buildings down will hear from *all* of us soon!"[1] Although exhausted from days of toil and grim responsibility, the hardhats found the energy to yell and scream their support of Bush's promise of retribution—they obviously took him at his word.

Bush went on to say, "The nation sends its love and compassion to everybody who is here. Thank you for your hard work. Thank you for making the nation proud. And God bless America."[2] Bush's plain, simple words seemed to touch the hearts of the men gathered around him, who seemed to sense that they were spoken with warm sincerity, without any political calculation for effect. Speaking as if to a friend, the hardhats called out such things as, "God bless you," and "We're proud of you, George." One of the men yelled, "Don't let 'em get away with it, George!" In the words of *Washington Times* Senior White House correspondent Bill Sammon, "The informality was astounding. These hardhats were addressing the most powerful man on the planet by his first name."[3] Bush had put aside the trappings of his high office and put himself on an equal plain with these hard-working, dedicated Americans, and they instinctively knew it—by his manner and message, they felt they were talking more to the rancher from Crawford, Texas than to the man who routinely spoke to national leaders about world peace, world economy, and world health.

President Bush's visit to Ground Zero was recalled by former New York City Mayor, Rudy Giuliani, in his speech to the Republican National Convention. He told how the Secret Service seemed concerned for the

President's safety. "With buildings still unstable," he said, "with fires raging below ground of 2000 degrees or more, there was good reason for concern." Giuliani next spoke of the "big, real big" construction workers on the scene, who were telling the President what he ought to do. A smile on his face, Giuliani shared this anecdote:

> Now each one of them would engage the President and I imagine like his cabinet give him advice. They were advising him in their own words on exactly what he should do with the terrorists. Of course I can't repeat their exact words. But one of them really went into great detail and upon conclusion of his remarks President Bush said in a rather loud voice, "I agree." At this point the guy just beamed and all his buddies turned toward him in amazement. The guy just lost it. So he reached over, embraced the President and began hugging him enthusiastically. A Secret Service agent standing next to me looked at the President and the guy and instead of extracting the President from this bear hug he turned toward me and put a finger in my face and said, "If this guy hurts the President, Giuliani you're finished." Meekly, and this is the moral of the story, I responded, "but it would be out of love."[4]

Later, when the cameras were turned off, George Bush and Laura Bush met with many of the family members of the missing and the dead. The President and First Lady spent hours talking with them, listening to stories about their loved ones, and looking at their pictures of the victims. It was an unstructured situation in which the Bushes tried to give comfort and support to grieving people. In the midst of such sorrow, it was not surprising that the President was moved to tears. But, as one person present put it, he has "a tough cry."[5] Bill O'Reilly wrote that Bush "felt deeply" for the 9/11 victims and "rose to the occasion" by taking "the fight to our enemies."[6]

Looking back about a year later on his visit to Ground Zero—following the murderous attacks of al Quaeda—Bush called it "a defining moment" in his presidency. Journalists also saw it as a defining moment, but they got it wrong. They wrote such lines as the "President finds his voice" and that he "began to look like a leader when he threw out the script." For one thing, there was no script to throw out. In an interview, Bush told Sammon that at Ground Zero, he spoke spontaneously. He said, "It wasn't planned, it wasn't thought about, it wasn't scripted. It just happened."[7] A journalist who heard the President speak, told Press Secretary Ari Fleischer that Bush's assertion, "The people who knocked these buildings down will hear from *all* of us soon!" was like Ronald Reagan's challenge, "Mr. Gorbachev, tear down this wall!" But, Sammon reminds us, "There was a major difference—Reagan's line had been written in advance."[8]

When Barbara Bush saw her son on television deliver this speech, she felt a mother's pride in his ability to meet the challenge of the moment. In her book *Reflections: Life After the White House*, she wrote, "Never have I been so proud." She continued, "It is one thing to give a talk that you have a little time to work on; but it is quite another thing to speak from the heart. When he put his arm around that firefighter—that was magic."[9]

Reported in January 2004 were the results of a National Archives initiative, "The People's Vote: 100 Documents That Shaped America," in which over 300,000 Americans cast votes. Voters gave the eighth-highest number of votes to Lincoln's "Gettysburg Address." And, having the option of "writing in" additional documents, many voters wrote in President Reagan's speech before the Berlin Wall and President Bush's speech at Ground Zero.[10]

Bush's masterful speech at Ground Zero demonstrated his ability to deal with, and adapt his speaking to, a difficult and challenging situation: He faced a scene of indescribable disaster and death, an environment that posed personal danger, a defective bullhorn and a crowd of hecklers, an audience that largely voted for Al Gore, tired men who didn't come to listen to a speech, and the need to present a short but appropriate message spontaneously. In meeting these challenges, the American public saw Bush's character and personality more intimately, although these were evident in previous presidential appearances. They saw a leader who could forget about himself and the impression he was making in focusing his full attention on the people he addressed and the situation that brought them together. This quality of selflessness is central to the charisma he projects as a person and as a speaker, as we shall see in upcoming chapters.

The majority of Americans like George W. Bush. He enjoyed the longest period of approval ratings above 60 percent of any president in 40 years. His popularity and leadership benefited his party in the midterm elections. But, on what basis have most Americans formed their opinions of President Bush as a person and leader? Or, how have they produced a mental picture of the man they believe George W. Bush to be? A likely answer to these questions is that, to a great extent, many Americans have drawn their opinions about President Bush from his public speeches and press conferences—they have come to know the man through his many televised platform appearances. They have observed him speaking on cable news, network news, or C-SPAN; possibly, they have sat in one of the many audiences he has addressed around the country to promote his domestic agenda and foreign policy; they may have heard him speak as members of a delegation, invited to the White House to supply him with fresh ideas on some issue; or they likely have heard sound bites from his speeches on radio or television that rallied the nation to fight against global terrorism, following the attacks on U.S. soil on September 11, 2001.

Sadly, the people who rely on the three major networks for opportunities to hear the President's speeches, are likely to hear only biased digests. For instance, these networks on May 24, 2004 did not carry Bush's address on the future of Iraq. The omission prompted *The Chicago Sun-Times* to state: "It is a shame that the three networks failed to carry his speech, because in a little more than half hour, he clearly summarized both the enormous task we face and the progress we have made in shepherding that nation from dictatorship to democracy."[11]

Assuming that platform utterances have provided a main avenue to many people's knowledge of George W. Bush as a person and a leader—which is a reasonable assumption—it becomes important to describe and appraise the leader of the free world's speaking and speeches. Whether his enemies like it or not, whenever he speaks, he makes news around the world! One is reminded of Albert Einstein's words: "With me, every peep becomes a trumpet solo." Recently, William F. Buckley, Jr. wrote, "Insufficient attention has been paid to the great volume of speeches and addresses by President Bush in the heavily altered theater, national and worldwide, since the great assault on the Twin Towers."[12] Previously, some writers have touched briefly on President Bush's public speaking, intending to give more attention to other aspects of his presidency; other writers have treated his speaking rather superficially, writing, perhaps, without the advantage of an in-depth background in the subject area. What is needed is a broader approach and one that is more thorough, which should open up an interesting and entertaining journey to discover the sources of George W. Bush's ability as a persuasive public speaker, an ability continually tested in waging war against terrorism—a war that calls for new paradigms to protect the homeland and fight the enemy in various countries. President Bush must keep his focus on this war as a leader and public speaker, while, in the background, there is a constant drumbeat of Democratic complaints, charges, and insults, politically motivated.

Unfortunately, there are some people in our society who rely solely on journalists' filtered pronouncements about the President's speeches, rather than listening to them themselves and forming their own opinions. An informal survey by the author during the past year found a number of such people. Here are a few examples of what they said. A self-identified Independent disclosed, "I voted for Bush, but I can't listen to him on TV; my husband won't let me." A college professor and Democrat commented, "Bush has difficulty expressing himself. He never gives speeches that focus on his agenda. His handlers are probably protecting him from much exposure. You never see him on TV." Here was someone teaching our youth saying that Bush had "difficulty expressing himself," but admitting that he had not heard him speak. He showed surprise in learning that Bush spoke often about his agenda and the war, and that such speeches, many times, could be seen on Fox News or C-SPAN. A union member on a large building project declared, "I didn't vote for Bush or Gore, even though I'm a Democrat. I care about the environment and Bush doesn't." He confessed, however, that he had never heard the President speak about the environment or anything else. "I hate Bush," remarked another respondent, "just like I hated his father. I don't have to hear Bush speak to know what he thinks. I get all the information I need from Peter Jennings on ABC." When it was suggested to him that he might be getting a narrow point of view, he looked flustered and changed the subject. One young man, who sounded like a conservative Democrat, said that he intended to vote for Bush's reelection, because he was voting against the candidates on the Democratic side. He mentioned that he had made his decision after hearing President Bush's "State of the Union Address" in 2003.

The majority of respondents—Republicans, Independents, and

Democrats—reported that they planned to vote for George W. Bush in 2004; these people tended to be those who had heard him speak one or more times. These individuals obviously liked and trusted President Bush. However, they generally had difficulty making specific comments about his speeches, which suggested that they would benefit from knowing more about persuasive public speaking.

Since the focus of this book is on George W. Bush's persuasive public speaking, the decision was made to give readers some helpful information on persuasive speaking in concise, interesting, and practical terms—the result is Chapter 3, "Political Leaders' Persuasive Speaking." Effectively used, five ingredients can enable politicians and political leaders to change audience members' attitudes and move them to action; persuasive public speaking is their stock and trade, which Chapter 3 underscores. As Robert Jackson, in *That Man*, his biography on Franklin D. Roosevelt, observed, "Speech today, as always, is a primary asset in politics. Public speaking is not an outmoded political weapon, although its style has been changed."[13] Jackson's words are a reminder that we should be able to evaluate the speaking of our leaders and would-be leaders in determining which ones to support. In making that determination, we must make every effort to select for support those persons who respect people and uphold truth.

Historically, in time of war great speech making flourishes. Powerful public speaking becomes the primary means of effectual leaders in marshalling forces to confront enemies of our country that have attacked and killed our citizens. At such a time, George W. Bush has emerged in the political process as an effectual leader at one of the most dangerous periods in our nation's history. He has distinguished himself as a powerful speaker, who has used his persuasive speeches to confront the danger, calling Americans and the international community to courage in waging war against global terrorism. His communications staff "provided support for the approximately 425 annual public remarks President Bush gave in 2001 and then in 2002."[14] He has expressed this call to courage with depth of feeling and persuasive eloquence. Many years ago, Ralph Waldo Emerson, with prophetic insight, observed, "Times of eloquence are times of terror."[15]

NOTES

1. Bill Sammon, *Fighting Back: The War on Terrorism from Inside the Bush White House* (Washington, D.C.: Regnery, 2002), 188-189.
2. Ibid.
3. Ibid., 185.
4. Rudy Giuliani, "Speech to the 2004 Republican National Convention," Madison Square Garden, New York City, August 30, 2004, www.gopconvention.com; *Republican National Convention*, Fox News, August 30, 2004.
5. Margaret Carlson, "A President Finds His Voice," *Time*, September 24, 2001, p. 50.
6. Bill O'Reilly, *Who's Looking Out For You?* (New York: Broadway, 2003), 50.
7. Sammon, *Fighting Back*, 191.
8. Ibid.
9. Barbara Bush, *Reflections: Life After the White House* (New York: Scribner, 2003), 390.
10. John McCaslin, "Inside the Beltway," *Washington Times* National Weekly Edition, January 5-11, 2004, p.6.
11. John McCaslin, "Inside the Beltway," *Washington Times*, National Weekly Edition, May 31-June 6, 2004, p. 6
12. William F. Buckley, Jr. quoted in ad "New from National Review Books," *National Review*, September 29, 2003.
13. Robert H. Jackson, *That Man: An Insider's Portrait of Franklin D. Roosevelt* (Oxford: Oxford University Press, 2003), 158.
14. Martha Joynt Kumar, "The Contemporary Presidency: Communications Operations in the White House of George W. Bush: Making News on His Terms," *Presidential Studies Quarterly*, June 2003, p. 381.
15. Edward W. Emerson and Waldo E. Forbes, *Journal of Ralph Waldo Emerson, III* (Boston: 1909-1914), 256.

Chapter 2
The Speech as a Vehicle for Truth

Life is short, but truth works far and lives long;
let us speak the truth.
— Arthur Schopenhauer, *The World as Will and Idea*

In every profession, organization, and institution of our society, public speaking plays an important role. It can turn topics into issues, create controversies through differences of opinion, trace positive or negative trends, offer information or interpretation, give an emotional outlet for tears or laughter, or persuade people to look inward at self or outward at the world. In fact, public speaking, in its capacity to persuade people, shapes many diverse situations, as is evident in court trials, evangelistic meetings, conventions, rallies, and political campaigns. Traditionally, Americans have made public speeches the central feature of ceremonial occasions that have great meaning for them, such as memorial services, college commencements, and presidential inaugurations.

While we may not always be aware of it, every speech we hear, may give us a fresh insight or a new slant on a subject of interest. This might hold true, even when we listen to a political speaker whose philosophy and agenda we reject. The writer-mathematician Bertrand Russell tells us, "It is important to learn not to be angry with opinions different from your own, but to set to work understanding how they come about." He adds, "If, after you have understood them, they still seem false, you can then combat them much more effectively than if you had continued to be merely horrified."[1] Whatever the speakers' opinions, those who demonstrate integrity in handling facts and ideas, born out of respect for their listeners' welfare, may bring to our attention some truth from their specialized knowledge of a topic. However, in the absence of these preconditions, we can, as Russell says, better understand and combat a speaker's false opinions—this applies doubly to political speakers, since they have, or seek, the power that enables them to preserve or pervert our cultural heritage.

Public speaking has become one of the principal ways in which people actively participate in the political process, both by presenting and listening to public speeches on local or national issues. Simply put, speaker and listeners create a forum for the examination of truth. This may be what Henry David Thoreau meant when he said, "It takes two to speak the truth—one to speak and another to listen." Speaking and listening to the truth is, in a sense, a requirement of the Constitution, since the first amendment provides great access to the public mind by guaranteeing freedom of speech, of the press, and of assembly. If democracy is to function as intended by the framers of our Constitution, "truth must become a democratic project."[2] For democracy cannot simply be a process for reaching decisions in a free society, it must find order and direction in a commitment to that which is good and true; so that, as citizens, we can make moral judgments about our choices in arriving at decisions.[3] When we assume that what is right is what we want to do, with no question of what we ought to do, we deny our obligation to the truth. "This is the threat of our time and indeed is the nature of our time."[4] In his "Iowa Republican Party Victory Luncheon Speech" in March, 2002, George W. Bush expressed a comparable view:

> I always used to say that one of my hopes was that this nation's culture would shift from one that said, if it feels good, just go ahead and do it, and if you've got a problem go ahead and blame somebody else, to a culture which says we are responsible for the decisions we make in life.[5]

In the interest of preserving our democratic society, we must give our support to politicians and political leaders who believe that people should take responsibility for their words and actions and that words and actions should be judged by standards of truth, which separate the proven, probable, and real from the unproven, improbable, and unreal. When politicians and political leaders fail to make this separation in order to assail political opponents in their speeches, knowing that a percentage of the audience will likely accept what they say as fact, they weaken our democratic society. To recall Samuel Johnson's words: "Without truth, there must be a dissolution of society."

Therefore, for democracy to work well, politicians and political leaders must make every effort to present the truth in their speeches—this must be the object of speakers and the expectation of listeners. In the words of 19th century speech theorist William Shedd, they should give speeches in which *"truth [is] clearly perceived, deeply felt, and strongly expressed."*[6] Truth teaches us what to value, how to plan, and what to guard against; as such, it is the single most important mainstay of liberty and freedom. The men and women who represent us in government, ideally, put the interests of the nation—a nation at war—above partisan politics, "they impose upon themselves certain restraints dictated by their control of facts and by their consideration of the welfare of others."[7] Whenever they fail to exercise such restraints, liberty and freedom in our culture are undermined. It follows then that we must hold our political leaders and politicians—in whom we invest power and influence—to the highest level of integrity. That the electorate does so, with some dissatisfaction, is suggested by the fact that surveys routinely show that Americans have a low level of trust in the integrity and honesty of politicians.[8] In the early 1990s, a survey by the *New York Times*/CBS News found that 71 percent of Americans agreed with the statement, "there is practically no connection between what a politician says and what he will do once he gets elected."[9]

Given this view of politicians, Americans are all the more impressed and appreciative when a political leader like George W. Bush appears on the scene and speaks to them honestly and forthrightly. His speeches focus on solutions rather than slogans, and policies rather than personalities; they appeal to the highest instincts of his listeners and not to their lowest; they encourage independent thought rather than groupthink; and, instead of pessimism, they express optimism that our democratic society can meet every challenge victoriously.

Ideally, political leaders seek people's support to advance a vision that promises a better future for Americans. However, for a leader to gain followers, he or she must, in the words of Ralph Waldo Emerson, be perceived "as a bringer of truth," especially if the realization of the vision requires patience, hard work, and sacrifice. Effective leaders are able to encourage faith in something that cannot be seen, but only visualized through the spoken word. As the 17th century poet-preacher, John Donne, observed, "Rhetoric [or persuasive address] makes absent and remote things present to our understanding." In a democracy like ours, political leaders multiply their efforts to bring about constructive change by gaining their listeners' help in transforming a vision into a reality. Ultimately, this requires a citizenry that can distinguish honest leaders from expedient demagogues. Jonathan Dolliver, 20th century U.S. Senator of Iowa, expressed confidence in the American citizenry when he declared, "The democracy of . . . America is no fierce mob, bewildered by the babble of tongues or the scribble of pens." Instead, he said, "It is an eager citizenship, anxious for the national welfare, having within it a tribunal of reason and conscience before which all causes are to be heard, and from which must emanate the final judgments that direct the progress of mankind."[10]

The citizens' search for truth in speeches, as a basis for giving support to a political leader, is made complicated, however, by hearing opponents disagree with each other, although each claims to speak the truth. For example, this occurs during a presidential campaign, when each candidate presents an alternative solution to a problem. Listeners (or voters), then, must make the effort to examine competing proposals to determine wherein the truth lies. By reflecting (or giving serious thought) about what each speaker has said in a speech, we ought to be able to perceive the truth with some degree of confidence.

Speakers of high character and competence encourage listeners to reflect on the message they present, so that those listeners may determine the truth of what they say; they are not afraid of the truth, unlike certain politicians. Take the case of the U.S. Senate Democrat, who, speaking to reporters, accused two members of the Bush administration of being connected with Enron prior to the Enron investigation. When, a short time later, this proved inaccurate, he could not give reporters on a television show a good explanation for making such a claim. But, speakers who have a reputation for being trustworthy, see truth as an ally in seeking to achieve their purpose in speaking.

Aside from our own instincts, the reflective discovery of truth is helped by focusing on these four questions: (1) Does the speaker rely mostly on sweeping generalizations with few, if any, facts, and if "facts" are given, are they questionable? (2) Does the speaker substitute emotional language—appealing to base motives, such as hatred of some group or class—for ideas about solving problems? (3) Does the speaker attack an opponent's proposals or policies without offering constructive alternatives, and do attacks become personal against an opponent (fallacy of *ad hominem*)? and (4) Does the speaker use fallacious reasoning to prove a point, or give inaccuracies to listeners that mislead them in their judgment of issues?

A positive answer to any of these questions signals an attempt to undermine the reflective discovery of truth. These four questions remind us that we have a responsibility to make the necessary effort, as working listeners, to separate solid promises from slick pretences, because we value truth as a basis for belief. But, are people generally willing to accept this responsibility? Henri Amiel, Swiss essayist and poet, expresses an opinion: "A lively, disinterested, persistent liking for truth is extraordinarily rare." The reason, he says, is that we don't want "to be troubled or inconvenienced by reflection."[11] Yet, if we fail to give serious thought to the truthfulness of what politicians tell us, we may pay a bigger price than trouble or inconvenience.

Excerpts from two speeches may illustrate the reflective discovery of truth. The first excerpt comes from George W. Bush's "Acceptance Speech" to The Republican National Convention on August 3, 2000. The second one comes from Al Gore's "Acceptance Speech" to The Democratic National Convention on August 17, 2000. We will see what each candidate said about Social Security and Medicare.

In Philadelphia, Governor Bush, on the subject of Social Security and Medicare, said:

> We will strengthen Social Security and Medicare for the greatest generation, and for generations to come.

> Medicare does more than meet the needs of our elderly, it reflects the values of our society.
>
> We will set it on firm financial ground, and make prescription drugs available and affordable for every senior who needs them.
>
> Social Security has been called the "third rail of American politics"—the one you're not supposed to touch because it shocks you.
>
> But if you don't touch it, you can't fix it. And I intend to fix it.
>
> To seniors in this country—you earned your benefits, you made your plans, and President George W. Bush will keep the promise of Social Security—no changes, no reductions, no way.
>
> Our opponents will say otherwise. This is their last, parting ploy, and don't believe a word of it.
>
> Now is the time for Republicans and Democrats to end the politics of fear and save Social Security, together.
>
> For younger workers, we will give you the option—your choice—to put a part of your payroll taxes into sound, responsible investments.
>
> This will mean a higher return on your money, and over 30 or 40 years, a nest egg to help your retirement, or pass along to your children.
>
> When this money is in your name, in your account, it's not just a program, it's your property.[12]

In his statement on Social Security and Medicare, Governor Bush recognized that the program needed an overhaul to keep it viable. He said that he wanted to "strengthen" it by putting it on "firm financial ground." He was careful to assure seniors that, as president, he would make "no changes, no reductions" in Social Security "no way." But, he warned, "Our opponents will say otherwise"—an easy prediction, since they already had. He promised to "make prescription drugs available and affordable for every senior who needs them." A key word in this promise is "available." Bush, in using this word, may have been responding to the Democrats who wanted the federal government to set legal limits on prescription drug prices. He opposed this idea, because, long term, price controls "invariably result in shortages, a black market, and—in this case—a curtailment of research on cures for dread diseases."[13]

Bush then spoke principally to younger workers in the audience about his innovative proposal to allow them to put some small portion of their payroll taxes into a fund that would invest in stocks and bonds. Speaking as a former businessman, Bush pointed out that such an investment over 30 to 40 years would yield a higher return than would Social Security alone. As a result, he said, younger workers could look forward to having "a nice nest egg" for retirement. The Cato Institute, an independent think tank, conducted research on the history of the stock market and examined Bush's claims for his proposal and—doing an analysis based on an individual earning a beginning salary of $20,000 and retiring at age 65—came to a conclusion that supported his claims. To prevent any misunderstanding, Bush stressed, "we will give you the option—your choice" about participating in this program. He could have mentioned that the "Social Security fund had yielded an extremely low return on its investments."[14]

Vice President Gore, talking about Social Security and Medicare two weeks later in Los Angeles, said:

> I'll fight for a new tax-free way to help you save and build a bigger nest egg for your retirement. I'm talking about something extra that you can save and invest for yourself, something that will supplement Social Security, not be subtracted from it.
>
> But I will not go along with any proposal to strip $1 out of every $6 from the Social Security Trust Fund and privatize the Social Security that you're counting on.
>
> That's Social Security minus. Our plan is Social Security plus. We will balance the budget every year and dedicate the budget surplus first to saving Social Security.
>
> In the next four years, we will pay off all the national debt this nation accumulated in our first 200 years. This will put us on the path to completely eliminating the debt by 2012, keeping America prosperous far into the future.
>
> And to me, family values means . . . putting both Social Security and Medicare in an iron-clad lockbox where the politicians can't touch them. To me, that kind of common sense is a family value.

> Hands off Medicare and Social Security trust fund money. I'll veto anything that spends it for anything other than Social Security and Medicare. . .
>
> A new prescription drug benefit under Medicare for all our seniors, that's a family value. And let me tell you, I'll fight for it and the other side will not. They give in to the big drug companies. Their plan tells seniors to beg the HMOs and insurance companies for prescription drug coverage.
>
> And that's the difference in this election. They're for the powerful. We're for the people.
>
> Judge for yourself. Look at the agendas. Look at the facts. Big tobacco, big oil, the big polluters, the pharmaceutical companies, the HMOs—sometimes you have to be willing to stand up and say no, so families can have a better life.[15]

In his statement on Social Security and Medicare, Gore promised to fight "for a new tax-free way" to enable people to "build a bigger nest egg" for their retirement. What he had in mind was "something extra" that people "can save and invest" for themselves. But, how could he promise that their own investments would produce "a bigger nest egg"? Gore stated that the "something extra" would "supplement Social Security, not be subtracted from it." Here, he was suggesting that Bush planned to subtract some portion of seniors' Social Security benefits in order to, as he claimed in the next paragraph, "privatize the Social Security that you're counting on." Yet, just two weeks earlier, Gore heard Bush emphatically promise seniors "no changes, no reductions, no way." He also heard him state that only younger workers—who had 30 to 40 years to see investments grow—would have the "option," the "choice" of investing a small percentage of their payroll tax in stocks and bonds. And, according to Bush's agenda, "The government will establish basic standards of safety and soundness, so that investments are only in steady, reliable funds . . . The money in this account may be used only for retirement, or passed along as an inheritance."[16] Gore's agenda makes no mention of such safeguards for personal investments of "something extra" money.

Describing how he would supplement Social Security for seniors, Gore said, "Our plan is Social Security plus." By this, he meant that he would "balance the budget every year and dedicate the budget surplus first to saving Social Security." Of course, Gore knew, as a former senator, that Congress would have to cooperate in keeping this promise, which would require showing restraint in spending and funding entitlements, something Congress has never been good at doing. Also, future budget surpluses would necessitate a robust and growing economy; however, by this point, the early signs of a recession were evident. And, there could not be large-scale terrorist attacks—like, but considerably worse than, the 1993 World Trade Center bombing—that would drain our economic resources, such as those that occurred on September 11, 2001. Moreover, with the phrase "saving Social Security," Gore conceded that the Social Security fund was in serious financial difficulty with a poor outlook, which was certainly the case. The Vice President did not explain how he expected to supplement Social Security for seniors *and* save Social Security by drawing from his projected budget surpluses.

Gore went on to make an astounding promise to his audience. He asserted, "In the next four years, we will pay off all the national debt this nation accumulated in our first 200 years." So, by 2004, as president, he would eliminate the national debt. But, then, in the next sentence, he said, "This will put us on the path to completely eliminating the debt by 2012, keeping America prosperous far into the future." Gore must have confused some members of his audience. Did they hear 2004 or 2012? He offered no explanation as to how he planned to provide seniors with a Social Security supplement, while saving the fund and paying off the national debt.

Speaking metaphorically, Gore told his listeners that he would put "both Social Security and Medicare in an iron-clad lockbox where the politicians can't touch them." But, simply saying that he would guard the fund for these programs did not address the problem. The fund would run out of money in due course, unless the President acted to put it on a sound fiscal basis. The audience response to the Social Security *lockbox* metaphor must have been sufficiently positive to cause Gore to use the term seven times in the course of the debates with Bush.

He described "A new prescription drug benefit under Medicare for all seniors" as "a family value." Then, going on the attack, added, "And let me tell you, I'll fight for it and the other side will not." Strangely, using present tense, he continued, "They give in to the big drug companies." Some specifics here would have helped to know what he meant. Once again Gore did not represent a Bush plan accurately when he said, "Their plan tells seniors to beg the HMOs and insurance companies for prescription drug coverage." What did he mean? Seniors, of course, would not have "to beg" companies for such coverage; they had it available.

Then, perhaps, to bolster a weak charge, Gore resorted to class warfare, saying, "And that's the difference in this election. They're for the powerful. We're for the people." Apparently, by Gore's definition, the rich who had important positions were not "the people." To support this assertion, he said, "Look at the facts." And then he listed the following: "Big tobacco, big oil, the big polluters, the pharmaceutical companies, the HMOs." By beginning his so-called "facts" with "tobacco" and including "polluters," he stigmatized the three other industries, which, he suggested were bad simply because they were "big." Several days before Gore delivered his convention speech, George Will wrote, "Gore, a creature of the 1960s, seems to consider hostility toward business a necessary ingredient in courtship of 'those people,' who are not 'the ones who think comfortably about their savings over scotch in the club.'"[17] If Gore read Will's article or heard about it, it did not deter him from the use of class warfare tactics.

In spite of Al Gore's sweeping generalizations, inaccuracies, appeals to irrational fear and class hatred, and lack of clarity of ideas, which obscured the truth about Bush's proposal concerning Social Security and Medicare, his speech was well received by a majority of Americans. Prior to his convention speech, he had trailed Governor Bush in the polls by several points—*Newsweek* polls had him down 38% to 48%. After his speech, the polls gave him a narrow lead over Bush.[18] Therefore, one must conclude that many people in the electorate found his speech persuasive. But, why?

First, Gore had the advantage of having greater national prominence than the governor of Texas, which likely prompted many people to give Gore's speech more weight than it otherwise deserved. He had, after all, spent a number of years in national politics, as a senator and as a vice president.

Second, because Gore spoke two weeks after Bush, he could respond to his opponent's convention speech, attacking his proposals—especially those on Social Security and Medicare—before a national television mass audience.

Third, his speech gave him the opportunity to claim his independence of former President Bill Clinton—he stated emphatically, "We're entering a new time. We're electing a new president. And I stand here tonight as my own man."[19] Presumably, he said this as a result of polls that found that 56% of people wanted him to say in his speech how he differed from former President Clinton.[20] While some of the 56% would have felt reassured by Gore's statement, others could have failed to see a distinction made in the speech between himself and Clinton.

Certainly, Gore did not deliver a great speech by the standards set forth in this chapter—it was not more persuasive than Bush's convention speech. These observations raise an important question: What characterizes a speech that an audience is likely to perceive as persuasive? In other words, assuming we knew what to look for, what are the ingredients that we would expect to find in such a speech? The answer to this question is presented in the next chapter, "Political Leaders' Persuasive Speaking."

NOTES

1. Bertrand Russell, *The Art of Philosophizing and Other Essays* (Totowa, NJ: Littlefield, Adams, 1974), 25.
2. James V. Schall, "Truth as a Democratic Project," *Modern Age*, Winter, 1998, p. 33.
3. Ibid.
4. Ibid., 40-43.
5. George W. Bush, *We Will Prevail: President George W. Bush on War, Terrorism, and Freedom*/Selected and Edited by National Review (New York: Continuum, 2003), 130.
6. Lester Thonssen and A. Craig Baird, *Speech Criticism: The Development of Standards for Rhetorical Appraisal* (New York: Ronald Press, 1948), 470.
7. Ibid., 468.
8. W. P. Robinson, *Deceit, Delusion and Detection* (London: Sage, 1996), 287.
9. James M. Kouzes and Barry Z. Posner, *Credibility: How Leaders Gain and Lose It, Why People Demand It* (San Francisco: Jossey-Bass, 1993), 35.
10. Jonathan P. Dolliver, "Oratory of the Stump," in Ashley H. Thorndike, ed., *Modern Eloquence*, vol. 10 (New York: Modern Eloquence Corp., 1923), xxii.
11. Van Wyck Brooks (transl.) *The Private Journal of Henri Frederick Amiel* (New York: Macmillan, 1935), January 22, 1874, 407.
12. George W. Bush, "Compassionate Conservatism," *Vital Speeches of the Day*, August 15, 2000, p. 643.

13. Jim Ryun, *America Strong: George W. Bush's Plan* (Ottawa, IL: Green Hill, 2001) 46-47.
14. Ibid., 44.
15. Al Gore, "Making America All It Can Be," *Vital Speeches of the Day*, September 1, 2000, p. 677. The two deletions in quote from Gore speech were digressions from social security; the first, of 32 words, dealt with family values, and the second, of 43 words, focused on keeping cigarettes from children.
16. Ryun, *America Strong*, 44-45.
17. George Will, "Relaxation by Exhaustion," *Newsweek*, August 7, 2000, p. 76
18. Howard Fineman and Bill Turque, "How Al Got His Bounce," *Newsweek*, August 28, 2000, p. 23.
19. Gore, "Making America All It Can Be," p. 675.
20. Howard Fineman, "Praying to Win," *Newsweek*, August 21, 2000, p. 24.

Chapter 3
Political Leaders' Persuasive Speaking

The leader, and the persuasive speaker (who is the best kind of leader), draws his power from his understanding of people and uses that power to draw them on to the achievement of their own best hopes and ideas.

—Robert T. Oliver, *The Psychology of Persuasive Speech*

What inclines an audience to perceive a speech as persuasive? The speech has convinced them that what the speaker has advocated will have positive results for them and others. What audience members have heard the speaker say has caused them to make a decision to act in accordance with the speaker's judgment on a particular issue. Such a decision requires people to open their hearts and minds to an understanding that they can affect change in the world around them, as the speaker has called them to do. The speaker has inspired them to see themselves as capable of making a difference, individually and with like-minded people. A persuaded person has realigned his or her thinking with that of the speaker—he or she shows a willingness to accept the speaker's view of reality.

The persuasive speaker seeks to awaken people from indifference and inactivity; to influence their attitudes, opinions, or beliefs—to strengthen those they have or lead them to adopt new ones. Sometimes the persuader tries to move them to replace one philosophy with another that is quite different. Persuading people to agree with a position that may be far from their own is not an easy task. In effect, the speaker asks them to rethink their belief and value systems in the process of forming new opinions. Some people are unwilling to do this—to admit that they were wrong. "Those who never retract their opinions love themselves more than they love truth," observed Joseph Joubert, an eighteenth-century French essayist. In listening to people say why they support one political party over another, one is led to believe that many do so, simply because they have adopted their parents' party affiliation, they have some emotional attachment to that party, or they think they must vote the same as other members of their group (for example, ethnic or special-interest group). One would rather see these people examine pertinent information, pro and con, and then decide which political party to support. As Robert T. Oliver, persuasion theorist and diplomat, reminds us, often people disbelieve, simply because they lack information needed to believe.[1]

The persuasive speaker draws many principles, concepts, and methods from a great classical heritage in developing speeches for particular audiences. Contemporary knowledge of persuasion builds on ancient Greek and Roman rhetoric. In modern usage the term "rhetoric" has taken on the derogatory meaning of inflated and insincere speech, usually applied to a politician by an opponent. But in ancient Greece, *rhetoric* emphasized the art of persuasive speaking, best defined by Aristotle as the faculty of discovering all the available means of persuasion in a particular situation.[2] The tradition of rhetorical effectiveness in Greece probably began with the political leader and orator Demosthenes (384-322 B.C.), who, in his speaking, powerfully exemplified Aristotle's definition of rhetoric. Demosthenes' reputation as the greatest of the Greek orators rests mainly on three speeches denouncing Philip II, King of Macedon and father of Alexander the Great, as a danger to the security of Athens. When Philip heard what Demosthenes, in his second speech against him (c. 344 B.C.), had said, he declared, "Had I been there, he would have persuaded me to take up arms against myself."[3] It would seem that Demosthenes' speeches warning Athens against Philip went too long unheeded. In 338 B.C., the powerful army that Philip had built easily crushed the Athenians. Demosthenes is a reminder that the foremost mission of the political leader is to persuade the national audience of impending danger or disaster.

The modern speaker who presents a speech that persuades an audience to a new point of view, likely has demonstrated knowledge of, and skill in using, five key ingredients, which make up the basic formula of the persuasive speech. These ingredients are: (1) Audience relevancy, (2) Effective organization, (3) Emotional appeals, (4) Animated delivery, and (5) Conversational style. We need to look at each of these ingredients in this chapter.

Audience Relevancy

For centuries, the centrality of the audience has been recognized in the rhetorical tradition, in theory if not always in practice. In the 4th century B.C., Plato, through "Socrates," observed that speakers must know the nature of the audience if they expect to be effective in speaking to its members. Socrates emphasized the diversity of types of audiences,[4] which is a principle recognized today. There are audiences that, at the outset, are friendly, hostile, or indifferent. This fact raises an interesting question: "What can speakers do to enhance their persuasiveness, whatever the attitudes of people in the audience?" One answer is that speakers must craft a speech that is relevant to the lives of people in a particular audience. A speaker has crafted a relevant speech for an audience when a large percentage of its members, on hearing it, perceive it as being closely related to their interests, needs, and aspirations. Once audience members have perceived this connection, it becomes easier for the speaker to persuade them to take the action that he or she advocates—perhaps, vote for a particular candidate, distribute campaign literature in one's neighborhood, donate money for a candidate's campaign.

Speeches that audience members find relevant do not just happen by luck, accident, or caprice. Rather, they are the result of design, as persuasive speakers select their subject, state their proposal, gather their evidence, plan their arguments, devise their illustrations, form their appeals, develop their organization, and phrase their thoughts and ideas, all in the light of one essential question: "What is the audience point of view—as shaped by interests, needs, and aspirations—that must be taken into account if one's proposal is to win acceptance?"

The answer to this question leads to another question: "How do persuasive speakers stay audience-centered so as to influence listeners, while at the same time, remain true to their ideals?" The behavior of every political leader reveals how he or she has answered this question. We can see that many such leaders answer by building their speeches on the shifting sand of expediency, saying what they think people *want* to hear. We can see other leaders answer by building their speeches on the solid rock of principle, saying what they believe people *need* to hear. If political leaders are to enjoy the high regard and respect of the people they represent, then they must, on the one hand, make their message audience relevant, and, on the other hand, strive to present the truth. Political leaders make a bad bargain when they buy audience applause with words that they don't really believe. In his famed "Oration on the Crown," Demosthenes asked: "What greater crime can an orator [or eloquent public speaker] be charged with than that his opinions and his language are not the same."[5]

In some situations, persuasive speakers can determine what might be relevant to the audience by taking their cue from the occasion of the speech. The occasion strongly suggests to speakers what is appropriate and inappropriate as a speech subject. For instance, Billy Graham would not give a sermon on famous people he has met to an audience in an evangelistic crusade; George W. Bush would not discuss the UN Security Council with an audience at a fund-raising banquet. The effective speaker selects and develops his subject with the audience in mind. When a commencement speaker talks about his own brand of politics, instead of a subject relevant to graduating students, he is self-centered, not audience-centered.

This was the charge against former MSNBC host Phil Donahue, in spring, 2003. He "was booed at North Carolina State University by students demanding that he get off the stage. Some walked out. Mr. Donahue, who was explaining 'what liberals believe' to new graduates, had also told them, 'No one in authority should tell you shush,' later adding, 'Take a liberal to lunch. Take a Dixie Chick to lunch.' "[6] When one of the graduates who had walked out of Donahue's audience was interviewed, she expressed the thought that he had focused on his own interests and not the interests of the graduates.

People tend to listen to speeches in the hope of hearing something relevant to their wellbeing. This holds true when they listen to televised political leaders' addresses. One study found that public opinion was more influenced by a U.S. president's foreign policy speeches, especially crises speeches, than economic speeches. And, "People who watch televised addresses have been found to be more politically active than those who do not watch the addresses."[7]

In the U.S., communication scholars nationwide were surveyed to determine the most important 100 American speeches of the 20th century, judged according to their impact and rhetorical artistry. "Given the historical affinity between rhetoric and politics, it is not surprising that the overwhelming majority were delivered in the political arena."[8] And most of these political speeches dealt with issues on foreign policy, national defense, and war and peace—speeches that focused on subjects relevant to people's survival. Of these top-chosen American speeches, 35—more than a third—were delivered by presidents in office.[9]

After Theodore Roosevelt (1858-1919) made the presidency a "bully pulpit," we saw that "the president became the dominant voice in American political discourse."[10] Then with the advent of radio and television, the rhetorical power of the presidency was increased tremendously. The new technology made it possible for the president to bypass Congress and speak directly to the entire nation.[11] Probably, no president has gone directly to the American people as much as President Bush in seeking to gain support for his domestic agenda and war on terrorism, often addressing the need for Congress to take action on both—his intent, clearly, was to show how these topics were relevant to people's lives. No other new president but Bush "traveled to so many states so early and no new president used this explicit strategy of appealing over the heads of particular Senators in order to affect their votes in Washington."[12]

At the beginning of President Bush's second term—the day after his "State of the Union Address"—he used the bully pulpit to promote his Social Security overhaul proposal. He spent two days campaigning in five states that he had won in the 2004 election. In Fargo, N.D., for example, he explained to his audience how his proposal would benefit younger workers in their retirement and leave seniors unaffected with no reason to take Democrats' fear appeals seriously. "I've heard all of the complaints—and you'll hear a lot more—how this is going to ruin Social Security," Bush told the large gathering in Fargo. "Forget it, it's going to make it stronger."[13] Importantly, seven Democratic senators in the five states would be up for reelection in two years; Bush's strategy involved the persuasion of people in those states to put pressure on the seven to support his Social Security plan in Congress.

George W. Bush has also used the power of the bully pulpit to counteract the liberal media's distortion, misinterpretation, and biased criticism of his remarks on various occasions. Even his "Second Inaugural Address" was seen by liberal journalists as an "opportunity to remonstrate, revile, and ridicule the president," wrote Peter Berkowitz, who teaches at George Mason University School of Law. "Only," he added, "they've had to rewrite the speech to do it."[14] Columnist Michael Barone, in *The American Spectator*, told how Bush triumphed over the Old Media's efforts to hurt his credibility during the presidential campaign by directly addressing his message to audiences created by the Republican National Convention, the second and third debates, and his stump speeches.[15] He sometimes had to make his speeches relevant both to people at home and abroad.

During the past few decades American presidents have had to confront the challenge of adapting their speeches to the interests, needs, and aspirations of mass audiences around the globe. Today, any mass audience has to be considered a composite of subgroups, distinct from one another, though they may speak the same language and share many cultural characteristics. Each subgroup has an agenda; and each seems to derive its identity from its agenda.

Television and radio broadcasts of the President's speeches into homes throughout the U.S. and the world mean that the mass audience is broken into still smaller units of family members and their friends. "Here we find the mass audience as the sum of innumerable small gatherings. A mass audience is not the same [anymore] as an audience of masses."[16] Given the divergent opinions of worldwide mass audiences on a host of issues from global warming to trade barriers, President George W. Bush needed to face a rhetorical problem every time he gave a major address. How to craft a speech that will be perceived as relevant to most of the listening audience; and, at the same time, be true to his goals and values. "The effort to conjure a mass (universal) audience at best yields a mix of segmented (particular) audiences," writes John Peters of the University of Iowa. "Discourse *ad humanitatem* never catches all humans, even though it may inspire or discipline a speaker's imagination; mass address or dissemination does not always imply mass reception."[17]

In spite of the hard reality that "mass address" does not always equal "mass reception," President Bush has done very well in gaining the trust and support of the majority of the people in the segmented audiences within the national mass audience of America. He has accomplished this primarily through his rhetorical skill as a political leader, while confronting an inherited recession, a war in many places against global terrorism, corporate scandal, the development of homeland security for an open society, and the personal attacks and carping criticism of Democrats seeking to regain political power in Congress and the White House. As David Brooks, senior editor of *The Weekly Standard*, concluded, "if you probe into the Democratic mind at the current moment [in June, 2003], you sense that the rage, the passion, the fighting spirit are all fueled not only by opposition to Bush policies, but also by powerlessness."[18]

George W. Bush's rhetorical skill was also up to the challenge of creating a coalition of over 90 nations—including Great Britain, Poland, Italy, Japan, and Australia—to enforce the UN Security Council resolutions in Iraq. During the brief stage of major conflict in Iraq, member nations of the multilateral force fulfilled a variety of roles, some of them behind the scenes, anonymously. Given the President's success in convincing leaders and majorities of many nations to oppose terrorist regimes multilaterally, it is disingenuous for Democrats to accuse Bush of acting unilaterally, as Senator John Kerry did in saying, "the Bush administration's blustering unilateralism is wrong, and even dangerous for our country."[19] At this writing, there are just under 30 countries participating in a coalition to rebuild and democratize Iraq, while seeking to make the country secure against terrorists. Obviously, the leaders of the nations that joined these coalitions could see how fighting terrorism was relevant to their country's interests, needs, and aspirations.

In modern times, assembly in the form of large audiences continues to be important for hearing our political leaders' messages. Americans who take politics and government seriously and understand that they impact the quality of their lives, will make an effort to be physically present in the audience of a political speaker whom they believe they should hear. Moreover, Americans generally value firsthand experience; the opportunity to see and hear for oneself seems to be a strong urge in our culture. For example, thousands of our citizens went to New York City to see Ground Zero for themselves. The decision of listeners to be physically present in an audience benefits the persuasive speaker. Studies show that such listeners may begin to change their opinions after they have committed themselves to listen to a speech that is opposed to those opinions. So, by choosing to listen to the speaker, people may indicate a willingness to change their attitudes.[20]

Effective Organization

Theophrastus (c. 372-c. 287 B.C.), philosopher, scientist and student of Aristotle, is quoted as saying an "unbridled horse ought to be trusted sooner than a badly organized speech."[21] Both might take you for an unpleasant ride. Effective organization means the rhetorical arrangement of points, ideas, and materials, logically and psychologically, for optimum persuasive effect. Just as the passenger of a plane expects the pilot to follow a carefully charted flight plan, a listener in an audience expects the speaker to follow a carefully organized speech plan.

The essential parts of a persuasive speech follow an order handed down from ancient Greek and Roman writers. Plato (c. 427-c. 347 B.C.) observed that "every speech ought to be put together like a living creature, with a body of its own, so as to be neither without head, nor without feet, but to have both a middle and extremities, described proportionately to each other and to the whole."[22] In other words, a speech needs to have a beginning, a middle, and an end. Each of the parts has a particular function that contributes to the whole.

First, is the *introduction* that seeks to gain the interest and attention of the listeners, enhance the speaker's credibility, and prepare the audience for forthcoming ideas by stating the proposal. Second, is the *body* (or discussion) that, through a series of divisions—usually three or four—headed by main points, argues for the validity and truth of the proposal. Third, is the *conclusion* that intends to amplify the topic, excite the listeners' feelings, recall the facts for the audience, or move the audience to focus on the subject, or act on the proposal.

Great persuasive speakers in history, especially political leaders, have known that the conclusion of the speech is their last opportunity in that setting to leave the audience inspired and motivated; they have known that the conclusion is not the end, instead, for the audience, it is their beginning as they leave the place and try to help realize the speaker's vision. Often persuasive speakers reach their highest eloquence in their closing remarks. Here are three examples of excellent conclusions:

Abraham Lincoln delivered his "Second Inaugural Address" in Washington, D.C. on March 4, 1865. As he spoke, the Civil War raged on. He concluded his speech as follows:

> Fondly do we hope, fervently do we pray, that this mighty scourge of war may speedily pass away. Yet if God wills that it continue until all the wealth piled by the bondsman's two hundred and fifty years of unrequited toil shall be sunk, and until every drop of blood drawn with the lash shall be paid by another drawn with the sword, as was said three thousand years ago, so still it must be said, that the judgments of the Lord are true and righteous altogether.
>
> With malice toward none, with charity for all, with firmness in the right as God gives us to see the right, let us finish the work we are in, to bind up the nation's wounds, to care for him who shall have borne the battle, and for his widow and his orphans, to do all which may achieve and cherish a just and lasting peace among ourselves and with all nations.[23]

On December 7, 1941, the Japanese attacked Pearl Harbor. Shortly afterward, Winston Churchill traveled to Washington, D.C. for a series of conferences with President Franklin D. Roosevelt. On December 26, 1941, Churchill delivered his "Address to the Congress of the United States." In his conclusion, he stated:

> Prodigious hammer strokes have been needed to bring us together today; or, if you will allow me to use other language, I will say he must, indeed, have a blind soul who cannot see that some great purpose and design is being worked out here below, of which we have the honour to be the faithful servants.
>
> It is not given to us to peer into the mysteries of the future;

> still I avow my hope and faith, sure and inviolate, that in days to come the British and American peoples will for their own safety and for the good of all, walk together side by side in majesty, in justice, and in peace.[24]

Nine days after the attacks on the World Trade Center and the Pentagon that took thousands of lives, on September 20, 2001, George W. Bush delivered his "Address to a Joint Session of Congress and the American People." In concluding his speech, Bush said:

> It is my hope that in the months and years ahead, life will return almost to normal. We'll go back to our lives and routines, and that is good. Even grief recedes with time and grace. But our resolve must not pass. Each of us will remember what happened that day, and to whom it happened. We will remember the moment the news came—where we were or what we were doing. Some will remember an image of fire, or a story of rescue. Some will carry memories of a face and a voice gone forever.
>
> And I will carry this. It is the police shield of a man named George Howard, who died at the World Trade Center trying to save others. It was given to me by his mom, Arlene, as a proud memorial to her son. This is my reminder of lives that ended, and a task that does not end.
>
> I will not forget this wound to our country, or those who inflicted it. I will not yield—I will not rest—I will not relent in waging this struggle for the freedom and security of the American people.
>
> The course of this conflict is not known, yet its outcome is certain. Freedom and fear, justice and cruelty, have always been at war, and we know that God is not neutral between them.
>
> Fellow citizens, we will meet violence with patient justice—assured of the rightness of our cause, and confident of the victories to come. In all that lies before us, may God grant us wisdom, and may He watch over the United States of America.[25]

Speech organization gives order and placement to facts, ideas, emotional appeals, arguments, supporting materials (such as illustrations, examples, anecdotes, analogies, statistics, and quotations), and transitions; it determines when and how such content emerges in the speech for maximum effect. Moreover, organization guides the speaker's line of reasoning to ensure logical consistency between what is stated early in the speech and what is stated later. It should be pointed out "that the most impressive and truthful matter conceivable can lose luster and attractiveness through faulty organization, and conversely that perfect organization can never transform drivel into truth."[26]

Political leaders who are persuasive know that through organization they can most effectively adapt their messages to particular audiences. They may depart from the conventional treatment of introduction, body, and conclusion in order to deal with, or make the most of, special conditions in the audience situation. For example, facing a resistant or indifferent audience, political leaders may state their proposal in the conclusion, rather than in the introduction. Or, confronting a potentially hostile audience, they may lengthen the introduction so as to devote more time to altering the audience's mood, while shortening the body by reducing the number of main points or supporting materials. (In Appendix A, see what Henry Grady, 19th century Southern orator and political leader, did in confronting a potentially hostile audience in the North, 21 years after the Civil War.)

In determining the order of arguments—an argument contains *evidence* (facts or testimony) and a *conclusion* drawn from it—persuasive political leaders again are guided by consideration of the kind of audience that they expect to address. When persuasive speakers know that the audience requires some convincing regarding their point of view, research suggests that attitude change becomes more likely if they place their strongest argument *first* or *last* in the body, rather than in the middle.[27] The "listener whose interest in a given topic is low may be induced to pay more attention if an interesting argument is presented first, but the listener whose interest is already high may respond better to the climactic order."[28]

Since many speakers produce poorly organized speeches that lack distinct parts, omit a proposal, include more than one topic, or present a rambling development, we should ask, does speech organization really make a difference in persuasion? Researchers answer that organization does make a difference. One study found that when two or more major parts of speeches—such as introduction, body, transitions—were rearranged, the listeners showed significantly less attitude change in line with the speaker's point of view, than when the parts were placed in the proper order.[29] Another study found that when sentences in speeches were rearranged out of their normal order, the listeners' attitude toward the speaker was significantly less positive.[30] Nobody should be surprised that researchers concluded that more logical and comprehensible speeches are more persuasive. Common sense should teach us that poor organization makes active listening more difficult, whereas good organization makes active listening easier and enhances retention of speech content. Speech organization helps the listeners to have a clear understanding of what the speaker advocates.

However, in modern times, for various reasons, speakers in many fields, including politics, have, to the detriment of persuasion, replaced speech organization with *essay* composition. This disregards the fact that a speech is designed to be *heard*, whereas an essay is designed to be *read*. By definition, an *essay* is "a short literary composition of an analytical, interpretive, or reflective kind, dealing with its subject in a nontechnical, limited, often unsystematic way and, usually, expressive of the author's outlook and personality."[31]

By contrast, a persuasive speech is a rhetorical instrument whose order of essential parts seeks, by the presentation of proofs, the listeners' acceptance of a proposal, which may require attitude change. A persuasive speech has an oral quality that has the flavor of dialogue—for example, it avoids complex sentences and wording that obscures the meaning of ideas. The great debater Charles James Fox (1749-1806), after addressing the British Parliament, asked the stenographer who took down his speech, "Did it read well?" When the stenographer said that it did, Fox responded, "Then it was a bad speech." Of course, Fox meant that it must have lacked the oral quality of a good speech. A persuasive speaker organizes the body of the speech around a series of assertions (or main points), which he or she then logically supports with evidence, arguments, and reasoning (or subpoints)—the pattern is *assert* something and then *support* it.

On the other hand, the speaker who delivers an essay instead of a speech, states ideas that lead to other ideas in a meandering development that is not guided by any strict form or logic.[32] While the essay may contain some persuasive elements, the persuasive speech focuses every part on convincing the audience to accept the proposal. Political leaders sometimes make presentations that have characteristics of both.

Emotional Appeals

Most people can remember a time when, as a member of an audience, they responded positively or negatively, to a persuasive speaker's emotional appeals. Carla recently attended a seminar on parenting. She said, "The main speaker had us laughing one minute and crying the next, but he always brought us back to his point, so that he fulfilled his purpose in speaking to us." She added, "Unlike some speakers on the subject who are negative and make you feel guilty and uncertain about your parenting, this speaker motivated you to be a better parent."

People are motivated to a large extent by emotions, so, for speeches to be persuasive, they must contain emotional appeals. Effective political speakers know and apply this principle.

The story is told about an advertising researcher in New York City who stationed a man in Central Park with dark glasses, a cup, and a sign that said, "I'M BLIND." During the day, the man collected $44.10 in his cup. The next day, the researcher put the man back in the park with the same dark glasses and cup, but this time his sign read, "IT'S SPRING, AND I'M BLIND." That day, he received $161.65 in his cup! Why was the man more successful the second day? One answer is because he appealed to people's feelings of empathy more compellingly—he was, in effect, more persuasive.

On the second day of the experiment, the man's sign contained a strong emotional appeal, which motivated passersby to give him money. We can define an *emotional appeal* as a statement that arouses or reinforces emotions in listeners, so as to impel them to behave in desirable ways. Part of what motivates people's behavior is the desire to experience certain emotions, such as the joy of completing an academic program, becoming a parent, or helping someone less fortunate than oneself.

A powerful motive for our behavior is our beliefs. Frequently, our beliefs determine what we say and do in a given situation, and how we feel about what others say and do around us. For example, when a

Republican political ad comes on television, many Democrats may use their remote control to turn off the sound with a feeling of satisfaction, lest they expose themselves to contrary beliefs that could create dissonance in their belief system. This behavior is known as the *audience-selection effect*.[33] Often, the very audience that persuasive political leaders are trying to reach with emotional appeals and arguments turn them off.

Emotion has always been viewed as a crucial element in persuasive speaking by ancient and modern writers on the subject. These writers have recognized that human beings are emotional as well as logical in the way they make choices, form likes or dislikes, or decide on a course of action. Certainly, how human beings feel about something affects what they think about it; often emotions lead the way in many of life's situations, such as getting married, selecting a college to attend, or even choosing a career. Understanding this, it is the persuasive speaker's task to arouse emotions in listeners that will encourage responsible behavior, insofar as human limitations permit. To achieve such a result, the persuasive political leader should have, as the Roman statesman and orator Marcus Cicero (106-43 B.C.) says, "A knowledge of . . . all the emotions of the mind, which nature has given to man, must be intimately known; for all the force and art of speaking must be employed in allaying or exciting the feelings of those who listen."[34]

For political leaders to have the knowledge Cicero recommends, they must have a clear, in-depth understanding of their audiences' interests, needs, and aspirations, since these may be the wellsprings of their emotions. However, political leaders should appeal to emotions that focus on listeners' better nature, rather than to use appeals that aim at base motives, such as hatred, envy, and selfishness. As President Woodrow Wilson advised, "see to it that the handsome passions are in a majority."

Emotions displayed by the political leader, too, should be appropriate to the message and occasion. A speaker who failed to do this, and appeared to lose votes as a consequence, was Governor Howard Dean. On January 19, 2004 in Des Moines, after having placed a disappointing third in the Iowa caucuses, Dean gave a farewell speech in which he seemed to lose control of himself. At one point, in tone and volume more akin to anger than confidence, he screeched out a list of states with primaries that he would enter—he finished the list with a scream. What disturbs one is that a speaker does not devote such intensity to a list of states. Also, did Dean forget that he was speaking to a mass audience?

Political leaders should appreciate the importance of appealing to emotions that produce positive rather than negative attitudes in their hearers. Jerome Frank, professor of psychiatry at Johns Hopkins University, speaks to this point:

> The emotional components of attitudes also deserve a special word. Attitudes that are connected with a sense of uncertainty, confusion or with the prediction of an unfavorable outcome of a course of action tend to generate unpleasant emotions such as anxiety, panic, and despair. Those that give the person a sense of security and promise a better future are related to feelings of hope, faith, and the like . . . . [For] these emotional states not only have direct bearing on a person's ability to modify his perceptions and behavior, but also largely determine his state of well-being.[35]

Frank's words offer insight into the strategy of Democratic politicians as they campaigned to regain the White House in 2004. The Democrats continually attacked George W. Bush; they tried to create uncertainty regarding his character, and predicted disastrous results from his wartime policies. This negative strategy to undermine the words and work of the Commander in Chief, aimed at producing a national mood of anxiety, panic, and despair. Democratic politicians hoped that this would modify voters' perceptions and behavior sufficiently to cause them to vote for the Democratic nominee for president in 2004, and, so, recover the sense of security that their negative strategy had presumably destroyed. They, of course, failed.

During the months preceding the Democratic primaries in 2004 and during the presidential campaign of 2004, the cause of public debate suffered. In Democrats' speeches, Americans saw emotional appeals degenerate into the fallacy of *emotional language*. This fallacy is one of several that invalidate reasoning by *begging the question* (or assuming that a statement is proven when, in fact, it needs to be proven). The emotional-language fallacy substitutes intense emotional wording for proof.

For example, in August, 2003, at a rally in Santa Fe, New Mexico,

Governor Howard Dean declared, "There are probably more members of al Qaida attacking America today in Iraq than before the war!"[36] (Dean did not seem to notice that he had conceded that al Qaida was in Iraq prior to the war, which many Democrats had disputed, including Al Gore. Dean offered no evidence to support this statement.)

In the course of a television debate with fellow Democratic contenders for the presidency, Senator Joe Lieberman said that if Dean were elected, the "Bush recession would be followed by a Dean depression."[37] (Lieberman should have known that Bush inherited the recession from the previous administration, and that the country was no longer in a recession. Lieberman did not support this statement with evidence.) A speaker who asks listeners to believe he can strengthen the economy better than his opponents because he connects one with the word "recession" and the other with the word "depression" is begging the question.

Another example comes from a campaign speech by Congressman Dick Gephardt, delivered in late July of 2003. In this speech, he stated, "I'm running for president because I believe George Bush has left us less safe than we were four years ago."[38] (Gephardt seems to have forgotten that the terrorists who flew the planes into the towers and the Pentagon were planning the attacks more than four years before, according to captured al Qaida leaders; he seems also to have forgotten the original attack on the World Trade Center in 1993 that took six innocent lives, but failed to move the Clinton administration to take action to prevent future terrorist attacks, such as 9/11. He also insulted the C.I.A. and its director George Tenet, appointed by Bill Clinton.)

It should be noted, however, that the use of emotional language in and of itself does not make it a question-begging fallacy. Acceptable emotional appeals are (1) directly related to the issues in dispute, and (2) supported by strong and relevant evidence.[39]

Politicians on the Left also use emotion with the fallacy of *ad hominem* ("to the man"). Common in the rhetoric of many politicians on the Left, its user seeks to stir up feelings of prejudice, suspicion, and dislike against an opponent by attacking his or her character, motives or personality, instead of debating the issue on logical grounds.

In his speech on August 7, 2003, at New York University, Al Gore shot some "bizarre and acidic accusations" at Bush. Grabbing onto a conspiracy theory peddled by assorted crazies, he suggested that the war in Iraq was planned and executed strictly to "benefit friends and supporters" of the President.[40] This charge is not only ludicrous, it is unconscionable that a former Vice President of the United States would make such a statement to people about the leader of their country in order to sow in their minds seeds of suspicion. One wonders if this was an expression of enmity by a bitter loser. The Harvard English scholar, Robert Gorham Davis, put it well: "If men are desperate enough they will listen to arguments proper only to an insane asylum but which seem to promise them relief."[41]

We should remember another target of *ad hominem* attacks—Katherine Harris. During the 2000 election, serving as Florida's Secretary of State, she endured an unrelenting barrage of attacks on her integrity, personality, and appearance. In a letter to this author, she wrote:

> Now I look back on my role in that critically important election with honor and satisfaction. Signing the document that legitimized the final tally of the Florida Presidential recount vote was the most profound moment of my life. I have no regrets. Still, for months on end, I paid a price for doing the right thing.
>
> The liberal media flooded the airwaves with lies regarding my authority to act, the desperate Democrats unleashed a torrent of personal attacks designed to make me a national villain, and the Hollywood elite made me the target of their jokes and scorn.[42]

Personal attacks on somebody's appearance is the last resort of opposing arguers who have no factual basis for their opposition. One particularly cruel personal attack came from *Washington Post* columnist Robin Givhan, who found Harris "easy to mock," since her "mouth is set in a jagged edge," and she "applied her makeup with a trowel."[43] She wrote, "At this moment that so desperately needs diplomacy, understatement and calm, one wonders how this Republican woman, who can't even use restraint when she's wielding a mascara wand, will manage to use it and make sound legal decisions in this game of partisan one-upsmanship."[44] Givhan's attempt here to move from insult to substance merely produced the fallacy of *false analogy*—surely, with a little thought, many of her readers could see that restraint in "wielding a mascara wand" can never be analogous to restraint in making "sound legal decisions." Such faulty reasoning can, however, fool people. Concerning false analogy, Davis points out, "Such arguments introduce assumptions in a metaphorical guise in which they are not readily detected or easily criticized. In place of analysis," he noted, "they attempt to identify their position with some familiar symbol which will evoke a predictable, emotional response in the reader [or listener]."[45] When Givhan got around to making remarks about Harris' clothing, she left no doubt about the feelings she sought to evoke in her audience: "Hate the suit. Hate the buttons. Hate you."[46] What is that term that liberals like to use? Oh yes, "mean-spirited."

Fear may be the most common emotion that human beings experience. Persuasive political speakers understand its power and reflect that understanding in their speeches. "So, first of all, let me assert my firm belief that the only thing we have to fear is fear itself . . .," spoke Franklin D. Roosevelt in his "First Inaugural Address" on March 4, 1933.[47] He used these words to try to inspire optimism in Americans struggling to survive the Great Depression.

However, speaking on September 2, 1940, at the dedication of the Great Smoky Mountains National Park, Roosevelt sought to arouse Americans to a new threat to their well-being—that they were slow to understand or admit—to which a reasonable response was fear. Appealing to fear, he asserted, "Today we no longer face . . . hard and lonely struggles with nature . . . If we are to survive, we cannot be soft in a world in which there are dangers far more deadly than those the frontiersmen had to face."[48] Then to remind his audience of the war in Europe, he warned, "The earth has been so shrunk by the airplane and the radio that Europe is closer to America today than was one side of these mountains to the other when the pioneers toiled through the primeval forest."[49] He emphasized that "close to us today" is the threat of "the airplane, the bomb, the tank, and the machine gun."[50] In using such fear appeals, Roosevelt sought to persuade Americans to wake up to the fact that war in Europe could engulf America and that complacency could prove dangerous. President Bush's appeals to fear have a similar purpose, as he seeks to arouse the nation to meet a new and equally-dangerous threat to our way of life.

One study found that a strong fear appeal—suggesting something is life threatening—will hurt the speaker's credibility if it evokes a high degree of emotional tension without adequately satisfying the need for reassurance. "The speaker, then, is well advised to present a specific plan of action and to demonstrate its feasibility and effectiveness whenever he uses a strong fear appeal."[51]

Political leaders can use a variety of emotional appeals that may, in appropriate audience settings, prove persuasive. They are likely to be more effective in selecting and presenting these appeals if they can empathize with people, that is, imagine how others feel and be supportive in response.[52]

Animated Delivery

Have you ever noticed that when reporters and news analysts comment on a presidential speech, they tend to focus on style or delivery? Focusing on delivery is a practice of long standing. Commenting in November, 1863 on Abraham Lincoln's "Gettysburg Address," a reporter for the *New York Times*, wrote: "President Lincoln's brief address was delivered in a clear, loud tone of voice, which could be distinctly heard at the extreme limits of the large assemblage." The reporter added, "It was delivered (or rather read from a sheet of paper which the speaker held in his hand) in a very deliberate manner, with strong emphasis, and with a most business-like air."[53]

Delivery and style, of course, are the most obvious aspects of the speech for reporters and news analysts. By focusing on delivery, such as the speaker's deportment, or style, such as distinctive lines, a speech can be reduced to simple, descriptive print-bites in publications and soundbites on television. Unfortunately, by focusing on delivery or style, and slighting content, such as ideas, organization, reasoning, arguments, facts, and illustrations, reporters and analysts limit themselves to fewer substantive comments.

This does not mean that delivery is unimportant—it is the source of the speaker's personal nonverbal communication. By definition, delivery is the transmission of content to the audience by voice and bodily action. A good speech has both worthwhile content and effective delivery. Yet, political speakers often fail to exemplify this truism in their speaking. The political speaker who offers worthwhile content without concern for delivery, discourages the audience from listening; the political speaker who uses effective delivery but lacks worthwhile content, adds little or nothing to the audience's knowledge.

However, speakers should bear in mind that what they think they have transmitted to audience members through various nonverbal cues may not be what those audience members have received. If speakers are ineffectual in their communication of vocal cues (such as tone, emphasis, pausing) and visual cues (such as posture, facial expressions, gestures), they may lead auditors to misinterpret their meaning or form wrong assumptions about their motives. For example, if listeners misinterpret the speaker's vocal cues used to convey subtle meanings, they may leave the speech occasion with an erroneous, negative impression of the speaker, or, at least, some confusion as to what he or she meant at some point.

The speaker faces a special challenge when he or she seeks to use nonverbal cues to communicate humor to an audience, whose first language is not that of the speaker. Even when speakers do their best in such a situation, they may not be satisfied with the results. The point is well illustrated by former President Ronald Reagan's experience in Mexico, which he described in a 1988 speech to the National Governors' Association:

> As you know, I recently visited Mexico to meet with President De la Madrid. And I was reminded of when I was governor of California and was asked by the then President to go down and represent him . . . . On this first visit to Mexico, I gave a speech to a rather large audience and then sat down to rather unenthusiastic and scattered applause. I was embarrassed and tried to cover all of that, because what made it worse was that the next speaker up was speaking in Spanish, which I didn't understand, but he was getting interrupted virtually every line with most enthusiastic applause. So, I started clapping before anyone else and longer than anyone else until our ambassador leaned over and said to me, "I wouldn't do that if I were you. He's interpreting your speech."[54]

Of course, Ronald Reagan was the consummate nonverbal

communicator, one key reason why he was such an effective public speaker. His nonverbal communication conveyed honest attitudes and sincere feelings, a rare quality among politicians.

Political speakers are often ineffectual in their nonverbal communication, because they try to fake sincerity and fail. Reporting on the persuasive effects of delivery, speech professor Gary Cronkhite pointed out that "the potential persuader is well-advised to be sincere or avoid a personal appearance." Why? "Audiences," he said, "are surprisingly perceptive in their judgments of emotion reflected in *each* of a number of nonverbal modalities [such as vocal patterns of inflection and rhythm], and when they have several of those modalities available to reinforce their judgments, it will take a very clever speaker to deceive them."[55] According to additional research, "a split-second delay or anticipation in timing [of postural shifts or gestures] can reveal a damning insincerity or ludicrous planning on the part of the speaker . . . . Whatever one's beliefs about the ethical necessity of sincerity, it can certainly be an aid to delivery."[56] The demeanor of political speakers can create an impression of sincerity or its opposite.

Complementing political speakers' demeanor are their facial expressions. The face is the most important channel of visual cues in the delivery of the persuasive speech. Changes in facial expression have a stimulating effect on audience members, and this reinforces their attention. The face and the head primarily transmit information about the speaker's emotions and attitudes during his or her presentation; facial expressions reveal to the audience what the political speaker thinks and feels about what he or she is saying at any given moment. When speakers do not respond facially to their words but hold one static expression—as is the case with many politicians—they appear to conceal what they really think and feel. Senator John Kerry of Massachusetts, for example, maintains essentially one "expression" on his face when he speaks publicly—it is a kind of somber-worried look. He had this characteristic look as he campaigned for the Democratic nomination for the presidential election of 2004. It is little wonder that audiences did not warm up to him—they probably, deep down, felt doubtful about the sincerity and conviction behind his words. An ancient Chinese proverb declares: "To see a person's face is better than to hear of his reputation." The wise person who coined that saying likely thought of the face's capacity to inspire trust or raise doubt in the mind of the observer.

Some interesting research suggests that a political speaker whose facial expressions contribute to his or her attractiveness and convey confidence and other positive personality traits, can, via the perception of such traits, change people's attitudes. These traits become *persuasion cues*, because, once activated, they can prove very influential.[57]

The eyes have it! Speakers who establish eye contact with listeners open channels of communication with them, and give them the feeling that the speech is intended for them personally. For political speakers to have this effect, they must perceive individuals in the audience as persons. When they see listeners as persons, they can scan their facial expressions for reactions to the speech. This feedback may suggest the need to change something, perhaps the rate of speaking. By "talking" with their eyes, political speakers can soften words that otherwise might be considered harsh. They can signal the audience to anticipate a change of pace—perhaps to settle back for a funny story. They can "eye-express" concern, involvement, or sincerity.[58] Eye contact is a particularly strong element of George W. Bush's delivery—more about that later.

The hand, with its flexible arrangement of 27 bones, can produce a great variety of gestures with grace and speed. Hand gestures can enhance the speaker's delivery when they are well-timed, appropriate to what is being said, and graceful in movement.[59] Most politicians fail on all three points. So, they would do better to keep their hands on the lectern, relaxed and ready for an occasional appearance. Politicians' lack of skill in gesturing may result from their frequent dependence on manuscripts of their speeches, which generally they insist on reading. Since politicians often deliver speeches on television, it is surprising that they often neglect the use of gestures, which are so appropriate for this medium and the viewers who represent a visually-oriented society.

The speaker's voice has a great deal to do with the effect his or her speech has on the audience. Certainly, vocal delivery can heighten or diminish the listeners' understanding of, and belief in, what is communicated. Essential elements in vocal delivery are pitch, loudness, rate, quality, and rhythm, plus articulation and pronunciation. A speaker enhances his or her persuasiveness by having the ability to control and vary pitch, loudness, and rate in conveying a wide range of meanings, including subtle shifts of attitude and emotion. Political leaders who speak with effective vocal variety are more likely to impress an audience positively than if they speak with monotonous pitch, loudness, and rate.

A political leader who lacked variety in all three elements, but especially in loudness and rate, was former Senator Thomas Daschle of South Dakota. One person, commenting about his speaking, put it this way: "He sounds as if he's trying hard to sound sincere and he thinks by talking softly and slowly that he will." Jon Lauck, a history professor at South Dakota State University, compared Daschle to former Senator George McGovern of South Dakota, who, he said, valued "rationality in democratic discourse." His "soft-spoken" delivery "moved" those who heard him. Lauck wrote, "Daschle tries to imitate the McGovern style, but he just sounds mousy."[60] Not a good campaigner, he lost his Senate seat to John Thune.

A number of studies from recent decades have shown how much vocal cues affect listeners' judgment of speakers. The findings of those studies have far-reaching implications. Speakers with good fluency and proper pausing were perceived as more competent, composed, sociable, and persuasive than speakers without. And, speakers who had a pleasant vocal quality and pitch variety were perceived as having greater competence, sociability, and persuasiveness than speakers who lacked them; also, speakers with these attributes enhanced their character (particularly trustworthiness) in the judgment of listeners.[61]

The speakers' rate of speaking has received a lot of attention by researchers. A too-slow rate lowers credibility. The speaker who talks too slowly may be perceived as hesitant, uncertain, or unprepared. A too-slow rate of delivery can tire or bore the audience. Studies of rate preference (using taped messages) found that subjects generally preferred speakers who spoke at an above-average rate (180-190 words per minute). The subjects considered those speakers more persuasive than those who spoke at an average rate (140-150 words per minute).[62] The fact that Kerry spoke at a faster rate than Bush did in their first presidential debate on September 30, may well have caused many viewers to have perceived him as more effective—to focus more on delivery than on content.

At times we listen more to vocal cues than to words because *how* the speaker says something may have more meaning for us than *what* the speaker says. The nonverbal-communication effect of inflections, pauses, vocal tone, word stress, changes in pitch, volume, and rate can change the way we understand words and phrases, something that politicians have long understood. In 1940, in a radio speech, Franklin D. Roosevelt ridiculed three of his enemies in Congress by creating a rhythmical phrase of their names: "Martin, Barton, and *Fisssh*"—drawing out the last name with a distasteful tone. This nonverbal bit of humor provoked laughter at the expense of the three congressmen throughout the country.

It is not so funny, however, when a political speaker uses such means to attack opponents with unfounded innuendo, as Gore did in his August 7th speech at New York University. He "seemed to suggest that the Bush administration itself might have been behind the forged Niger documents," wrote Stephen Hayes in *The Weekly Standard.* Hayes quotes Gore's words from his speech and points up his nonverbal innuendo: " 'And on the nuclear issue of course, it turned out that those documents were actually *forged* by somebody—though we don't know who,' he said, drawing out the last phrase for dramatic effect." Hayes added, "The audience of activists from *MoveOn.org* laughed loudly and traded knowing looks."[63] The forged documents became an issue when President Bush, before discovering they were forged, in his 2003 "State of the Union Address," referred to their contents by saying, "The British government has learned that Saddam Hussein recently sought significant quantities of uranium from Africa." However, on July 14, 2004, Britain's Commission report on prewar intelligence concluded that there was ample evidence from many sources that Saddam Hussein had tried to buy uranium from Niger, and that President Bush's statement was "well founded." The Senate Select Committee on Intelligence reached the same conclusion five days before.[64]

The political speakers who want to be persuasive in their speaking, must, in their delivery, effectively coordinate words, vocal cues, and body motions to symbolize their speeches. Their faces, for example, cannot communicate one thing, and their words another. In the *Brutus,* Cicero praised the statesman and orator Marcus Antonius (143-87 B.C.) by saying that he made every action "correspond to the meaning of every sentence, without beating time to the words."[65]

The meaning of the term *animate* is "to bring to life." Animated delivery brings to life the content of the speech, as it blends with conversational style.

Conversational Style

Over the centuries, the word "style" has come to mean many things. It is applied to behavior, fashions, taste, objects, trends, writing, and speaking. It has even been applied to character, as when the 18th century French naturalist George de Buffon said, "Style is the man himself." The origin of the word "style" is very different. It comes from the Latin *stilus*, meaning a sharp, slender, pointed instrument used by the ancient Romans in writing on wax tablets.

In time, the word *style* came to mean the way a speaker chose and arranged words in speeches. It takes only a little imagination to see how the "sharp, slender, pointed instrument" that made the right impression on the wax tablet, became the precise word that made the right impression on the mind of the listener. Jonathan Swift, English-Irish writer and master of satire, said simply, "Proper words in proper places, make the true definition of style."[66] Philip Stanhope, Earl of Chesterfield, in a letter to his son, used a metaphor and said, "Style is the dress of thoughts."[67] But, whatever definition we use, an effective rhetorical style can have a strong persuasive effect. "Give me the right word and the right accent," observed the English novelist Joseph Conrad, "and I will move the world."[68]

Down through history, political leaders have exhibited more than one kind of speech style. A precedent for different styles is centuries old. In Cicero's *Orator*, to name but one source, the author describes and analyzes the plain, moderate, and grand styles that speakers might use. Cicero taught that the skilled speaker should be able to employ all three. His own speeches provide excellent examples of the three styles. Cicero wrote that those who listen to the speaker who has a *plain style* may feel confident that they could speak in the same manner, even though they lack skill in speaking. This mode of address, he pointed out, appears easy to imitate, but, in fact, is quite difficult. It is a relaxed style of speaking, he said, that, while it follows certain rules, allows considerable freedom. Moreover, its arrangement of content is clear and plain, with appropriate language. Humor is admissible, either to enhance expression or provoke laughter at an opponent.[69]

Cicero's description of the plain style sounds a lot like what has come to be called the "conversational style." Writing in 1898, Thomas Higginson, in his essay on "Hints on Speech-Making," advised, "Always speak in a natural key, and in a conversational manner. The days of pompous and stilted eloquence are gone by, and it was perhaps Wendell Phillips more than anybody else who put an end to it in this country, and substituted a simpler style . . . . There is no question," he noted, "that within thirty years our American public speaking has been pitched upon a far more natural key."[70] According to Higginson, then, the emergence of the conversational style—or possibly the rediscovery of the ancient plain style—dates back to the late 1860s through the influence of Wendell Phillips, the most effective antislavery speaker of the Civil War era. Someone who heard him speak many times, reported, "You are looking for a man who is all art and thunder. Lo! A quiet man glides upon the platform and begins talking in a simple, easy, conversational way . . . . You listen, believe and applaud. And that is Wendell Phillips." This admirer added, Phillips' style aimed "to produce the greatest effect by the simplest means."[71]

The shift from the oratorical to the conversational crystallized in the first half of the 20th century. Public speaking, as a result, did not decline in importance or quality as some academics had predicted. It simply evolved to meet the dynamics of a new age. This occurred rapidly in America's political arena, as great speakers such as Theodore Roosevelt, Woodrow Wilson, William E. Borah, and Franklin D. Roosevelt appeared on the scene. As the 20th century advanced, politicians found the conversational mode a way to accommodate to the faster pace of life—the listeners in their audiences were busy people with more and more options about how to spend their time. They wanted politicians and political leaders to speak clearly, concisely, and interestingly—they did not want them to take an hour to say what could be said in 25 minutes.

Today, there are politicians—sadly not many—whose conversational style marks them as having outstanding leadership qualities. They communicate confidence in the vision that they present, conviction as to the rightness of their cause, and trust in the people's capacity to rise to the challenge to which they have called them. They do not talk down to their audiences, but, rather, they talk to them as one friend talks to another. And they stay on their course without regard for media views or opinion polls. They would have agreed with Winston Churchill when, in 1941, to the House of Commons, he declared, "Nothing is as dangerous in wartime than to live in the temperamental atmosphere of a Gallup poll, always feeling one's pulse and taking one's temperature."[72]

During the 2004 presidential campaign, candidate Kerry seemed to adjust his style to suit the dictates of the elite press and their polls. According to journalists' reports after the election, early in the campaign, a well-known speech coach in Washington advised him to "shift to a more conversational style, to vary the pace, to sound more casual in his speech."[73] Either he would not or could not take the good advice.

For many years, speech teachers have stressed that effective persuasive speaking—and public speaking in general—is not "oratorical," that is, the emphasis is not on beauty of expression, but on clarity of expression that facilitates immediate comprehension of main points and ideas. However, this does not mean that the conversational style of persuasive address is characterized by uninteresting language and dull content. The best persuasive speakers deliver speeches with memorable phrases and impressive anecdotes and illustrations, which build attention and increase the speaker's credibility. Since the persuasive speech seeks to convey a lasting impression, it should present, in addition to audience-relevant content, key thoughts with *vividness* of style (or striking language that engages the imagination and memory). Elements of vividness of style can touch both the heart and mind. For example, in a speech before Parliament after becoming Prime Minister in 1940, Winston Churchill gave a frank and bitter appraisal of the situation the British faced in its war with Germany. He said:

> We shall defend our island whatever the cost may be; we shall fight on beaches, landing grounds, in fields, in streets and on the hills. We shall never surrender and even if, which I do not for the moment believe, this island or a large part of it were subjugated and starving, then our empire across the seas, armed and guarded by the British Fleet, will carry on the struggle until in God's good time the New World, with all its power and might, sets forth to the liberation and rescue of the Old.[74]

While public speaking in the conversational mode shares some characteristics with everyday conversation, it also differs in important ways. "Rather than resulting from spontaneity and artlessness [as conversation does], the conversational mode of public speaking reflects a calculated rhetorical choice designed to enhance the audience's perception of the speaker and acceptance of his or her ideas by incorporating into the speech stylistic and nonverbal attributes associated with conversational discourse."[75]

Probably, the biggest difference between the conversational mode of public speaking and everyday conversation is that "the best modern speeches, like those of traditional oratory, grow out of serious thought, extensive preparation, and a substantial dose of rhetorical creativity."[76] This is particularly true of persuasive speeches that defend a position or oppose one. When such speeches are delivered by U.S. presidents on state occasions as, for example, Inaugural Addresses, State of the Union Addresses, and speeches to the United Nations, they are polished instruments with key points that strive for eloquent expression, suggestive of the grand style, which, in Cicero's words, "sometimes forces its way into and sometimes steals into the senses; which implants new opinions in men, and eradicates others which have been long established."[77]

War tends to elevate the quality of presidential rhetoric. Perhaps President John F. Kennedy had this in mind when, according to Arthur Schlesinger, Jr., he "observed that war made it easier for a president to achieve greatness."[78] During wartime, a great deal is demanded of the rhetorical performance of presidents—concepts such as victory, heroism, sacrifice, sorrow, faith, morality, security, morale, and tactics become the substance of rhetorical eloquence. In the tradition of wartime presidents Abraham Lincoln, Woodrow Wilson, and Franklin D. Roosevelt, George W. Bush has used the power of public speaking to prepare Americans for, and lead them during, war with a determined enemy—a war forced on America with the brutal attacks of September 11, 2001. On special occasions, as when addressing Congress, the American people, our allies, and foes, President Bush has presented speeches that contain some elements of the grand style of the classical period. He and his speech writers have given us addresses that refine and make memorable the spoken word.

While many of the addresses Bush has delivered are of high rhetorical quality, one might ask if they have had a positive impact on his presidential approval. One study suggested that they have. Researchers analyzed the content of President Bush's 2002 "State of the Union Address" and then matched it with responses in a laboratory experiment and a nationally representative survey. The researchers concluded that the President can use rhetoric to influence substantially his job approval by promoting issues that then become the basis of Americans' approval evaluations. For instance, when media are led by the President's rhetoric to present news stories on, say, national defense, people will tend to assess the President's overall approval on the basis of his job performance on defense. The researchers found that 87 percent of those who watched his "State of the Union" on television, believed "Bush is a strong leader."[79] He has created the same impression in his less-formal speech situations.

The hallmark of Bush's presidential rhetoric, as seen on most occasions, is his conversational style of speaking, which has rarely been matched in effectiveness by predecessors in the White House during the past century. His style of address makes him truly a modern leader. He seeks to inspire Americans to build a stronger America—spiritually, economically, and militarily—in an increasingly dangerous world in which innocent men, women, and children are targeted by terrorists. Speaking to an audience on October 17, 2001, President Bush said:

> Our nation has felt great sorrow. Yet this can be a time of great achievement. A great evil can be turned to a greater good. The terrorists did not intend to create a new American spirit of unity and resolve, but they are powerless to stop it.[80]

Referring to Bush's style, a friend of the author observed, "He speaks his mind from the heart." We believe the words he speaks because we believe in the character of the man who speaks them—George W. Bush.

NOTES

1. Robert T. Oliver, *The Psychology of Persuasive Speech*, 2nd ed. (New York: David McKay, 1963), 218.
2. Lane Cooper, *The Rhetoric of Aristotle* (Englewood Cliffs, NJ: Prentice Hall, 1960), 7.

3. George F. Hoar, "Eloquence," in Ashley H. Thorndike, ed., *Modern Eloquence*, vol. 5 (New York: Modern Eloquence Corp., 1923), xiii.
4. John D. Peters, "Audience," in Thomas O. Sloane, ed., *Encyclopedia of Rhetoric* (Oxford: Oxford University Press, 2001), 70.
5. Oliver, *The Psychology of Persuasive Speech*, 31.
6. John McCaslin, "Inside the Beltway," *Washington Times* National Weekly Edition, May 26-June 1, 2003, p. 6.
7. Reed L. Welch, "Was Reagan Really a Great Communicator? The Influence of Televised Addresses on Public Opinion," *Presidential Studies Quarterly*, December 2003, pp. 872-873.
8. Stephen E. Lucas, "Public Speaking," in Thomas O. Sloane, ed., *Encyclopedia of Rhetoric* (Oxford: Oxford University Press, 2001), 643.
9. Ibid.
10. Ibid.
11. Ibid.
12. Corey Cook, "The Contemporary Presidency: The Permanence of the 'Permanent Campaign': George W. Bush's Public Presidency," *Presidential Studies Quarterly*, December 2002, p. 760.
13. Richard W. Stevenson, "Bush on Road, Pushes Warning on Retirement," *New York Times*, February 4, 2005, p. A1.
14. Peter Berkowitz, "They Always Bash Bush First," *Weekly Standard*, February 7, 2005, p. 12.
15. Michael Barone, "Republican Rout," *American Spectator*, December/January 2005, p. 13.
16. Peters, "Audience," 70.
17. Ibid., 69.
18. David Brooks, "Democrats Go off the Cliff," *Weekly Standard*, June 30, 2003, p. 24.
19. Stephen F. Hayes, "Gore Goes Gaga," *Weekly Standard*, August 18, 2003, 16.
20. Gary Cronkhite, *Persuasion: Speech and Behavioral Change* (Indianapolis: Bobbs-Merrill, 1969), 148-149.
21. Thonssen and Baird, *Speech Criticism*, 392.
22. Ibid., 397.
23. Lewis Copeland, ed., *The World's Great Speeches* (New York: Garden City, 1942), 316-317.
24. Bower Aly and Lucile F. Aly, *Speeches in English* (New York: Random House, 1968), 238.
25. George W. Bush, "Address to a Joint Session of Congress and the American People," *Vital Speeches of the Day*, October 1, 2001, p. 763.
26. Thonssen and Baird, *Speech Criticism*, 404.
27. Cronkhite, *Persuasion*, 195-196.
28. Ibid., 196.
29. Ibid., 191-192.

30. Ibid., 192.
31. Victoria Neufeldt, ed., *Webster's New World Dictionary of American English*, 3rd ed. (Cleveland: Webster's New World, 1988), 464.
32. George G. Williams, *Creative Writing* (New York: Harper and Brothers, 1954), 180.
33. John M. Darley et al., *Psychology*, 4th ed. (Englewood Cliffs, NJ: Prentice Hall, 1988), 667.
34. Marcus Tullius Cicero, *De Oratore*, J. S. Watson, trans. (Philadelphia, 1897), I, v.
35. Jerome D. Frank, *Persuasion and Healing*, rev. ed. (New York: Shocken Books, 1974), 28.
36. Roger Simon, "A Sense of Panic in the Pack," *U.S. News & World Report*, September 15, 2003, p. 20
37. Ibid.
38. Hayes, "Gore Goes Gaga," p. 16.
39. Douglas Ehninger and Wayne Brockriede, *Decision by Debate* (New York: Dodd, Mead, 1968), 171.
40. Hayes, "Gore Goes Gaga," p. 16.
41. Robert Gorham Davis, "Reason and Emotion," in Wilfred H. Stone and Robert Hoopes, eds., *Form and Thought in Prose*, 2nd ed. (New York: Ronald Press, 1960), 86.
42. Katherine Harris, Letter to the Author, July 28, 2003.
43. Sammon, *Fighting Back*, 126-127.
44. Ibid.
45. Davis, "Reason and Emotion," 81.
46. Sammon, *Fighting Back*, 127.
47. Aly and Aly, *Speeches in English*, 212.
48. Oliver, *The Psychology of Persuasive Speech*, 135-136.
49. Ibid.
50. Ibid.
51. Cronkhite, *Persuasion*, 184.
52. LeRoy L. Lane, *By All Means Communicate*, 2nd ed. (Englewood Cliffs, NJ: Prentice Hall, 1991), 164.
53. "Ghettysburg Cemetery Dedication," *New York Times*, November 21, 1863, p. 1.
54. "Remarks at a White House Meeting with Members of the National Governors' Association," *Weekly Compilation of Presidential Documents*, 24 (February 29, 1988), 239-242.
55. Cronkhite, *Persuasion*, 210.
56. Ibid., 211.
57. Douglas A. Bernstein et al., *Psychology*, 4th ed. (Boston: Houghton Mifflin, 1997), 581.
58. Lane, *By All Means Communicate*, 296.
59. Ibid., 297.
60. Jon Lauek, "Daschled Hopes," *Weekly Standard*, December 29, 2003/January 5, 2004, pp. 44-45.

61. Judee K. Burgoon et al., "Nonverbal Behaviors, Persuasion, and Credibility," *Human Communication Research*, Fall, 1990, pp. 146-148.
62. James MacLacklan, "What People Really Think of Fast Talkers," *Psychology Today*, November 1979, pp. 113-117.
63. Hayes, "Gore Goes Gaga," p. 16.
64. Bill Sammon, "British Report Bolsters Bush," *Washington Times* National Weekly Edition, July 26-August 1, 2004, p. 31.
65. Thonssen and Baird, *Speech Criticism*, 442.
66. Jonathan Swift, Letter to a Young Clergyman, January 9, 1720.
67. Philip Dormer Stanhope, Letter to His Son, November 24, 1749.
68. Thonssen and Baird, *Speech Criticism*, 86-87.
69. Wolfgang G. Müller, "Style," in Thomas O. Sloane, ed., *Encyclopedia of Rhetoric* (Oxford: Oxford University Press, 2001), 748.
70. Thomas W. Higginson, "Hints on Speech-Making," in Ashley H. Thorndike, ed., *Modern Eloquence*, vol. 2 (New York: Modern Eloquence Corp., 1923), xiv.
71. Charles Morris, *The World's Great Orators and Their Orations* (Chicago: John C. Winston, 1902), 301.
72. Winston Churchill, Report on the War, House of Commons, September 30, 1941.
73. Evan Thomas and the staff of *Newsweek*, *Election 2004: How Bush Won and What You Can Expect in the Future* (New York: Public Affairs), 2004), 57.
74. Winston Churchill, Speech on the War, House of Commons, May 13, 1940.
75. Lucas, "Public Speaking," 643.
76. Ibid.
77. Thonssen and Baird, *Speech Criticism*, 88.
78. Arthur Schlesinger, Jr., "The Democrat Autocrat," *New York Review of Books*, May 15, 2003, p. 18.
79. James M. Druckman and Justin W. Holmes, "Does Presidential Rhetoric Matter? Priming and Presidential Approval," *Presidential Studies Quarterly*, December 2004, pp. 755, 774.
80. Bush, *We Will Prevail*, 45.

Chapter 4
Credibility: The Man Behind the Message

Just as good character (according to Aristotle) is antecedent to effective rhetoric, virtue must precede responsible leadership. This must be an article of faith with us.
— Josiah Bunting III, *An Education for Our Time*

Character Becomes Credibility

Whenever anyone tries to sell us something—whether it is a new car, an insurance policy, or a campaign promise—our natural inclination may be to ask ourselves, "Can I believe the person behind the message?" The credibility of the person adds value to what he or she has communicated. Credibility is the modern term for what the ancient Greeks called *ethos*, which meant "character." The Greeks considered ethos or character to enhance the speaker's ability to influence others through public presentations. In his book *Rhetoric*, Aristotle related ethos to the speaker's "habit of choice," as well as to the good or bad motives that listeners might perceive behind the speaker's message.[1] As it would likely be in the Greek world of Aristotle's day, credibility is the degree to which people believe and respect the speaker.[2]

This chapter focuses primarily on George W. Bush's credibility in relation to his leadership abilities, and reveals attacks by the Left to besmirch his character in an effort to lower his credibility. Character upholds the credibility of leaders, whose performance may carry them to greatness.

In recent decades, researchers have sought to isolate specific qualities of leadership credibility. The extensive research of James Kouzes and Barry Posner, as reported in their book *Credibility: How Leaders Gain and Lose It, Why People Demand It*, has produced strikingly consistent findings. "Time and again," they write, "people sent a clear message about the qualities leaders must demonstrate if they want others to enlist voluntarily in a common cause and to commit themselves to action freely."[3] This, of course, is the goal of the persuasive public speaker, whether he or she is a defense attorney, a sales person, the president of the company, or the president of the country.

Kouzes and Posner found in their research that most people admire and look for leaders who are (1) competent, (2) forward-looking, (3) inspiring, and (4) honest.[4] Surveys showed that respondents ranked these qualities way above any other qualities. As Kouzes and Posner put it, "If the qualities alone were running for office, these are the ones that would achieve consensus and victory."[5] It so happens that these are the qualities that put George W. Bush in office as governor of Texas and president of the United States—qualities that people detected as they heard him speak.

Aristotle taught that the speaker is a source of proof in the speech, "that his character [ethos] is the most potent of all the means of persuasion."[6] Providing more information, Aristotle confidently stated, "we yield a more complete and ready credence to persons of high character not only ordinarily and in a general way, but in such matters as do not admit of absolute certainty but necessarily leave room for difference of opinion."[7] For example, if Senator Orrin Hatch of Utah or former Senator Zell Miller of Georgia—both men of integrity—were to voice an opinion on a controversial subject, fair-minded people who knew them would likely give their views credence, especially if their opponents could not claim the same high credibility.

When audience members perceive the speaker as a credible source, they believe that (1) his opinions are conclusions based on careful examination of data; (2) his facts are reliable in so far as verification is possible; (3) his emotions and attitudes are sincerely represented by his nonverbal communication; and (4) his personality is such that they can attribute qualities to him that inspire trust and likeability.

Left Attacks on Bush's Credibility

Sadly, the Left in our society is unwilling to apply such points as the above in appraising President George W. Bush—fairly and logically—as a credible leader. Instead, they resort to hate-speech in their attacks to regain the political power they once enjoyed. The Bush-haters come from such groups as politicians, Hollywood types, journalists, writers, and college professors. Lacking substance, cogency, and rationality, they rely on cruel, bizarre charges in their attacks on the President's ethics, religious faith, patriotism, and humanity. Some of the Bush-haters have entombed these charges in books, which, as Andrew Ferguson, writing in *The Weekly Standard*, puts it, "show no sign of having been written for people who read books. They have found their audience."[8]

Because the hatred that the Left feels toward President Bush has become so consumingly-intense, we need to ask, what drives this emotion? Ferguson raises the same question: "Why do they hate him so?" While not finding a definitive answer in what the Bush-haters have stated, he observes, they "hate Bush for the least articulable reasons, the visceral kind that never quite rises to the level of rationality."[9] Then Ferguson points us to where the explanation for their hatred lurks, when he writes that it is "something much deeper than policy, much deeper even than politics, plunging down and down into the mysteries of cultural identity in fractured America."[10]

Yes, the explanation for the Bush-haters' hatred lies at a deep level in the country's cultural identity that is moving—with the help of a liberal media, judiciary, and teaching profession—ever Leftward. The Left views George W. Bush as an obstruction to this movement. To the Left, Bush is the embodiment of traditional, conservative beliefs and values, which it rejects. Bush's rhetoric emphasizes such beliefs and values as individual responsibility, national pride, military superiority, and right to life; it also gives expression to his Christian faith in God.

President Bush frequently makes statements that evince his Christian faith and its importance in his life, which seems to intensify the animosity that his enemies feel toward him. In his speeches—especially since the attacks of September 11—he expresses his religious philosophy openly and naturally in order to inspire, encourage, and embolden the American people during a time of war—something that liberals do not like. David

Limbaugh, in *Persecution: How Liberals Are Waging War Against Christianity*, writes, "A reporter asked Michael Gerson, President Bush's chief speechwriter, if the president understood how offended many people were by the closing lines of the State of the Union address in January 2003."[11] The supposedly objectionable words were: "The liberty we prize is not America's gift to the world, it is God's gift to humanity." Limbaugh noted that Gerson reportedly replied by referring the reporter to a clause in the Declaration of Independence that states essentially the same idea.[12]

The attack by the fanatical cheerleaders for the Left have sounded downright anti-Christian as well as anti-Bush. For example, Michael Moore, a filmmaker, has called the President a "nitwit" for having a belief in Providence (or God).[13] Presumably, T.S. Eliot, Martin Luther King, Jr., Mother Teresa, John F. Kennedy, and C.S. Lewis who shared the same belief were also nitwits. Al Franken, a writer, on hearing that Bush believed that Christian faith was necessary for salvation, accused him of being one of those who "like to exclude others from heaven."[14] Surely, Franken would agree that if one is to be a good Christian, he should practice the teachings of Christ. And, Christ Himself said: "I am the way, and the truth, and the life; no one comes to the Father, but through Me."[15] Molly Ivins, a journalist, "seems to harbor a special animus toward Christians, at least those Christians with the gall to believe Christianity is true. She scoffs at Franklin Graham's prayer 'in Jesus' name' at the president's inauguration."[16] Ivins recoiled in horror in response to President Bush's declaration that he could not have given up alcohol so readily without the grace of God.[17]

The President's Christian faith is a reminder to those on the Left that his vision of America differs greatly from their own. They see his vision as judgmental, restrictive, out-moded, and controlling; they fear that it will undermine the gains they have made in establishing cultural mores and laws (and interpretations of laws) that are consistent with, or promote, their secular worldview. The Left is bent upon the transformation of American culture into one that is completely secular—the word *secular* is defined as "not sacred or religious; temporal; worldly." One wonders if the model for such a culture is not France.

Those supporting a secular vision of America want to see someone in the White House whose vision matches their own. All of the Democrats who campaigned for the 2004 presidential nomination courted the political

Left in their speeches and bashed Bush at every opportunity to curry favor. For example, prior to the primaries, Democrats leading the pack for the nomination attacked the President with unhinged hostility:

> Howard Dean compared President Bush to the Taliban and calls him "the enemy" and "despicable."
>
> Dick Gephardt calls the President "a miserable failure" and the worst President he's ever worked with.
>
> John Kerry compared President Bush to Saddam Hussein, called for "regime change" and accused him of fraud.
>
> Joe Lieberman said President Bush is a "segregationist," compared him to "a felon" and called the Administration "nearly as dangerous" as Iraqi terrorists.[18]

Why would prominent politicians in the Democratic Party resort to such nasty, vicious attacks? The only logical answer—to attempt to lower Bush's credibility and popularity in the eyes of the American public through character assassination.

The special interest groups on the Left that foster a secular culture, gave particular support to the Democratic candidates who seemed likely to scrap President Bush's policies—foreign and domestic—even when those policies appeared to be working well—of course, they have their own definition of success. In his *Who's Looking Out for You?*, Bill O'Reilly warned that secular forces have campaigned to persuade Americans that "public spirituality is 'noninclusive' and therefore offensive. They have succeeded mightily in burying the true tenor of this country."[19]

Bush's Qualities of Credibility

On December 15, 2003, following the capture of Saddam Hussein, President Bush held a press conference and took a question from Bill Sammon, senior White House correspondent for *The Washington Times*. Sammon stood up and said, "Mr. President . . . Howard Dean recently seemed to muse aloud whether you had advance knowledge of 9/11. Do you agree or disagree with the RNC that this kind of rhetoric borders on political hate speech?" The President was silent for a moment; he shook his head with an expression of mixed anger and sadness and then, speaking softly, he replied, "There's time for politics" He paused. "Time for politics." His tone becoming disdainful, he added, "It's an absurd insinuation."[20]

Obviously, George W. Bush knew what Dean and other Democrats had said about him to win the support of Leftward voters, and so might have used Sammon's question as an opportunity to counterattack. But, he refrained from doing so. Such restraint is the style of the man, who characteristically takes the high road and still hopes to change the tone of Washington politics. In spite of daily attacks on him or his policies by Democrats seeking to regain the White House, Bush refused to fire back, even when their denunciations became extremely insulting. The American public saw a man too busy serving the country and awakening the world to the dangers of terrorism to divert attention from leading to campaigning. In occasional speeches he made to raise funds for the Bush-Cheney reelection campaign, he made it clear that politics would have to wait on the work of keeping Americans and other freedom-loving people as safe as possible in a dangerous world.

Consistent with Bush's leadership style, the Bush-Cheney reelection campaign strategy for 2004 delegated the responsibility of responding to attackers to the Republican National Committee (RNC), while the President and Vice President remained above the Democrats' political posturing until the last several months of the campaign when they focused their counterattacks on Kerry's record. Basic to this strategy was the recognition that there was an obvious "stature gap" between Bush and Kerry. During the Democratic primaries, a White House source close to the President observed, "If he gets down with the Lilliputians, he is going to look like another one of them."[21] Speaking of his credibility, the same source commented, "People might not always agree with the president, but they see him as a strong, principled leader and they respect him for that. Having him—or his official spokesmen or even his campaign—responding to, you know, Howard Dean, would reduce that stature."[22]

We can give substance to this word "stature" by showing how Bush measures up as a credible leader by being competent, forward-looking, inspiring, and honest, qualities often reflected in his speeches. For as Kouzes and Posner assert, "Credibility is the foundation of leadership."[23]

Competent

For many years, researchers have studied the role of competence in leadership. They have found that leaders show that they are competent by looking out for the welfare and security of those they lead; serving, inspiring, and uniting people; and praising the work of others.[24] They possess the requisite intelligence and knowledge to handle their responsibilities and the know-how to make smart decisions in the face of changing circumstances. Herein is a profile of the competent leader—it is also a good description of the leadership of George W. Bush.

What else identifies a competent leader? Howard Gardner, Hobbs Professor of Cognition and Education at Harvard, who pioneered research on multiple intelligences, tells us, "leaders are people who can change the thoughts, feelings, and/or behaviors of a significant number of other people."[25] He adds, "leaders lead *directly*, by speaking (or, occasionally, writing) to their audiences and thereby seeking to bring about changes."[26] Focusing more on the interpersonal, Kouzes and Posner write: "Leadership is a relationship, one between constituent and leader that is based on mutual needs and interests."[27] Collectively, these writers remind us that leaders influence people's behavior through communication that positively affects their thoughts, feelings, needs, and interests, which creates a sense of relationship with them. This is competent leadership in action.

A good test of a leader's competence is to see how he interacts with people he does not know, in a situation that requires spontaneity and adaptability. President Bush met such a test, according to a newsletter (Fall 2001) published by the offices of the internationally-known ophthalmologist Dr. I. Howard Fine. The newsletter's cover story featured a meeting in Washington, D.C. between 20 physicians that represented the Coalition of Medical Specialty Societies and President Bush, former Secretary Tommy Thompson, and Secretary Elaine Chao. The physicians had been invited by the President to discuss the Patients' Bill of Rights. As current president of the American Society of Cataract and Refractive Surgery, Dr. Fine had been invited to the meeting. In the newsletter, he wrote: "I was immensely impressed with how personable the President is. He was gracious in his dealings with all of the people present, as well as his staff, elevator operators, clerks, and everyone with whom he came into contact." He went on to say, "I was also tremendously impressed with how knowledgeable he is with respect to health care issues and health care policy. He was looking for feedback from those present regarding the failures of HMOs to provide needed care."[28]

Although he did not use the term, Dr. Fine's impressions of George W. Bush convey much about the President' competence, which he apparently rated highly. In the way the President related to others, demonstrated technical knowledge, discussed issues, sought feedback, and set the tone of the meeting, Dr. Fine observed the man behind the message and "had the delightful experience of meeting with the sitting president."

A competent leader solicits feedback from the people he represents and in whose behalf he makes decisions. George W. Bush understands, "By being open to influence . . ., leaders encourage people to provide more information." He practices the principle, "We trust them, and they trust us. We listen to them, and they will be more likely to listen to us." If this principle is to be made practical, however, "informal and formal feedback opportunities need to be structured."[29]

In creating such opportunities and being directly involved with the people providing feedback, Bush shows confidence in his ability to discuss serious policy issues in a public forum. One way he does this is by inviting ordinary people to join him on a platform before an audience and tell him the effects of certain policies on their lives and, sometimes, what new policies they would like to see enacted. Bush seats himself on a high stool, microphone in hand, with participants on either side of him, who are also seated on stools and holding microphones. This was the format on March 16, 2004 in Washington, D.C. when, under the auspices of the U.S. Chamber of Commerce, Bush brought together small-business owners to discuss affordable health care for their employees. Each participant on the platform had the opportunity to tell the President about his or her experience with rising health insurance costs. Bush then responded to each person, adding technical information, emphasizing certain of their points, and calling for Congressional action—for example, on Associated Health Plans.

Throughout this program, President Bush remained energetic, attentive, knowledgeable, and expressive; he was in his element as he talked and joked with these entrepreneurs and spoke to a responsive audience about something close to his heart. "It's that vibrancy in the private sector," he declared at one point, "that really defines a strong economy."[30]

Obviously, President Bush can think on his feet, answering questions making comments, introducing humor. But how capable is he behind the scenes, working with his Cabinet members, getting the most value from their input? One answer to the question comes from Secretary of Defense Donald Rumsfeld, who after impressive careers in the military and government, operates with high expectations of himself and those with whom he works. In March '04, he granted an interview to Bret Baier of Fox News who asked him how he would characterize President Bush's interaction with him and other Cabinet members. "First of all, he's very much engaged," Rumsfeld said, which, one could tell, was important to him. "He is available to talk about things that are important; he is interested in them. I was in a meeting with him [and Condoleezza Rice] the other day, this week, on a national security issue and—I'm going to guess—in 45 minutes, he asked 40 questions." Impressed, Baier checked his hearing, "Forty questions in 45 minutes?" Rumsfeld verified the number, chuckling with admiration for Bush, as he recalled the situation. "And he was totally engaged in it," continued Rumsfeld. "And he wanted to know; he wanted to peel the onion; he wanted to get down several layers in the thing, and [see] pieces of it. And it forced the discussion and the consideration. And," he noted, "it elevated a whole host of things that he obviously believed that he needed to know and wanted to reflect on and consider." Baier then interjected, "So, it's not micromanaging is it." Rumsfeld emphatically responded, "No, no, quite the contrary. It's developing sufficient knowledge of something, so that you can provide policy guidance and direction, and you know exactly how long the string ought to be on the key people, who are managing that piece of it for you. And then stepping out and letting them do it."[31]

Rumsfeld's description of Bush at work and at war is that of a strong leader, whose questions are geared to press his advisors to get beneath the surface of issues and give him in-depth analysis that he needs in order to make important decisions. Surrounding himself with bright, confident people has led some in the liberal media to suggest that they are the ones calling the shots on key issues. Setting the record straight, Ann Coulter, in *Slander*, writes, "There was no question that it was he who was calling the shots. It was he who made the central decision to go after the entire Al

Qaida terrorist organization after CIA director George Tenet raised the 'sobering thought' that Al Qaida was a '60-country problem.'" Emphasizing her point, she noted, "Not Secretary Donald Rumsfeld, not National Security Advisor Condoleezza Rice, not Secretary of State Colin Powell."[32]

Writing from the perspective of an insider, Ari Fleischer, former White House Press Secretary, noted that while Bush's critics portrayed him as a man who lacked intelligence, thoughtfulness, and even curiosity, he was, in fact, quite the opposite. Fleischer found him keen-minded and quick-witted, a leader with the instincts of a CEO who saw the "big picture" and who kept his advisors focused on its realization.[33]

In spite of the fact that President Bush has assembled one of the finest Cabinets in American history, the liberal media have used every pretense to criticize how they work together. They seemed to have assumed that if two or more members disagreed on a course of action, the Cabinet was dysfunctional. This assumption seems to have prompted *New York Times* columnist Thomas Friedman to write: "A lot of people say that Mr. Bush, while he knows little foreign policy, has hired smart advisors. Oh, really? Well what happens when his two smartest advisors disagree?"[34]

To answer Friedman's question, one thing that would happen is that Bush would make a decision after comparing alternative courses of action from two "smart advisors." Certainly, the President's MBA studies at Harvard would have taught him that effective leaders seek divergent points of view from department heads and advisors before making crucial decisions. Peter F. Drucker, called the father of modern management, in his classic *The Effective Executive*, stated, "Decisions of the kind the executive has to make are not made well by acclamation. They are made well only if based on the clash of conflicting views, the dialogue between different points of view, the choice between different judgments." He added, "The first rule in decision-making is that one does not make a decision unless there is disagreement."[35] In the same context, Drucker observed, "Every one of the effective Presidents in American history had his own method of producing the disagreement he needs in order to make an effective decision. Lincoln, Theodore Roosevelt, Franklin D. Roosevelt, Harry Truman—each had his own ways."[36]

George W. Bush compares well with great U.S. presidents of the past in his ability to respond effectively to crises, whether domestic or foreign in origin. The way he responds—sometimes against conventional political wisdom—reveals a long-term perspective, as opposed to a knee-jerk reaction to satisfy a segment of the electorate. Of course, his response to the attacks of 9/11 stands as the most crucial in his presidency, demonstrating, as it did, a keen understanding of what the attacks portend for the future of America and the world. His response evolved into a new foreign policy that broke with the past and came to grips with a dangerous present, a present foreshadowed by terrorist atrocities against the U.S. over a period of years.

President Bush's foreign policy is designed to combat global terrorism, which he sees as the first war of the 21st century. "For him," says Tony Blankley, *Washington Times* Editorial Page Editor, "the terrorism menace is corporeal, ominous and imminent. If he is right—and almost every technical terrorism expert believes he is—I believe his obsessive, sustained focus on the danger is a sign of greatness." Blankley further says that while most political leaders "have long since tired of the mental and emotional strain of staring into the terrorism abyss, the president continues to focus and to act."[37] Bush realizes that the early stages of the struggle may be the toughest, because terrorist groups are not convinced that we have the fortitude to fight them, Blankley asserts.[38] They have reason to doubt our resolve in remembering the failure of U.S. policy following, for example, the bombings of the World Trade Center in 1993 and the *USS Cole* in 2000.

The Bush doctrine that underlies President Bush's foreign policy is only the third grand strategy in U.S. history, according to John Lewis Gaddis, Yale historian "whom many describe as the dean of Cold War studies and one of the nation's most eminent diplomatic historians."[39] In his new book, *Surprise, Security, and the American Experience,* Gaddis identifies three American statesmen who have distinguished themselves as grand strategists—they are John Quincy Adams, Franklin D. Roosevelt, and George W. Bush. As a *Boston Globe* article describes in an interview with Gaddis: "Grand strategy is the blueprint from which policy follows. It envisions a country's mission, defines its interests, and sets its priorities. Part of grand strategy's grandeur lies in its durability: A single grand strategy can shape decades, even centuries of policy."[40] Roosevelt's grand strategy remained in effect through the Cold War. "The end of the Cold War changed all that—and found the United States without a grand strategy."[41] President Bill Clinton, Gaddis maintains, believed that "globalization and democratization were irreversible processes, therefore we didn't need a grand strategy. Clinton said as much at one point. I think that was shallow. I think they were asleep at the switch."[42]

After September 11, 2001, Gaddis says in his book, George W. Bush underwent "one of the most surprising transformations of an underrated national leader since Prince Hal became Henry V."[43] The President, only about eight months in office, "undertook a decisive and courageous reassessment of American grand strategy following the shock of the 9/11 attacks. At his doctrine's center, Bush placed the democratization of the Middle East and the urgent need to prevent terrorists and rogue states from getting nuclear weapons." In addition, "Bush also boldly rejected the constraints of an outmoded international system that was really nothing more than a 'snapshot of the configuration of power that existed in 1945,' Gaddis says."[44]

President Bush's speech to the graduating cadets at West Point on June 1, 2002, contained a key statement pertaining to his grand strategy, according to Gaddis. Bush stated, "We will defend the peace against threats from terrorists and tyrants. We will preserve the peace by building good relations among the great powers. And we will extend the peace by encouraging free and open societies on every continent."[45] Gaddis quotes this statement in his new book and then informs his readers: "It's worth comparing these priorities with the three the Clinton administration put forth in its final report on national security strategy, published in December 1999: To enhance America's security. To bolster America's economic prosperity. To promote democracy and human rights abroad." Gaddis says:

> The differences are instructive. The Bush objectives specify defending, preserving, and extending peace; the Clinton statement seems simply to assume peace. Bush calls for cooperation among the great powers; Clinton never uses that term. Bush specifies the encouragement of free and open societies on every continent; Clinton contents himself with "promoting" democracy and human

> rights "abroad." Even in these first lines, then, the Bush NSS [National Security Strategy of the United States] comes across as more forceful, more carefully crafted, and—unexpectedly—more multilateral than its immediate predecessor. It's a tip-off that there [are] interesting things going on here.[46]

Concerning the Bush administration's performance in applying its grand strategy, Gaddis stresses, "I do take them very seriously. I do think Bush is in charge himself, and has been very underrated as a leader in all of this just as Ronald Reagan was underrated."[47]

If Americans knew how demanding the job of U.S. president is in the 21st century, there might be even more people impressed with President Bush's competence in that office and more people critical of an untried candidate who seeks to replace him. Someone who is a former governor of a large state is probably the best prepared candidate for the biggest position on the planet. "Within the first few months I discovered," said former president Harry S. Truman, "that being a president is like riding a tiger. A man has to keep riding or be swallowed." One of the few people who knows what the presidency involves is Secretary of Defense Donald Rumsfeld. In a March 19, 2004 interview, he told Bret Baier of Fox News about the difficulty of serving as Chief of Staff to former president Gerald R. Ford. He mentioned that when Ford came to the presidency he had a lot to learn, since his background in governmental leadership was limited to Congress. By contrast, Rumsfeld suggested, George W. Bush, having served as governor of Texas, was better prepared. "He came in at the place where some presidents arrive after being in office a few years."[48]

Forward-Looking

A forward-looking leader is a person who sees how present circumstances can be altered to give direction toward a new destination that promises people greater security and opportunity. In short, such a leader has a vision of a desired future state. The leader's vision has little impact however, unless it is communicated effectively to constituents. In this connection, Warren Bennis and Burt Nanus, in their book *Leaders*, point out, "There are a lot of intoxicating visions and a lot of noble intentions . . . . but without communication nothing will be realized."[49]

Leaders must communicate their vision compellingly and consistently to their constituents to elicit their enthusiasm and commitment.

To illustrate the importance of leaders' ability to communicate their visions, Bennis and Nanus compared former President Ronald Reagan with former President Jimmy Carter. They noted that Reagan made abstract topics and ideas meaningful and graphic. "According to an ABC poll, support for the U.S. invasion of Grenada *doubled* immediately after Reagan's explanatory speech." Conversely, these writers point out, Carter's communicative ability was "unimpressive," both in "form of presentation" and clarity of meaning. They quoted a cabinet officer that Carter had appointed who said that "she never knew what he stood for. As she talked about Jimmy Carter, she conjured a beautiful metaphor of her own: 'Working for him was like looking at the wrong side of a tapestry—blurry and indistinct.'"[50]

In the Reagan tradition, President Bush communicated his vision clearly and forcefully. His vision focused on the nation's security with three objectives (1) winning the war against global terrorism, (2) protecting our homeland, and (3) reviving our economy. In his 2002 "State of the Union Address," his vision found expression: "Our first priority must always be the security of our nation, and that will be reflected in the budget I send to Congress. My budget supports three great goals for America: We will win this war; we'll protect our homeland; and we will revive our economy."[51] In his 2003 "State of the Union Address," he expressed his vision more succinctly: "We will work for a prosperity that is broadly shared, and we will answer every danger and every enemy that threatens the American people." He underscored the priority of his vision by further stating: "This country has many challenges. We will not deny, we will not ignore, we will not pass along our problems to other Congresses, to other presidents, and other generations. We will confront them with focus and clarity and courage."[52]

When people hear the leader present a vision that is undergirded by a clear, "uplifting philosophy that dares everyone to take risks to realize its challenge," it can prove energizing and compelling.[53] President Bush's vision is undergirded by the Christian philosophy of good versus evil with the call—to which people of all faiths can respond—to join the mission to work for good and defeat evil. Given his strong religious beliefs, his duties that continually reinforce images of death and destruction of 9/11, and his concentration on waging war against global terrorism, it is not surprising that his rhetoric has a moral tone, that he sees the realization of his vision as victory of right over wrong.

The Left has been critical of Bush's moralistic rhetoric. Perhaps the President had this in mind when, on June 1, 2002, he spoke to the graduating class at West Point. In his speech he made it clear that he would continue "to speak the language of right and wrong," even though some people thought it was "undiplomatic or impolite."[54] He stated, "Moral truth is the same in every culture, in every time, and in every place. Targeting innocent civilians for murder is always and everywhere wrong. Brutality against women is always and everywhere wrong." Then, in a resolute tone, he said, "We are in a conflict between good and evil, and America will call evil by its name . . . . And we will lead the world in opposing it."[55] Jawaharlal Nehru, former Prime Minister of India, spoke of the consequences of not opposing evil. "Evil unchecked grows," Nehru argued, "evil tolerated poisons the whole system."

The vision that President Bush has set forth reminds one of Peter Drucker's "Six Rules for [U.S.] Presidents" in which he stated: "The president's top priority has to be something that truly needs to be done. If it is not highly controversial, it is likely to be the wrong priority . . . . But it also has to be important enough to make a difference if done successfully."[56] The President's vision meets all of Drucker's rules. Certainly, nothing could be more important than the nation's security, and to be successful in maintaining that security, the country needs a forward-looking leader. Such a leader is George W. Bush, who can visualize potential dangers and has the courage to act before they become a present reality. Speaking on January 29, 2002, in his "State of the Union Address," he said to America and the world: "We'll be deliberate, yet time is not on our side. I will not wait on events, while dangers gather. I will not stand by, as peril draws closer and closer." And then he seemed to sound a warning to potential enemies: "The United State of America will not permit the world's most dangerous regimes to threaten us with the world's most destructive weapons."[57]

President Bush's ability to anticipate future developments based on present conditions is characteristic of a forward-looking leader. This ability is enhanced when Bush uses his imagination to raise a variety of possibilities in grappling with long-term effects of problems. Kouzes and Posner make the point: "If leaders are to be admired and respected, they must have the ability to see across the horizon of time and imagine what might be."[58] Imagination is the creative side of planning that finds more options for solutions, but requires more taking of risks than playing it safe. Nobody less than Albert Einstein remarked, "Imagination is more important than knowledge." Leaders thus gifted, draw new conclusions from data, discover overlooked implications in facts, and "define what has previously remained implicit or unsaid."[59]

Establishing long-range goals for NASA, Bush "has set America on a bold new course for exploration and our aging, lethargic space program—a bold step into the cosmos that could help expand our presence in the solar system within a lifetime."[60] The President has shown again his ability to look beyond present circumstances to future opportunities. One is reminded of a bit of wisdom from Wayne Gretzky, the leading hockey player of his generation, who said that it's not as important to know where the puck is now as to know where it will be.

President Bush's plan for NASA is to retire the space shuttle by the end of the decade; develop a new space vehicle for travel to the moon by 2014; and build stations on the moon as points of departure for travel to Mars by 2020. His plan resolves a number of problems that have bogged down the space agency and hindered its progress; it gives NASA a new and challenging mission and purpose, which the space agency's top officials clearly recognize. NASA's new charter will doubtless produce important scientific breakthroughs that will enhance America's economy and the quality of life for our citizens. On January 13, 2004, at NASA, President Bush said, "We do not know where this journey will end, yet we know this: Human beings are headed into the cosmos."[61] President Bush, in common with other great leaders, has the ability to set challenging goals that inspire people to make a reservation with destiny.

Inspiring

People respect and admire leaders who are dynamic, enthusiastic, positive, uplifting, and optimistic. These are the qualities that fair-minded people must attribute to George W. Bush. He inspires others to believe in themselves, in the importance of the tasks they perform, and in the ultimate success of what they seek to accomplish—one can see evidence of this in the nonverbal behavior of audience members when he speaks to parishioners in a church, workers at a plant, teachers and students at a school, police officers at a police department, or soldiers and their families at a base. He communicates confidence in his ability to lead effectively toward the realization of his goals and vision; he projects a courageous attitude that is contagious. Kouzes and Posner rightly observe, "Without courage, there can be no hope. People are inspired by leaders who take initiative and who risk personal safety for the sake of a cause. Only those leaders who act boldly in times of crisis and change are willingly followed."[62]

When President Bush made his surprise visit to Baghdad in 2003, so that he could eat Thanksgiving dinner with his troops, he personified what these authors said about courage and inspired our brave military serving in Iraq and elsewhere. *The Weekly Standard* received an email from a captain who gave a firsthand account of the President's unexpected visit and what it meant to the 600 soldiers seated in the mess hall awaiting dinner:

> [Ambassador Paul] Bremer thanked us all and pulled out a piece of paper as if to give a speech. He mentioned that the President had given him this Thanksgiving speech to give to the troops . . . . Bremer then said that we should probably get someone more senior to read the speech.
>
> Then, from behind the camouflage netting, the President of the United States came around. The mess hall actually erupted with hollering. Troops bounded to their feet with shocked smiles and just began cheering with all their hearts. The building actually shook. It was just unreal. I was absolutely stunned. Not only for the obvious, but also because I was only two tables away from the podium. There he stood, less than thirty feet away from me!
>
> The cheering went on and on. Soldiers were hollering, cheering, and a lot of them were crying. There was not a dry eye at my table. When he stepped up to the cheering, I could clearly see tears running down his cheeks. It was the most surreal moment I've had in years . . . . Here was this man, our President, came all

> the way around the world, spending 17 hours on an airplane and landing in the most dangerous airport in the world, where a plane was shot out of the sky not six days before. Just to spend two hours with his troops. Only to get on a plane and spend another 17 hours flying back [when he would be in danger again]. It was a great moment, and I will never forget it.
>
> He delivered his speech, which we all loved, then . . . he stepped down and was just mobbed by the soldiers. He slowly worked his way all around the chow hall and shook every last hand extended. Every soldier who wanted a photo with the President got one. . . .
>
> You could tell he was really enjoying himself. It wasn't just a photo opportunity. This man was actually enjoying himself! . . . As he passed and posed for photos, he looked me in the eye and said, "How you doin', Captain." I smiled and said, "God bless you, sir." To which he responded, "I'm proud of what you do, Captain." Then moved on.[63]

President Bush has several personality traits, that, in their influence on his rhetoric, inspire people in his audiences—that is, have an animating effect on them. One of these traits is *optimism*. Kouzes and Posner tell us, "Optimism is essential to strengthening credibility." The reason? "Leaders with their eyes on an ideal and a strong image of tomorrow reflect optimistic outlooks. In expressing their convictions that it will work out for the best and be better than the past, optimists instill confidence in others."[64] This is an apt description of President Bush. His optimistic rhetoric lifts his listeners' spirits, puts difficulties and setbacks into perspective, and draws others to share his faith in the course he has charted to success. We see an example of his optimistic rhetoric that inspired the troops during his Thanksgiving visit to Baghdad in the following lines:

> We will prevail. We will win because our cause is just. We will win because we will stay on the offensive. And we will win because you're part of the finest military ever assembled. (Applause, hollers, and whistles.) And we will prevail because the Iraqis want their freedom. (Applause, hollers, and whistles.)[65]

People with nonverbal expressive social skills, who consistently inspire those to whom they speak, often find themselves in positions of leadership and social influence. These people are popularly labeled "charismatic." In observing George W. Bush's effect on individuals, small groups, and large audiences, one would assume that he has charisma. The dictionary defines *charisma* as "a special quality of leadership that captures the popular imagination and inspires allegiance and devotion."

Does President Bush fit the profile of a charismatic person? Research findings suggest that he does. According to psychologists, persons who have a charismatic personality "seem emotionally healthy and are not necessarily anxious or concerned with control, deception, manipulation of others, or self-monitoring." They communicate their feelings nonverbally with ease; they appear animated with head movements and smiles. Charismatic people are extroverted, "dominant, and fast-moving, but are in control, coping well, and sociable." Moreover, "they are just naturally expressive rather than characterized by excessive striving, hostility, and competition."[66] Leaders perceived by followers as charismatic, communicate an ideological vision that differs from the status quo, emphasize high expectations, have followers willing to think in new ways, show confidence in followers and recognize their efficacy and worth, and demonstrate exemplary behavior as role models.[67]

What does Bush gain as a charismatic leader? one might ask. One answer comes from Bennis and Nanus: Leaders with charisma "are granted a certain amount of respect and even awe by their followers, which increases the bond of attraction between them."[68] While Bush's charismatic personality doubtless increases his effectiveness as a persuader and leader, it is not the sole basis of his leadership ability; he derives this ability from other qualities as well, such as honesty and intelligence.

Honest/Trustworthy

In virtually every survey conducted by researchers in various parts of the world—United States, Western Europe, Japan, Latin America—honesty was selected more often than any other leadership quality. Moreover, it was usually the top quality.[69] It makes good sense to want an honest leader. When people follow a leader and work to realize his or her vision, they want to be sure that the person is worthy of their trust. Leaders with credibility keep their word—what they say they are going to do, they do. Such leaders have a reputation for being trustworthy.

George W. Bush has a reputation for being trustworthy. We can read or watch a video of his address to the Republican National Convention in 2000, and discover that nearly every agenda item discussed in the speech has been transformed into legislation or policy through his leadership—Medicare and prescription drugs, education, and tax-code reform included. He promised, "We will confront the hard issues—threats to our national security, threats to our health and retirement security—before the challenges of our time become crises for our children."[70] Unlike most politicians, President Bush kept his campaign promises, something that even some political opponents concede.

A political leader is seen as trustworthy, because he or she speaks the truth, even when he or she knows that some citizens may find the truth unpleasant and, therefore, difficult to accept. For example, as far back as September 20, 2001, in his "Presidential Address to a Joint Session of Congress," Bush told Americans: "Our war on terror begins with al Qaida, but it does not end there. It will not end until every terrorist group of global reach has been found, stopped, and defeated."[71] Then at a later point, he warned, "This war will not be like the war against Iraq a decade ago, with a decisive liberation of territory and a swift conclusion. It will not look like the air war above Kosovo two years ago, where no ground troops were used and not a single American was lost in combat."[72] Rather than indulge in wishful thinking as some leaders might have done, he provided a realistic assessment when he said, "Our response involves far more than instant retaliation and isolated strikes. Americans should not expect one battle, but a lengthy campaign, unlike any other we have ever seen."[73]

People generally seem to prefer leaders whom they believe are honest, trustworthy, and of high moral integrity. By definition, morality is the character of being in accord with the principles or standards of right conduct. When a candidate violates one of these standards, some portion of the electorate may lower its estimation of his or her credibility. During the 1988 "presidential primaries, married candidate Gary Hart was photographed with his girlfriend, Donna Rice, sitting on his lap on the yacht *Monkey Business*. His campaign was ruined with charges of womanizing and his presidential aspirations dashed."[74] It would seem that when people have assigned a credibility rating to a candidate, they don't like to feel fooled. Research shows that a quality strongly associated with leadership capacity is moral responsibility. People also tend to rate individuals they like, higher in leadership capacity.[75]

As Governor of Texas and President of the United States, George W. Bush has been an exemplar of moral integrity in both his private and public life. His morality, founded in his faith, gives him a sense of calling and purpose. Stephen Mansfield, Churchill biographer, studied how Bush's Christian faith has impacted his life and work, and concluded that it gives him an "inner moral compass" that he obeys by doing what he thinks is "the right thing."[76] What has impressed supporters and detractors alike has been the President's determination to follow what he believes is the right course of action, in spite of inducements or pressures to do otherwise. Many of his decisions have angered liberals, some have angered conservatives, and a few have angered both, such as the Medicare prescription-drug package. In signing the bill into law, he kept a campaign promise. Obviously, Mr. Bush did not need the advice that Harry Truman gave newly-elected John F. Kennedy: "*Once you're elected you stop campaigning.*"

During the latter half of 2003, some journalists and academics advanced the theory that President Bush acted expediently and changed the rationale for going to war with Iraq from destroying weapons of mass destruction to liberating Iraq. Presumably, Bush made this shift as a result of not finding WMDs that Saddam Hussein was known to have. His supporters explained this as an attempt to expand his vision to meet changed circumstances in Iraq. His detractors saw Bush's liberation language as an indication of moral inconsistency and "accused him of becoming a man in search of a rationale for an unnecessary war."[77]

If one accepts this theory, one must assume that the President temporized his original position for attacking Iraq by adopting a new rationale that now emphasized Iraq's liberation. If this theory were true, it might make the President appear less honest. However, it is not true. His speeches clearly show that, in addition to locating and destroying Hussein's WMDs—his most pressing objective—and transforming the Middle East into a more stable region, early on he spoke of the plight of Iraqis and their need of liberation and freedom. Therefore, such an emphasis was not a new rationale, but one that Bush had clearly stressed in his rhetoric. The U.S. and our coalition partners are now actively and sacrificially engaged in the process of reconstructing Iraq, and fighting terrorists so that its people can establish a democracy, as purposed by the President in his speeches.

A number of Bush's speeches give evidence of his Iraqi-liberation rationale. For example, on October 7, 2002, in his "Speech at the Cincinnati Museum Center," he said, "America is a friend to the people of Iraq . . . . The long captivity of Iraq will end, and an era of new hope will begin."[78] On January 28, 2003, the President, in his "State of the Union Address," to the Iraqis, declared, "Your enemy is not surrounding your country—your enemy is ruling your country. And the day he and his regime are removed from power will be the day of your liberation."[79] On February 6, 2003, in his "Statement Regarding the UN Security Council and Iraq," Bush asserted, "The United Nations can renew its purpose . . . And we can give the Iraqi people their chance to live in freedom and choose their own government."[80] On February 26, 2003, the President addressed the American Enterprise Institute and predicted, "A liberated Iraq can show the power of freedom to transform that vital region, by bringing hope and progress into the lives of millions."[81] He noted, "Iraq . . . is fully capable of moving toward democracy and living in freedom."[82] On March 17, 2003, Bush delivered his "Presidential Address to the Nation," which was also a translated radio broadcast to Iraq. At one point, he spoke to Iraqis: "We will tear down the apparatus of terror and we will help you to build a new Iraq that is prosperous and free . . . . The tyrant will soon be gone. The day of your liberation is near."[83] On March 19, 2003, President Bush, on the commencement of military operations in Iraq, talking to our troops, stated, "The enemies you confront will come to know your skill and bravery. The people you liberate will witness the honorable and decent spirit of the American military . . . . He added, "And helping Iraqis achieve a united, stable, and free country will require our sustained commitment."[84] On April 3, 2003, in a speech to military personnel and their families, the Commander in Chief emphasized, "And the liberation of millions is the fulfillment of America's founding promise . . . . Once again, we are applying the power of our country to ensure our security and to serve the cause of justice."[85] On April 10, 2003, in his "Presidential Message to the Iraq People," the President assured Iraqis: "The government of Iraq, and the future of your country, will soon belong to you . . . . We will help you build a peaceful and representative government that protects the rights of all citizens."[86]

When, on May 1, 2003, President Bush's plane landed on the carrier *USS Abraham Lincoln* in preparation for delivering a speech on the cessation of major combat operations in Iraq, it caused Democrats considerable consternation—Senator Robert Byrd, of West Virginia, snarled, "To me, it is an affront to the Americans killed or injured in Iraq for the president to exploit the trappings of war for the momentary spectacle of a speech."[87] The "trappings" that inspired Byrd's attack on the Commander in Chief's credibility, was a simple flight suit that a passenger in a small jet plane would be required to wear. Of course, before Bush spoke, he changed into a business suit, something that Byrd's statement left out.

Democrats such as Congressman Henry Waxman of California failed to see the importance of this message to our troops and Coalition forces. He saw only "clear political overtones" in the President's speech.[88] However, this charge was refuted by General Tommy Franks in his autobiography *American Soldier* (2004) when he wrote that he told Secretary of Defense Donald Rumsfeld: "There's a lot of work to be done over here [in Iraq], but major combat operations are over." Franks said that he would like to have this fact acknowledged by the President for the troops. He concluded, "I was grateful on the first of May for the President's words. Little did I know the criticism he would face for doing what I recommended."[89]

In his *Lincoln* speech, Bush declared, "The transition from dictatorship to democracy will take time, but it is worth the effort. Our coalition will stay until our work is done. Then we will leave, and we will leave behind a free Iraq."[90]

These several examples attest to the President's consistency of purpose and principle in respect to the liberation of Iraq. Such an emphasis was a natural extension of his philosophy of compassionate conservatism, which, in his "Acceptance Speech" to the 2000 Republican National Convention, he defined: "It is to put conservative values and conservative ideas into the thick of the fight for justice and opportunity."[91] The year before, in his autobiography, he said, "we must use our power in a strong but compassionate way to help keep the peace and encourage the spread of freedom."[92] It is clear that Bush's rationale to liberate Iraq—along with his other rationales—is consistent with his personal values and aims that are grounded in his philosophy, and influence what he says and does. Consistency is integrity in action. And, in the words of President Reagan's motto, President Bush is committed to "stay the course."

Whether liberals talk about President Bush's foreign policy, including his stand on Iraq, or domestic policy, including his efforts to improve the economy, they attack his honesty in every imaginable way. Academics are among those who want to question his honesty. In a recent issue of *Social Philosophy & Policy*, Robert Weissberg, a professor of political science at the University of Illinois, writes about "lying in politics." In his article, he says, "something believed to be fraudulent by the speaker may in fact turn out to be true."[93] Then, to provide an example, he states the following:

> For example, in his 2000 presidential campaign George W. Bush said that the U.S. economy stood in danger of a recession, which many took to be a lie at the time since it seemed contrary to all available evidence and respected opinion. That such a downturn did follow Bush's victory unexpectedly absolves Bush from mendacity: he told the truth, though for reasons of campaign expediency, not because it was true. Plainly, the addition of a verification requirement regarding "what was really known" at the time makes certifying lies arduous.[94]

Apparently, Weissberg assumed that Governor Bush had no way of knowing "that the U.S. economy stood in danger of a recession," and so concluded that he deceived the electorate. For according to Weissberg's assessment, "all available evidence and respected opinion" indicated no recession.

But, the truth is, Governor Bush received information about the economy from individuals who could offer "respected opinion." During the winter of 1998 and the spring of 1999, in preparation for the campaign, he hosted fifteen policy sessions at the governor's mansion, including some on the economy—participating in these and other sessions were leading experts from around the country. Karen Hughes recalled, "At our economics sessions, we were warned that the economic bubble of the 1990s was about to burst, and that the taxes being collected from Americans totaled 32 percent of the gross domestic product—the highest tax burden the American economy had ever seen." She emphasized that the experts agreed that tax cuts were needed.[95]

Early in 2000, ominous signs of a softening economy were evident. For instance, U.S. stock markets on April 14 had record-day losses, the Dow Jones falling 617.78 points, down 5.66% from the close of the day before; the Nasdaq, even worse, plummeting 355.49 points, down 9.67 from the previous day's close. The Nasdaq's drop was the worst in its history. The April 14 losses ended a volatile week for the markets, when investors lost $2 trillion. The Nasdaq had been in continual fall since mid-March, with investors dumping technology stocks seen as overvalued.[96]

An editorial in *The Wall Street Journal* analyzed the April 14 sell-off, and warned that figures suggested that price increases were "indeed spreading into 'core' inflation," which limited "the Fed's room for maneuver if the financial crash does start to infect the real sector." And, it stressed, "if recession does start to develop—because of this latest crash or any other catalyst—limits on monetary policy may force us to think again about fiscal policy."[97]

On March 2, 2000, George Marotta, Research Fellow at the Hoover Institution, Stanford University, and a person of "respected opinion," in a speech to The Channel City Club in Santa Barbara, said, "The bad news is that we could be in a stock market bubble that if corrected quickly could bring to a halt, not only the prosperity of our country, but could seriously affect the world economy."[98] He concluded by saying, "The Japanese believe that the U.S. is now in a huge bubble."[99]

In a December 5, 2000 speech to America's Community Bankers Conference in New York, Alan Greenspan, Chairman of the Federal Reserve Board, shared some gloomy facts about the economy, such as, "During *the past couple of years*, however, the widespread optimism that was apparent in financial markets has given way to some reassessment of risks and opportunities. The process has been underway ever since the global financial crisis of 1998."[100]

Governor Bush, having access to such evidence and opinions

concerning the economy, and being himself a successful investor who made millions in business, could certainly "read" the signs that pointed to an impending economic downturn. Moreover, he had the opinion of a trusted financial authority in the person of his running mate, Dick Cheney, former head of the large global corporation Halliburton.

Therefore, Governor Bush, in telling "what was really known," did not deceive the electorate regarding the economy. He told the truth as an honest leader who wanted to prepare Americans to understand the need of new fiscal policies in Washington. Weissberg might have noted that Bush, in his campaign speeches, gave voters facts to support his concerns about the economy. For example, he would provide such facts as the following:

> In the final quarter of 2000, the American economy grew at a sluggish, 1.1 percent pace. In that same quarter, there was no growth at all in new business investment. Industrial production began dropping last October [2000], and almost every week brings us reports of layoffs, especially in manufacturing. Michigan has been hit especially hard. According to the latest figures, unemployment has risen more in Michigan over the past year than in any other state of the Union. Some regions of America, and some industries are doing better, but the trend is clear, and the need for action is urgent. (Applause.)[101]

President Bush is the kind of credible leader who tells the hard truth to his listeners, and risks—as Weissberg revealed—having people take what he says "to be a lie at the time." George W. Bush continues to tell it like it is as a competent, forward-looking, inspiring, and honest leader, who faces facts rather than fabricates myths.

Most of the American electorate saw in the President the characteristics and character of a person of credibility and entrusted him with four more years in the Oval Office. Zell Miller, former Democratic Senator from Georgia, expressed his high regard for George W. Bush, who, he said, has effectively "led America in a time of recession, terrorism, and war," always "guided by principles—aided by his strong faith," committed to keeping the nation secure and promoting opportunity for all Americans.[102]

NOTES

1. Cooper, *The Rhetoric of Aristotle*, 8.
2. Lane, *By All Means Communicate*, 288.
3. Kouzes and Posner, *Credibility*, 13.
4. Ibid., 13-14.
5. Ibid., 14.
6. Cooper, *The Rhetoric of Aristotle*, 9.
7. Thonssen and Baird, *Speech Criticism*, 59.
8. Andrew Ferguson, "That Man in the White House: Reading the Bush Bashers," *Weekly Standard*, December 8, 2003, p. 28.
9. Ibid., p. 32.
10. Ibid.
11. David Limbaugh, *Persecution: How Liberals Are Waging War Against Christianity* (Washington, D.C.: Regnery, 2003), 200-201.
12. Ibid.
13. Max Goss, "Cruel Batch of 'Liberals'," *Washington Times* National Weekly Edition, December 1-7, 2003, p. 28.
14. Ibid.
15. *Bible*, John 14:6.
16. Goss, "Cruel Batch of 'Liberals'," p. 28.
17. Ibid.
18. Marc Racicot, Letter to the Author, November 26, 2003.
19. O'Reilly, *Who's Looking Out for You?*, 188.
20. President's White House Press Conference, Fox News, December 15, 2003.
21. Bill Sammon, "High Road? Bush Won't Get 'Down with the Lilliputians'," *Washington Times* National Weekly Edition, December 15-21, 2003, p. 12.
22. Ibid.
23. Kouzes and Posner, *Credibility*, 22.
24. John M. Darley et al., *Psychology*, 4th ed. (Englewood Cliffs, NJ: Prentice Hall, 1988), 690.
25. Howard Gardner, *Intelligence Reframed: Multiple Intelligences for the 21st Century* (New York: Basic Books, 1999), 126.
26. Ibid., 130.
27. Kouzes and Posner, *Credibility*, 11.
28. I. Howard Fine, "Meeting with the President," *Fine View*, Fall 2001, p. 1.
29. Kouzes and Posner, *Credibility*, 103.
30. "Remarks by the President with a Panel of Entrepreneurs, on Access to Health Care," U.S. Chamber of Commerce, Washington, D.C., March 16, 2004, www.whitehouse.gov.
31. *Rumsfeld at War*, Fox News, March 19, 2004.

32. Ann Coulter, *Slander: Liberal Lies about the American Right* (New York: Three Rivers Press, 2002), 187-188.
33. Ari Fleischer, *Taking Heat: The President, the Press, and My Years in the White House* (New York: William Morrow, 2005), 32.
34. Thomas L. Friedman, "Foreign Affairs: George W.'s Makeup Exam," *New York Times*, November 7, 1999, p. wk 15.
35. Peter Drucker, *The Effective Executive* (New York: HarperBusiness, 1993), 148-149.
36. Ibid.
37. Tony Blankley, "Unless the Terrorists are Appeasable, Bush Is Right," *Washington Times* National Weekly Edition, November 3-9, 2003, p. 30.
38. Ibid.
39. Laura Secor, "Grand Old Policy," *Boston Sunday Globe*, February 8, 2004, p. H1.
40. Ibid.
41. Ibid., p. H5.
42. Ibid.
43. John Lewis Gaddis, *Surprise, Security, and the American Experience* (Cambridge: Harvard University Press, 2004), 82.
44. Secor, "Grand Old Policy," p. H5.
45. Gaddis, *Surprise, Security, and the American Experience*, 83.
46. Ibid., 83-84.
47. Secor, "Grand Old Policy," p. H5.
48. *Rumsfeld at War*, Fox News, March 19, 2004.
49. Warren Bennis and Burt Nanus, *Leaders: The Strategies for Taking Charge* (New York: Harper & Row, 1985), 33.
50. Ibid., 36.
51. Bush, *We Will Prevail*, 108-109.
52. Ibid., 214.
53. Tom Peters, *Thriving on Chaos: Handbook for a Management Revolution* (New York: Harper & Row, 1987), 485-486.
54. Bush, *We Will Prevail*, 161.
55. Ibid.
56. Peter F. Drucker, *Managing in a Time of Great Change* (New York: Truman Talley/ Dutton, 1995), 60.
57. Bush, *We Will Prevail*, 108.
58. Kouzes and Posner, *Credibility*, 16.
59. Peters, *Thriving on Chaos*, 484.
60. Donald Lambro, "To Mars and Beyond," *Washington Times* National Weekly Edition, January 26-February 1, 2004, p. 29.
61. "Remarks by the President on U.S. Space Policy," NASA Headquarters, Washington, D.C., January 13, 2004, www.whitehouse.gov.
62. Kouzes and Posner, *Credibility*, 226.
63. "Bush's Baghdad Surprise," *Weekly Standard*, December 15, 2003, p. 4.

64. Kouzes and Posner, *Credibility*, 230.
65. *Bush's Thanksgiving Surprise Trip*, Fox News, November 27, 2003.
66. Howard S. Friedman and Judith E. Hall, "Nonverbal Expression of Emotion: Healthy Charisma or Coronary-Prone Behavior," in Craig Van Dyke et al., eds., *Emotions in Health and Illness: Applications to Clinical Practice* (New York: Grune & Stratton, 1984), 158-160.
67. Jane M. Howell and Boas Shamir, "The Role of Followers in the Charasmatic Leadership Process: Relationships and Their Consequences," *Academy of Management Review*, vol. 30, No. 1, 2005, p. 99.
68. Bennis and Nanus, *Leaders*, 223-224.
69. Kouzes and Posner, *Credibility*, 14-15.
70. Bush, "Compassionate Conservatism," p. 642.
71. Bush, *We Will Prevail*, 14.
72. Ibid., 14-15.
73. Ibid., 15.
74. Irving J. Rein, "Campaigns," in Thomas O. Sloane, ed., *Encyclopedia of Rhetoric* (Oxford: Oxford University Press, 2001), 80.
75. Nicholas Emler and Tina Cook, "Moral Integrity in Leadership," in Brent W. Roberts and Robert Hogan, eds., *Personality Psychology in the Workplace* (Washington, D.C.: American Psychological Association, 2002), 290.
76. Stephen Mansfield "How the President Found God," *Charisma*, October 2003, p. 59.
77. Suzanne Fields, "Standing on Lincoln's Shoulders," *Washington Times* National Weekly Edition, December 15-21, 2003, p. 29.
78. "Remarks by the President on Iraqi Threat," Cincinnati Museum Center, Cincinnati, Ohio, October 7, 2002, www.whitehouse.gov.
79. Bush, *We will Prevail*, 220.
80. Ibid., 224.
81. Ibid., 225.
82. Ibid., 226-227.
83. Ibid., 233.
84. Ibid., 236.
85. Ibid., 251.
86. Ibid.
87. Oliver North, "Byrd Droppings Stain Democrats," *Washington Times* National Weekly Edition, May 19-25, 2003, p. 33.
88. Ibid.
89. Tommy Franks, *American Soldier* (New York: Regan Books, 2004), 523-524.
90. Bush, *We Will Prevail*, 260.
91. Bush, "Compassionate Conservatism," 645.
92. George W. Bush, *A Charge to Keep* (New York: William Morrow, 1999), 236.
93. Robert Weissberg, "Mr. Pinocchio Goes to Washington: Lying in Politics," *Social Philosophy & Policy*, Winter 2004, p. 177.

94. Ibid.
95. Karen Hughes, *Ten Minutes from Normal* (New York: Viking, 2004), 113-114.
96. "U.S. Stock Markets Suffer Record Losses," *Editorials on File*, April 1-15, 2000, p. 544.
97. Ibid., 545.
98. George Marotta, "Is the U.S. on a Huge Bubble?," *Vital Speeches of the Day*, April 15, 2000, p. 413.
99. Ibid., p. 414.
100. Alan Greenspan, "Structural Changes in the Economy and Financial Markets," *Vital Speeches of the Day*, December 15, 2000, p. 130. Italics added.
101. "Remarks by the President to Southwest Michigan First Coalition/Kalamazoo Chamber of Commerce Joint Event on the Economy," Western Michigan University, Kalamazoo, Michigan, March 27, 2001, www.whitehouse.gov.
102. Zell Miller, *A Deficit of Decency*, (Macon: Stroud & Hall, 2005), 32-33.

Chapter 5
The Bush Intelligence Factor Reappraised

We seek individuals who not only can analyze but also will do the right thing; individuals who will be admirable not only as thinkers or creators but also as human beings.
— Howard Gardner, *The Disciplined Mind*

What kind of person does America need in the White House in the first decade of the 21st century? Well, someone who knows that we and our allies are at war with a formidable enemy—an enemy that hates our values, culture, form of government, and, most of all, freedom and liberty that stem from a democratic process; someone who truly understands that an enemy that targets civilians for terrorist attacks cannot be bought off, negotiated with, appeased, or restrained by discussions at the United Nations; someone who grasps the reality that Islamic extremist groups, like al Qaeda, are motivated by a political-theological ideology that can influence young men and women to commit suicide; someone who has enough common sense to know that cutting taxes strengthens the economy and, in the long run, creates jobs, whereas increasing taxes—the Democrats' propensity—has the opposite effect; and someone who takes on the tough, and politically risky issues, such as immigration, social security, tax-code reform, traditional marriage protection, and health care, instead of burying such issues after the campaign speeches are over.

That "someone" must be a person who has certain capacities that enable him to shift cognitively from one issue or subject to another with energy and concentration to meet the demands of high-stakes decision-making. Moreover, that "someone" must have developed a worldview that sees America's interests in the world from a broad perspective, that recognizes the opportunities and dangers in a world that, seemingly, grows smaller with every high-tech breakthrough. In other words, the nation needs a leader in the White House whose character, mind, personality, and style are a good fit for the leadership challenges of the present age in which we live.

That "someone" is George W. Bush who has demonstrated, in dealing with several national crises, that the knowledge and skills that he has brought to the office of the president are those that are needed at this time in our country's history. He appears to possess the requisite kinds of intelligence that, according to Howard Gardner's research, contribute significant characteristics and abilities to persons in leadership positions. George Santayana, the American philosopher, defined intelligence in a way that makes one think of President Bush. He said, "Intelligence is quickness in seeing things as they are."

Howard Gardner, Harvard professor of cognition and education and the leading exponent of the theory of multiple intelligences, posits four intelligences that he says "are crucial to leaders." These are (1) *linguistic intelligence*, (2) *interpersonal intelligence*, (3) *intrapersonal intelligence*, and (4) *existential intelligence*.[1] They provide—along with *space intelligence*—a framework for discussing Bush as an intelligent leader who engenders confidence in his leadership.

Bush's Linguistic Intelligence

According to Gardner, *linguistic intelligence* is displayed in several ways, including the ability to gain "useful information" through "skilled questioning and discussion with others;" and by the ability "to convince others of a course of action through the use of stories, speeches, or exhortations."[2]

First, President Bush has the required linguistic intelligence that he shows by his ability to present a story that frames events and possibilities that help followers to see the world and their places in it differently. "In telling stories, leaders create dramatic narratives about themselves, their families, their people, and their nations," writes Gardner. "Such narratives can be compelling, for they draw listeners into the sweep of history, causing them to identify with and make common cause with their leader."[3]

President Bush brings together various elements to create the story of the fight against terrorists—scattered across 60 countries, he reminds us—which he has compellingly presented as "the first war of the 21st century." The rhetorical challenge that he faces is to make the story of the fight against terrorists relevant to the interests, needs, and aspirations of his audiences. Bush strives to keep the memory of the story of the 9/11 attacks in the minds of people who may think they have the luxury of forgetting them, since homeland security, so far, has prevented further attacks. Gardner says stories have a protagonist, goals, obstacles to overcome, and strategies for achieving the goals.[4] Each of these elements is evident in a speech Bush delivered to the nation on November 8, 2001, in Atlanta, Georgia. Notice in the following excerpt, how he wove them together with the thread of American values:

> Our great national challenge is to hunt down the terrorists and strengthen our protection against future attacks. Our great national opportunity is to preserve forever the good that has resulted. Through this tragedy, we are renewing and reclaiming our strong American values.
>
> Both Laura and I were touched by a recent newspaper article that quoted a little four-year-old girl, who asked a telling and innocent question. Wondering how terrorists could hate a whole nation of people they don't even know, she asked, "Why don't we just tell them our names?" (Laughter) Well, we can't tell them all our names—but together we can show them our values.
>
> Too many have the wrong idea of Americans as shallow, materialistic consumers who care only about getting rich or getting ahead. But this isn't the America I know. Ours is a wonderful nation, full of kind and loving people; people of faith who want freedom and opportunity for people everywhere. One way to defeat terrorism is to show the world the true values of America through the gathering momentum of a million acts of responsibility and decency and service.

> I'm encouraging schoolchildren to write letters of friendship to Muslim children in different countries. Our college students and those who travel abroad for business or vacation can all be ambassadors of American values. Ours is a great story, and we must tell it—through our words and through our deeds.[5]

In his 1999 book *Intelligence Reframed: Multiple Intelligences for the 21st Century*, Gardner selected the former British prime minister (1979-1990) Margaret Thatcher as a good example of a leader with linguistic intelligence. According to Gardner, Thatcher's leadership brought renewal to Great Britain, so that it became once again "a nation proud, independent, patriotic, and capable of acting on its own energies and values." She inspired the British to buy into her story of renewal. "Thatcher did not just tell a story well;" Gardner emphasized, "she embodied the story." He would have us know, "She also proved courageous, by taking a risky course in the 1982 Falkland-Malvinas War and by surviving a terrorist bomb attack . . . in Brighton. As the contemporary phrasemakers put it, she 'walked the talk'."[6]

By contrast with this world leader, Gardner said of our 42nd president: "President Bill Clinton is a brilliant storyteller, but he tends to tell too many stories, and it is not clear which ones he truly believes and genuinely embodies."[7] Much the same could be said of John Kerry, as he campaigned for the presidency in 2004.

For Bush, there is no pretense or playacting; he genuinely embodies the story of the fight against terrorists that he communicates to a world slowly awakening to its lessons. The attacks of 9/11 and his subsequent visit to Ground Zero shortly afterward has had an indelible impact on his mind, heart, and soul. Fighting terrorists while protecting America has become a sacred commitment for George W. Bush.

Gardner warns against the practice of some leaders who "craft a story simply to satisfy an audience." Such leaders "are likely to be seen as inauthentic or, worse, hypocritical."[8] As research cited in Chapter 3 showed, audiences are quite adept at detecting sincere speakers from insincere speakers. When you listen to President Bush speak, you realize that, whether he or a speechwriter originated his remarks, his words are in tune with his beliefs. Americans appreciate a president who says what he believes.

"Like [President] Reagan," Jay Nordlinger, Managing Editor of *National Review*, observes about President Bush, "he speaks as though he believes what he is saying—because he actually does."[9]

A linguistically-intelligent leader also is able to use language to achieve important goals. Certainly, Bush has shown this capability in a variety of ways. One way he has used his linguistic skills is to get important legislation passed in Congress. In lining up votes for key bills that reflect his agenda, he has had to make his arguments to both liberal Republicans and liberal Democrats. Some readers will remember how he worked with Senator Kennedy in drafting the "No Child Left Behind Act," which he signed into law. Of course, as the '04 election drew nearer, Kennedy became increasingly hostile in his remarks against the Commander in Chief. Vice President Dick Cheney, who has held important positions in three presidential administrations, told *U.S. News*: "A lot of what a president does is to exercise shared responsibility—most of the time, with Congress, whether it's getting a budget approved or a major piece of legislation authorized."[10] This is not an easy task for a president who wants to get things done. Convincing members of the House of Representatives and the Senate to put aside political caculations and share in that responsibility, is a major test of a president's verbal skills and leadership in general. In spite of the obstructiveness of the Democratic leadership, President Bush has met this test well. For example, when it came to cutting taxes—something that Democrats are reluctant to do—he effectively exercised his influence. Speaking on February 19, 2004 on the economy, he said, "I convinced the Congress to cut the taxes."[11]

Cheney also made the point in his *U.S. News* interview that when the president gets "into the military arena . . . , in effect, as commander in chief, that's not a shared responsibility." Then, he noted, "You've got to bring the Congress along."[12] When, in the fall and winter of 2002, President Bush began to prepare for war with Iraq, he mustered up strong support among Democrats and Republicans. A majority of the Democratic senators voted for the resolution that authorized the President to use force against Iraq, including John Edwards and John Kerry. Doubtless, this outcome required much behind-the-scenes persuasion by the President.

Another way President Bush has used his linguistic skills is to establish close working relationships with other national leaders. He invites presidents and prime ministers of various countries to the White House, where he and Laura Bush meet with them in formal and informal situations. During such visits, Bush can get better acquainted with his foreign counterpart and work out agreements and deal with areas of disagreements. Often at the close of the visit, both leaders hold a combined press conference. Bush usually begins by paying tribute to the visiting president or prime minister. In March 2003 at Camp David, Maryland, President Bush introduced Tony Blair as follows:

> Thank you all. It's my honor to welcome my friend and Prime Minister of Great Britain, Tony Blair, back to Camp David. America has learned a lot about Tony Blair over the last weeks. We've learned that he's a man of his word. We've learned that he's a man of courage, that he's a man of vision. And we're proud to have him as a friend.[13]

When Blair spoke, he said:

> Thank you, Mr. President, and thank you for your welcome. Thank you for your strength and for your leadership at this time. And I believe the alliance between the United States and Great Britain has never been in better or stronger shape.[14]

Toward the end of his remarks, Blair noted, "It is, indeed, often overlooked that President Bush is the first U.S. President publicly to commit himself to a two-state solution, an Israel confident of its security and a viable Palestinian state."[15]

Bush has also traveled to other nations to meet with their leaders and give speeches on his post-9/11 vision for America and the world. He has visited such nations as Russia, Japan, Spain, Australia, and Great Britain and, in speeches delivered, stressed the unity and cooperation that has existed between America and the nation visited. He has retained the friendship and support of the leaders who joined the coalition against Iraq, even though they have faced the opposition of protesters and politicians in their countries for standing with America in the war against terrorists.

Doubtless, the fact that the Bushes periodically entertain world leaders at their ranch in Crawford, Texas stems from their desire to create a calm, relaxed atmosphere, conducive to developing relationships that produce straight talk and clear reflection. The ranch provides a shirt-sleeve environment that encourages a guest to be himself. The first world leader invited to the "Texas White House" was Russian President Vladimir Putin. It has been reported that Bush felt that the visit deepened their friendship. At a local school where the two briefly appeared, Putin remarked that he had learned that he could count on what President Bush said. Since Putin's visit, Bush has hosted several foreign leaders at the ranch, including Blair, Saudi Crown Prince Abdullah, Jiang Zemin, President of China, Mexican president Vincente Fox; and, at Camp David, Pakistani President Pervez Musharraf. In an appearance on *Special Report with Brit Hume*, in February 2004, prize-winning journalist Charles Krauthammer commented that Bush's relationship with Musharraf has proven to be vital in the war on terrorism. Bush "feels that inviting someone to his home—the White House and especially the ranch—is something very special and personal,"[16] a senior White House official observed.

A third way that President Bush has shown a high level of linguistic ability to achieve his goals is by his management of meetings with Republican leadership, Cabinet and Congressional. Former Treasury Secretary Paul H. O'Neill—who was fired in December 2002 by President Bush—made a statement in a recently-published book *The Price of Loyalty* that takes issue with this assessment. He said that Bush ran his Cabinet meetings "like a blind man in a room full of deaf people."[17] He soon repudiated the statement on television. Frankly, the style of this remark does not sound like it originated with O'Neill, an opinion that must be shared by anyone who has heard him speak—rather, it sounds as if someone supplied it to a man embittered by the embarrassment of public failure. Former National Economic Council Director Lawrence Lindsey, who was let go at the same time as O'Neill, writing in the *Wall Street Journal*, said, "his bitterness, some would say, is quite understandable. But bitterness is a bad basis for objectivity, and any of Mr. O'Neill's views regarding President Bush and the conduct of economic policy do not comport with my recollection or with the public record."[18] To refute O'Neill, Lindsey went on to say:

> Every night, the president goes home with a two-inch binder known as the Briefing Book. It contains the background material for each of the president's numerous meetings the next day. Having been grilled on the details in those briefing memos, I can personally attest that Mr. Bush does his homework. Woe is any official who is not prepared, because the president will be.[19]

Karen Hughes, former Communications Director for President Bush, who gives evidence of having high linguistic intelligence herself, recalls meetings with, then, Governor Bush. She writes,

> I've sat in on countless policy briefings and discussions with him; he always asks the best questions, the ones that get right to the heart of the matter. We used to joke in the 1994 campaign that no matter how much we all studied and tried to know every fact before a new policy announcement, Governor Bush could always find one question to stump us.[20]

We also have the testimony of an outsider, Dennis Prager, a nationally syndicated radio talk show host, columnist, and author, known to be tough-minded and not easily impressed. In January 2004, he and President Bush were the main speakers in Philadelphia at the annual meeting of Republican senators and congressmen, sponsored by the Congressional Institute. Prager later wrote about the qualities he observed in President Bush:

> I realize that I open myself to ridicule by saying that everything I had suspected about the man was reinforced in a little over a minute and in the subsequent behind-closed-doors speech to the Republican congressional leadership. But it was. And that is not all.
>
> There is also his calm and dignity. After eight years of the look-at-me-and-adore-me presidency of his predecessor, it is almost too good to be true that a president does not make himself or regard himself as the center of the world in every encounter. It is clear that he knows the awesome responsibility resting on his

> presidential shoulders and that he believes that it is the presidency, not he, that must be the focus of admiration and attention.
>
> But what most impressed me—given that I assumed those qualities prior to meeting him—was the president's intelligence and clarity of vision.
>
> In his hour-long talk, including a long question and answer session, I watched a man speak on the widest variety of domestic and international issues without any notes, without any teleprompter, without any hesitation, and with passionate conviction.
>
> Those who believe that a Bush re-election is indispensable to a better world can only pray that the Democrats continue to regard George W. Bush as intellectually challenged. He never was, and he has grown in these past four years . . .[21]

Chris Wallace, who went from ABC to Fox News, was interviewed on October 31 by Brian Lamb on C-SPAN's *Booknotes*. He told about attending a White House luncheon for reporters to hear George W. Bush preview his 2004 "State of the Union Address." He said that the popular image of the President "portrayed in the press that he does not have a mastery of detail" was exploded by hearing him speak. "He was very conversant in the details of policy, very conversant," Wallace emphasized. He demonstrated "a command and a professionalism of a person who ran the show that I had never seen before." Americans rejected the elite press' false image of Bush's linguistic intelligence, and voted for his reelection.

Bush's Interpersonal Intelligence

Second, Bush has the required *interpersonal intelligence*, which political leaders often lack in their competence makeup. As this kind of intelligence predicts, Bush has interpersonal skills that he enjoys using in relating to others; and an understanding of the feelings and aspirations of people, which enhances his ability to influence them. "Interpersonal intelligence," Gardner emphasizes, "denotes a person's capacity to understand the intentions, motivations, and desires of other people and, consequently, to work effectively with others."[22]

President Bush shows that he understands people's feelings and aspirations by praising them for their contributions. Ralph Reed, former head of the Christian Coalition, speaking with radio talk-show host Tom Sullivan, sitting in for Rush Limbaugh, in November 2003, observed, "Wherever President Bush goes to speak, he honors someone, including those who may have voted against him . . . . He has elevated the tone of public discourse."[23] A search of the President's speeches revealed numerous complimentary references to political leaders in Congress and around the country. Such leaders included Gephardt, Daschle, and Senator Ted Kennedy, who subsequently made outrageous statements about him, possibly attempting to put him on the defensive, which failed.

Basic to the use of effective interpersonal skills is the trait of empathy that we see when a person has a deeply-felt understanding of what others might be thinking and feeling. Such a person instinctively knows what to say when others face a difficult situation. By all reports, President Bush has this trait.

For example, Lisa Beamer, in her book *Let's Roll*, describes the meeting that the President and First Lady Laura Bush had with the families of the victims of Flight 93—her husband, Todd Beamer, had yelled, "Let's roll!" when he led passengers in a fight to defeat the terrorists by crashing Flight 93 before it could be used as a guided missile. Beamer says that the meeting was a private one, without reporters or cameras. She writes; "President Bush spoke kindly and compassionately to the entire group [of surviving family members of Flight 93] in the East Room of the White House. He used no notes and spoke from the heart, almost conversationally."[24] Beamer tells how the President spent time with each family. "The President and first lady met with our family for eight to ten minutes, greeting each one of us and offering words of encouragement. In a rather refreshing twist, President Bush didn't offer the usual condolences, such as 'I'm sorry for your loss,' or something similar. Instead," she said, "he offered words of praise and appreciation, thanking us for the way we were handling the situation dropped in our laps as a result of September 11. As he spoke, however, his eyes were moist with tears." She adds, "Beyond the President's kind and inspiring words, the fact that he would take time to meet with us in the midst of such a serious crisis spoke volumes to our family."[25]

As we see George W. Bush interact with individuals, we sense that he genuinely likes to relate to people, unlike politicians who must force themselves to show interest in others in seeking votes. Bush seems always ready to help young and old to aspire, such as when he talks with entrepreneurs, or to give support to people when tragedy has struck them. Karen Hughes gives an insider's view of the charismatic leader when he was governor of Texas:

> I've seen Governor Bush stay for an hour after a graduation speech to shake the hand of every graduate. I have waited as he talked with every one of the hundreds of people who came to see him at huge community receptions. I've walked through countless hotel kitchens and back door entrances to buildings with him; he always stops to talk with the cooks, janitors, and elevator operators. He smiles, shakes hands, and establishes a warm and immediate connection. I never know how he does it; the people know it is genuine and heartfelt. He has hugged and comforted people after terrible floods, tornadoes, and fires. He attended church in Jarrell the Sunday after the devastating tornado there; he didn't speak or grandstand, he simply attended the service to lend his prayers and comfort.[26]

In word and action, we see President Bush reaching out to people, not for favors, but in friendship.

From the beginning of his presidency to the present, George W. Bush has devoted his linguistic and interpersonal skills to the task of unifying the nation, as he had done in Texas with considerable success. He has reached out to Democrats in Congress and groups that have traditionally voted Democratic in seeking support for his agenda, including his Faith-Based and Community Initiative. His appointees in the Cabinet and federal agencies are representative of many groups in American society. He seeks to select the best people for government posts or the judiciary, without regard for gender, race, ethnicity, or age. "Bush appointed women to more influential positions than any prior president." And he "appointed substantially more minorities than all three predecessors, and at the highest echelons . . ."[27] He doubtless prefers to have as many groups represented as possible, so that a pluralistic society can identify with its government. After George W. Bush was elected Governor of Texas, he made his friend

Clay Johnson his Appointments Director. In his autobiography, Bush writes: "Diversity is another consideration. I don't believe in quotas or racial preferences, but I instructed Clay to seek and recruit qualified appointees who reflect the diversity of Texas."[28] He assembled an excellent administrative team in Texas, as he has in Washington, D.C.

However, not long after he took office, he became the target of attacks by Congressional Democrats, the Democratic National Committee (DNC), and the liberal media, which sought to undermine his efforts to bring people and political parties together. The attacks have continued, except for a brief interruption following the terrorist attacks of 9/11. In other words, the Democrats started their campaign in 2001 to retake the White House in 2004. Their tactics would make someone with the ethics of the late Senator Huey Long blush. Yet in spite of the low level to which their tactics have sunk, President Bush has maintained his emphasis on national unity and bipartisanship in Congress which the passage of a number of key bills demonstrates.

Not surprisingly, when the 2004 election was about eight months off, the liberal media sought to label Bush a "divisive president."[29] On CBS, Bob Schieffer called the President "a polarizing president," and on ABC, correspondent Terry Moran, sitting in on *This Week* for George Stephanopoulos, said that Bush, in 2000, campaigned as "a uniter, not a divider" and failed.[30] On ABC, in answering a question from Moran, Leon Panetta, former Clinton Chief of Staff, declared, "For many Americans, this is a divisive president."[31] Schieffer acknowledged that, as Texas Governor, Bush did apparently bring the people together, but now, the newscaster said, he "seems to have become someone you either love or hate."[32] *Time* carried the same slogan on its cover of December 1, 2003. However, by separating the electorate into just two camps, the result is a classic *black-or-white* fallacy, often based on a disjunctive premise: "Either you love Bush or you hate Bush." Doubtless, there are lovers and haters, but there are also switchers, the undecided, the uninformed, and the third-party supporters. One also might consider the significant number of citizens who decide not to vote for president for a variety of reasons.

The death of former President Ronald Reagan inspired a number of journalistic comparisons between Reagan and George W. Bush. Kenneth Walsh in *U.S. News* authored such an effort. He wrote, "Bush, his opponents contend, is more divisive than Reagan, who worked with Congressional Democrats and tried to avoid making enemies."[33] Contrary to what these unnamed "opponents" charge, Bush, like Reagan, reached out to Democrats in Congress. Writing in *Presidential Studies Quarterly*, Corey Cook stated:

> Promising to "change the tone" in Washington, Bush initially reached out to members of Congress. In the first three weeks of his term, before traveling outside the district, Bush invited scores of members of Congress to the White House, including both majority and minority party leaders, key congressional education policy makers [such as Ted Kennedy], members of the House and Senate Budget committees, the Congressional Black Caucus, and freshman members . . .[34]

During the eight months leading up to 9/11, President Bush continued to make an effort to work with both Democrats and Republicans in Congress. In a *National Journal* article of September 22, 2001, Carl Cannon and Alexis Simendinger, recorded:

> Bush has repeatedly said he wants to lower the volume and vitriol of partisan dialogue in this city. This determination turns out to be worth more than just style points. Much has been made in the days since the [9/11] crisis about how Democrats and Republicans have set aside their differences and rallied around the nation and the President. But the fact that during his first eight months in office Bush eschewed personal attacks—even while some were directed at him—has made this easy for Democrats to do, both politically and personally.
>
> In other words, the bipartisan airs weren't just for show; the cooperation has brought tangible results.[35]

Unfortunately, the bipartisan cooperation that Bush sought and briefly enjoyed after 9/11, soon disappeared as the Democrats with their friends in the media began to revise history by accusing the President of divisiveness.

Democratic candidates adopted the divisive tactic with enthusiasm. Primary contender Senator John Edwards suggested that Bush had divided the country into "two Americas," one rich and one poor. On February 3, 2004, Kerry, speaking in Seattle, portrayed Bush as divisive, saying that he had driven "a wedge between people."[36]

President Bush's detractors know that if they label him a "divider" rather than a "uniter" and repeat it "long enough," as columnist Cal Thomas observed, "some people will believe it."[37] In politics, an old and mean tactic is to try to portray an opponent's strength as being just the opposite to what it actually is—so a president who seeks to unite people is portrayed as one who divides them. The Left has tried to do the same thing regarding George W. Bush's intelligence.

A politician who finds close contacts with the public difficult and must, therefore, force himself to meet and talk with individuals, reveals nonverbally a lack of interpersonal intelligence. Most unbiased observers would likely say that John Kerry is weak in this kind of intelligence; he appears stiff and aloof, which became evident during his campaign for the White House. But, the same observers would likely say that George W. Bush is strong in this kind of intelligence. Even some people who retain and present negative images of Bush imply this. For example, journalist Mike Stanton at Brown University, in September 2003 on C-SPAN, after characterizing Bush's image at the beginning of his 2000 campaign against Gore as "this shallow playboy, frat [type]," conceded that he "did know how to work a room . . . . People liked him."[38] One might add that the voters in Texas who elected Bush twice as their governor by healthy margins, would not have stereotyped him in college-freshman terms.

Rather than to acknowledge Bush's interpersonal skills by saying he can "work a room," it would be truer to say that he has the natural ability to relate to people wherever he encounters them, and they instinctively know it; he can adapt to individuals' moods and feelings instantly, with a sincere desire to recognize their worth as fellow human beings—moreover, his interpersonal contacts are enhanced by the charismatic charm of his personality.

We saw this adaptive ability illustrated at the memorial service for the crew of the space shuttle *Columbia*, when President Bush showed sensitivity and kindness by assisting Evelyn Husband and her son Matthew in a simple but revealing act. Her husband, Rick Husband had commanded the lost space shuttle *Columbia*. The President provided moral support by sitting next to her in the front row of the audience. "At one point in the service," she recalled, "Matthew sneezed, and I could see out of the corner of my eye that he needed a Kleenex." Her young daughter Laura was sitting between her and Matthew and unable to help. Under the glare of many cameras, she reached across Laura and tried inconspicuously to rub her son's nose, which did not solve the problem. She was feeling helpless and embarrassed, when President Bush asked, "Do you need a handkerchief?" She whispered, "That would be great." Husband recounts, "The president took his handkerchief out of his pocket and handed it to me, and I slid it across Laura to Matthew . . . . I never once in my life thought that the president of the United States would help me wipe my son's nose on national television, but he was very gracious."[39] Minutes later, the President got up to deliver an address to a world audience. Bush's ability to shift his attention from the big presidential problems that he faced, to a problem that he did not feel was beneath his notice since it was big to the young widow beside him, revealed an interpersonal intelligence that looked deeply into people's needs.

In his interesting book *Changing Minds* (2004), Howard Gardner offered the following assessment: "George W. Bush seems to have been skilled at an early age in what I call *interpersonal intelligence*—the part of our intellectual equipment that is engaged in understanding and motivating other people. He likes other people, and he prides himself in getting to know them." He added, "Like other interpersonally skilled persons," President Bush has "confidence in his ability to get along with foreign leaders and to convince them to work together."[40]

The ability to communicate one-on-one effectively gives the political leader who has it a great advantage over opponents who do not have it. Of course, during a presidential campaign, a candidate must appear to be able to interact with voters to show that he is one of them. By "pressing the flesh," as President Harry Truman called handshaking, a candidate tries to convey the impression that he has similar interests, needs, and aspirations as those with whom he interacts. For their part, voters look for personal reasons to like and trust the candidate for the highest office on earth.

Bush's Intrapersonal Intelligence

Third, George W. Bush has the required *intrapersonal intelligence*, which involves a knowledge of one's strengths and weaknesses and their possible effects on others. Leaders endowed with this kind of intelligence "have an effective working model of oneself—including one's own desires, fears, and capacities—and to use such information effectively in regulating one's own life."[41] Such leaders get a lot done. They are able to reflect on the personal course they have charted, as well as on decisions they have made; they have the courage to make tough decisions.[42]

Gardner rightly combines intrapersonal intelligence with interpersonal intelligence as "two forms of personal intelligence."[43] Their relationship becomes obvious in the act of communication with other persons. Before we communicate interpersonally with another person, we communicate intrapersonally with self—in a kind of inner dialogue. "The way we present ourselves to others, what we think of ourselves, our moral and ethical judgments, and our perception of, and adjustment to, people all involve intrapersonal communication."[44]

We see evidence of leaders' intrapersonal intelligence in their ability to show consistency of purpose and belief in their decisions, which reflect an effective inner model of self. And they do so with the confidence born of a strong sense of personal identity, rooted in a healthy emotional life. Leaders need such qualities to withstand the complaints and criticisms that a high intrapersonal intelligence is likely to generate.

A leader who has a strong sense of identity based on an effective working model of self is likely to be someone who is consistent, even predictable. This is an apt description of George W. Bush. Upon seeing him in person or on television, one feels that this man knows who he is—that the inward model and the outward man have a close correspondence. This is because the model and the man are joined by core values that sensitize, motivate, prioritize, and energize Bush's actions in respect to others, whether individuals in particular or human beings in general.

A leader like Bush with high intrapersonal intelligence knows himself well enough to keep certain emotions and attitudes in check, so that they do not cloud his judgment concerning what actions are required in dealing with a particular situation. Presidents who lack such intelligence, may, for example, miss an opportunity to act due to the interference of certain emotions and attitudes that rise in defense of their ego. This may be especially the case when their policies come under attack. But President Bush has stood firm on his domestic and foreign policy agenda, in spite of critical reviews and dire predictions by politicians and pundits, who often see his policies from a twentieth-century worldview. Jay Ambrose, Director of Editorial Policy of Scripps Howard Newspapers, insightfully speaks to this point: "In what he has done in Afghanistan and Iraq, Mr. Bush has had to shake free of all sorts of attitudes and concepts that may have made sense in other eras, but not in the wake of September 11, 2001."[45] Ambrose understands what it has taken to accomplish this. He says, "He had to have the courage and determination to stay the course despite endless second-guessing at home and sniping by self-interested allies." He notes, "It is when you listen to his critics that you most keenly see what he has been up against."[46]

A president endowed with linguistic, interpersonal, and intrapersonal intelligences, has an enhanced capacity to make decisions for the protection of our nation and the spiritual, social, and economic well-being of our society; he can competently decide to take any action deemed necessary. Since taking office, President Bush has demonstrated that capacity many times. He understands that not to decide is a decision in itself, that hesitation in decision-making may prove disastrous in a world in which cause and effect have become almost simultaneous. Bush, intellectually, is prepared to use, with the backing of Congress, the full authority of his position in dealing with or preventing crises. When he had been in office for about a year, an aide asked him if the crises that had occurred had changed him, to which he answered that they had not. "Presidents either come to the Oval Office equipped and ready to deal with crises or they don't," Bush said, and then added, "If you're strong and firm, people follow."[47] Condoleezza Rice, while national security advisor, observed, "He wasn't born somebody else on September 11."[48] A highly-respected Democratic senator, Zell Miller of Georgia, in his book *A National Party No More: The Conscience of a Conservative Democrat*, wrote:

> I like the fact that the Bush White House is not timid about making a decision and does not suffer from "analysis paralysis,"

> the malady that is common to those learned people "who know so much and can see all sides." Unfortunately, these mostly well-intentioned persons see so many shades of gray, they often miss the black and white. And that is what is called for today.[49]

A leader with a strong intrapersonal life is likely to know when he is in the right, which then may lead him to the courage to act. For presidents to act in many of today's situations takes moral courage, since whatever he decides is likely to prove controversial in some quarters, especially in an election year. Take President Bush's decision to endorse an amendment to the Constitution stating that marriage in the U.S. shall consist only of the union of a man and a woman. Democrats were quick to condemn the President's decision. Kerry, in a February "debate" with Edwards in Los Angeles called Bush a "polarizing president" for taking such a stand. He said that states should decide the issue, but he voted against the Defense of Marriage Act of 1996 that would allow states to do just that.[50]

In contrast to Kerry's position on the issue, Dr. Jerry Falwell, minister and founder of Liberty University, on Fox's *Hannity and Colmes*, enthusiastically supported the President's stand on a marriage protection amendment, calling it a "courageous decision." He ranked it as one of two important events of the week of February 22, 2004—the other was the release of the film *The Passion of the Christ*.[51] On Liberty University's website, for February 25, 2004, Dr. Falwell stated: "Those who believe in the sacred foundations of marriage lauded Mr. Bush's willingness to enter the present controversy by boldly voicing his support of the man-woman institution of marriage that has been at the core of civilization."[52]

Great national leaders with demonstrated intrapersonal intelligence can reflect on the personal course they have charted and make difficult, sometimes unpopular decisions that rise above thoughts of personal or political risk—such leaders have the courage of their convictions, in the tradition of Margaret Thatcher, Ronald Reagan, Tony Blair, and George W. Bush. When President Bush took the fight to the terrorists in Afghanistan and Iraq, he displayed high moral courage. For attacking Iraq, he was accused by his Democratic rivals of playing politics, even of exaggerating the threat of terrorism. But, in fact, they have it backwards. Bush would have played politics had he stopped the war against terrorism after the impressive victory in Afghanistan, given a speech to the U.N., and waited and waited and waited for inspectors in Iraq to locate illegal weapons, programs for their development, and facilities for such. (If anyone is in doubt about the necessity of war in Iraq, he or she should read "The Right War for the Right Reasons" by Robert Kagan and William Kristol in *The Weekly Standard*, February 23, 2004.) General Douglas MacArthur, who spoke from experience, asserted:

> Last, but by no means least, courage—moral courage, [is] the courage of one's convictions, the courage to see things through. The world is in constant conspiracy against the brave. It's the age-old struggle—the roar of the crowd on one side and the voice of your conscience on the other.[53]

Leaders whose intrapersonal intelligence enhances their ability to regulate their own lives, accomplish a lot. Whether or not one approves of all of President Bush's legislation and initiatives, one must admit that he gets things done. As any humane person ought to see, he focuses on citizens who need help—the ban on partial-birth abortion, accountability in educating our children, tax cuts to foster jobs and assist low-income families, assistance for millions of seniors who can't afford prescription drugs, establishment of a Department of Homeland Security to help make us safer, a faith-based and community initiative to assist religious organizations to help children and adults, to name a few. Are all of them perfect? No. Can some of them be improved? Yes, in time. Is it better to do something about the problems they focus on, rather than to do nothing? Yes! Samuel Johnson, the great English author and critic, reminds us, "Nothing will ever be attempted if all possible objections must be first overcome." George W. Bush is probably the most results-oriented president in modern history. Concerning leaders' intelligence, Gardner says, "What matters enormously is the kind of work they carried out and how they carried it out, for that is the arena in which their ultimate contributions lie."[54] Bush agrees. In his news conference on November 4, 2004, he said that he was "focused on results." He emphasized, "I came here to get things done. And we are doing it."[55] Likely his achievements prompted Gardner to write, "I would say that [George W.] Bush has exhibited an impressive growth in intrapersonal intelligence during his years in high office."[56]

Bush's Existential Intelligence

Fourth, George W. Bush has the required *existential intelligence* that enables him to address existential questions about the meaning of individuals' existence, and thus "help audiences to understand their own life situations, clarify their goals, and feel engaged in a meaningful quest."[57] Gardner says that "the most effective leaders" can think and communicate in these terms. Moreover, they have the capacity to see their work in relation to "such existential features of the human condition as the significance of life, the meaning of death, the ultimate fate of the physical and psychological worlds, and such profound experiences as love of another person . . ."[58] Bush is typical of wartime presidents who draw on their faith in God in dealing with existential issues to which war naturally gives rise.

In prosecuting a war, presidents must make decisions that mean life or death, defeat or victory and live with the consequences. With the weight of such decisions on their shoulders, their belief in a higher power, a divine presence in their life gives them "the peace of God that passeth all understanding," as Paul writes in the "Epistle to the Philippians."[59] One president who led the country in a time of economic crisis and war was also a man who found strength in his religion—that man was Franklin D. Roosevelt. Rarely remembered as a leader with faith, nevertheless, "He held sincere religious convictions, and it was no mere gesture that led him to take his Cabinet, on the morn of his first inauguration, to divine service at St. John's."[60] Eleanor Roosevelt, looking back on her husband's religious faith, in *This I Remember*, wrote, "I think he actually felt he could ask God for guidance and receive it. That was why he loved the Twenty-third Psalm, the Beatitudes, and the thirteenth chapter of First Corinthians."[61] Roosevelt suggested good naturedly that the Lord, on occasion, would cause little things to go well to encourage him on and give him hope. When American and British troops hit the beaches of Normandy in June 1944 in the Allied invasion of Europe, Roosevelt led the nation in prayer in a radio broadcast.[62] Allan Nevins, Pulitzer Prize winning biographer and historian of Columbia University, in his essay on Roosevelt, found that his "most important quality of effective greatness lay in his ability to imbue Americans, and to some extent even citizens of other lands, with a new spiritual strength."[63] Roosevelt could help audiences to "feel engaged in a meaningful quest," because he lifted Americans, Nevins believed, "on the wings of the greatest adventure of our history [to that time], the effort to rescue democracy from totalitarianism, and to organize the world to safeguard freedom."[64] For F.D.R., "democracy" and "freedom" were words with existential meaning. In his last "Inaugural Address," he told Americans:

> The Almighty God has blessed our land in many ways. He has given our people stout hearts and strong arms . . . He has given to our country a faith that has become the hope of all peoples in an anguished world. So we pray to Him now for the vision to see our way clearly.[65]

Like Roosevelt, Bush finds his meaning in life in his Christian faith; he believes that God's purposes are realized in man's humble efforts to make life spiritually significant for other people. Unlike Roosevelt, however, Bush's faith is not only a resource of strength that inspires and emboldens him, it is the source of his commitment to his office and the primary influence on his outlook, policies, and rhetoric. His faith gives him a sense of mission in respect to his presidency. As Stephen Mansfield, in *The Faith of George W. Bush*, writes: "Bush continues to let faith frame his presidency. Indeed, it seems at times that politics takes a back seat to the religious imprint he hopes to make on the nation."[66] His mission—to make the nation more secure, including economically, and the world more peaceful by defeating terrorists—transcends politics, party, power, and personalities, all of uppermost importance to most political leaders. Always the gentleman, George W. Bush, called Kerry to congratulate him, following his sweep of the super Tuesday Democratic primaries. He told Kerry that he looked forward to their forthcoming debate. His mission is motivated by one driving force—to fulfill God's purpose for his life, which now is to serve the nation as president. Mansfield learned in an interview that, in a small gathering of ministers in the Oval Office, Bush said, "I'm not after the votes . . . . I am here, and I am in this room sharing concerns because someday I am going to stand before God, and I want to hear him say, 'Well done!' I hope that's why we're all here."[67]

The existential realm infuses Bush's rhetoric as a natural outcome of his faith. When he gave his "First Inaugural Address," he used a Biblical reference to the parable of the Good Samaritan, which Jesus told in response to the question, "Who is my neighbor?" Then describing America as compassionate, Bush pledged: "When we see that wounded traveler on the road to Jericho, we will not pass to the other side."[68] In offering that pledge, Bush knew that people's life situations were marked by suffering due to their own actions, or to the actions of others as in the case of the wounded traveler helped by the Samaritan. But, whatever the cause, he made it plain in his address that "Where there is suffering, there is duty."[69] Audiences can anticipate that Bush, much like a minister giving a benediction, will conclude his speeches by saying, "May God bless you all, and may God bless America."

Given the fact that the great majority of Americans believe in a divine being that most refer to as God, Bush's references to God's blessing doubtless brings comfort to many people in a time of war, when now the oceans no longer protect us from attacks as they did in Roosevelt's time. Many of us will recall how church attendance went up and liberals calmed their discordant complaints immediately after the 9/11 attacks. Even the A.C.L.U. showed some unusual restraint. Religion enjoyed new respectability in American social and political life. On our television, we saw leaders in Congress sing hymns on the Capitol steps and we heard that they introduced legislation that would make "God Bless America" the official national hymn. "What followed was a freer reign for religion in American society. Bush seemed to embody it. He prayed publicly and spoke of faith, divine destiny, and the nation's religious heritage more than he ever had."[70]

In a relatively brief time, however, many Americans lapsed into complacency about future attacks and regressed to a business-as-usual attitude; Democrats in Congress and in the press with the help of the D.N.C. made up for lost time by slinging mud at the Commander in Chief. There is an old Spanish proverb that says: "He who is in the mud likes to pull another into it." Unwilling to answer in kind, Bush continued to give his attention to the war, the economy, and key domestic issues. In each one of these, he, doubtless, saw God at work, given his belief "that God is in providential control over all that happens, including in his own life."[71]

In respect to the war on terrorism—more pointedly al Qaeda and related groups—Bush has the unalterable conviction that the Lord of hosts will enable America and her allies to defeat an obviously-evil enemy that justifies the mass murder of innocents on religious grounds—it is, in fact, a war between one ideology that values life and another one that glories in death. On September 20, 2001, President Bush, in his "Address to a Joint Session of Congress," warned America about the nature of the terrorist enemy: "Al Qaeda is to terror what the mafia is to crime. But its goal is not making money; its goal is remaking the world—and imposing its radical beliefs on people everywhere." He made his statement more concrete by saying, "They are the same murderers indicted for bombing American embassies in Tanzania and Kenya, and responsible for bombing the *USS Cole*."[72]

Does the goal that Bush imputes to al Qaeda sound overstated? Daniel Philpott, political science professor at the University of Notre Dame, states the following:

> In forming the ideology of the al-Qaeda movement, [Osama] bin Laden drew from radical revivalist themes in both Qtub's thought and Saudi Wahabbism. Al-Qaeda is exceptional among revivalists in proclaiming the goal of establishing a pan-Islamic caliphate throughout the world . . . . It proposes to accomplish its goal by working with allied Islamic extremist groups to overthrow regimes it deems "non-Islamic" and expelling Westerners and non-Muslims from Muslim countries. In February 1998 it issued a statement under the banner of "The World Islamic Front for Jihad against the Jew and Crusaders," proclaiming ["In compliance with God's order"] it is the duty of all Muslims to kill U.S. citizens—including civilians—and their allies everywhere. Al-Qaeda, then, translates radical Islamic revivalism into a nation of jihad that is more ambitious and more violent than that of almost any other radical revivalist group.[73]

President Bush's intellectual capacity to think in existential terms—a Gardner requisite intelligence of leadership—intensified by his personal faith, is exactly what is needed in understanding and, ultimately, defeating al Qaeda and other Islamic extremist groups. He understands that the war must not only be fought with tactics, military forces, and weapons, but with powerful existential ideas of life and liberty that contradict ideas of control and death. On the day after the attacks on our homeland, Bush met with the press in the Cabinet Room with his security team present. In the course of his remarks, he cast the forthcoming conflict in religious language when he said, "This will be a monumental struggle of good versus evil, but good will prevail."[74] Mansfield makes the point that "If Bush had simply spoken of 9/11 as a 'terrorist act,' he would have left Americans believing that the whole matter could be handled by the FBI and local police."[75] That is probably what the previous occupant in the White House would have done. But, instead, Bush saw the big picture and understood that this was not simply a terrorist act, 9/11 was, as Prime Minister Tony Blair, on March 5, 2004, in Sedgefield, England, stated, "a declaration of war by religious fanatics." At the same time, Blair said that the threat of Islamic extremism "is real, dangerous, and existential."[76]

The liberal Democrats have been unwilling to recognize the nature and the threat posed by Islamic extremism, which, Philpott writes, has established itself as an "international system" in countries around the globe,[77] likely including the U.S. The liberal Democrats talk as if a policy of disengagement is preferable to the war Bush and Blair wage against an intractable enemy, political and theological in nature. The liberals accuse Bush—and, by extension, Blair and other national leaders—of exaggerating the threat of terrorism. John Kerry, the Democratic senator from Massachusetts, has been most direct in making this charge. When asked, during the Democratic presidential debate on January 29, 2004, whether President Bush has overstated the threat of terrorism, Kerry answered, "I think there has been an exaggeration. They are misleading all Americans in a profound way." He added, "This administration's arrogant and ideological policy is taking America down a more dangerous path."[78] In all fairness to Kerry, he may not be playing politics in taking a position that flies in the face of reality—the reality of more than 3,000 people killed on 9/11—it may be, instead, that he simply does not have the needed existential intelligence to understand the scope and nature of the terrorist threat, that Islamic extremism presents to U.S. security and world peace.

In Bush's "Whitehall Palace Speech" on November 19, 2003, in London, he reviewed the terrorist attacks on 9/11 and those in Bali, Jakarta, Casablanca, Bombay, Mombassa, Najaf, Jerusalem, Riyadh, Baghdad, and Istanbul.[79] Since then, Moscow and Madrid and London must be added to the list, and doubtless the list will grow.

Fortunately, Bush and Blair have the capacity to grasp the magnitude of the threat posed by terrorists and the underlying ideology that serves to recruit and motivate them. As Philpott emphasizes, "Most importantly, we must come to understand that these [Islamic extremist] groups are defined, constituted, and motivated by religious beliefs, beliefs about the ultimate ground of existence."[80]

As President Bush speaks to audiences all over the U.S. and addresses the nation on formal occasions, he often brings together the existential concerns of purpose and significance of life with the presidential issues of public policy. He sees the latter as good when it enhances the value of the former—policy that is "good" shows compassion for those citizens in our society who need help. For example, in 2001, when he signed his first tax-cut bill into law, Bush stated that "tax relief is compassionate," because it assists "families struggling to enter the middle class" and "middle-class families squeezed by high energy prices and credit-card debt."[81] Then, in December 2003, at the time he signed the new prescription-drug benefit into law, he declared, that the reforms the bill enacts "are the act of a vibrant and compassionate government." By it, he said, "We show our concern for the dignity of our seniors by giving them quality health care" and "our respect for seniors by giving them more choices and more control over their decision-making."[82] When Bush signed into law the Partial Birth Abortion Ban Act of 2003, he said, in a tone of obvious pleasure, this bill "protecting innocent new life from [partial-birth abortion] reflects the compassion and humanity of America."[83] The majority of Americans could finally rejoice in seeing this horrendous "medical" practice outlawed in a bill similar to those Bill Clinton vetoed. In 2004, President Bush added another compassionate policy—"defending the sanctity of life," which may provide some of the rationale for his endorsement of a constitutional amendment declaring marriage the union of a man and a woman.[84]

Bush also makes it clear in his speeches that compassion is not just the government's responsibility, but it is also the people's as they join private "armies of compassion." Speaking to New York Police Department personnel on February 6, 2002, the President said:

> People ask me all the time what can I do to help fight terror, fight the evil ones. Well, I believe since this is a struggle between evil and good, the best way to do it is to do some good in your neighborhood; is to mentor a child who may be lost; is to help a shut-in; is to walk across the street to a neighbor in need and say, what can I do to help you?
>
> Many of you are already doing that—by loving the widows and the children of those who lost their lives. It's these thousands and millions of acts of kindness all across America on a daily basis that define the character of our nation. The way you fight evil is with millions of acts of good. It's the cumulative effect of the heart and soul of America that stands tall against the evil ones. Not only will we prevail militarily in the long run, but we will have overcome evil by being a nation that is more compassionate, more decent, more loving to our fellow citizens.[85]

One also witnesses an existential emphasis in Bush's rhetoric that is devoted to a leader's vital duty—to give the people who follow him a sense of hope, hope in the future and a belief in the success of the vision that charts the nation's course. Kouzes and Posner, after studying credibility of leaders, report, "Constituents look for leaders who demonstrate an enthusiastic and genuine belief in the capacity of others, who strengthen people's will, who supply the means to achieve, and who express optimism for the future."[86] Such leaders, they suggest, instill hope in their listeners. They assert, "Leaders must keep hope alive."[87] Bush knows the importance of keeping hope alive. In the spring of 2002, he told an audience, "we are called to defend freedom against ruthless enemies. And, once again, we need steadfastness, courage, and hope."[88] In his speeches, he conveys a genuine belief that Americans are up to any challenge, ready to meet any threat with courage and confidence.

He conveyed this belief in a speech at a time when death was on every mind. The *time*: September 14, 2001; the *place*: the National Cathedral in Washington, D.C.; the *occasion*: the remembrance for the victims of the terrorist attacks; President Bush's *purpose*: to give Americans assurances to bolster their hopes, so that Ground Zero did not bear bitter fruit of hopelessness.

He had words of assurance for Americans who hoped that the nation would remember the victims of 9/11. He reminded his listeners that, when the attacks came, the victims were beginning their day, "busy with life." Some of the victims, he said, knew they "faced death" and "called home to say, be brave, and I love you."[89] Then there were the plane "passengers who defied their murderers, and prevented the murder of others on the ground."[90] Bush also paid tribute to the rescuers, "whom death found running up the stairs and into the fires to help others."[91]

He had words of assurance for those who hoped for retribution: "War has been waged against us by stealth and deceit and murder. This nation is peaceful, but fierce when stirred to anger. This conflict was begun on the timing and terms of others. It will end," he assured his listeners, "in a way, and at an hour, of our choosing."[92]

He had words of assurance for persons who hoped to receive spiritual comfort. He spoke of a woman at St. Patrick's Cathedral who told him, "I prayed to God for a sign that He is still here." He drew on his personal faith in his response: "God's signs are not always the ones we look for. We learn in tragedy that His purposes are not always our own."[93] Perhaps he was thinking of the death of his younger sister Robin who died of leukemia when he was seven years old. Likely many listeners recognized his words from Scripture (Romans 8:38-39) when he declared, "As we have been assured, neither death nor life, nor angels nor principalities nor powers, nor things present nor things to come, nor height nor depth, can separate us from God's love."[94]

Many U.S. presidents' existential intelligence has been best expressed through their religious faith. It has been for them and for those they have led a source of wisdom, direction, and comfort, especially in times of national crisis. In his autobiography *A Charge to Keep*, George W. Bush wrote, "I have also learned the power of prayer. I pray for guidance. I do not pray for earthly things, but for heavenly things, for wisdom and patience and understanding. My faith gives me focus and perspective."[95]

Bush's Spatial Intelligence

In addition to having the four intelligences that, according to Gardner, "are crucial to leaders," George W. Bush has, what Gardner calls, *spatial intelligence*. Concerning this kind of intelligence, Gardner writes that it "features the potential to recognize and manipulate the patterns of wide space (those used, for instance, by navigators and pilots) as well as the patterns of more confined areas (such as those of importance to sculptors, surgeons, chess players, graphic artists, or architects)."[96]

The persons with this kind of intelligence can detect emerging patterns in their endeavors, on the basis of specific events or features, that to those who lack such intelligence may seem unrelated; moreover, they can reason how certain actions on their part can produce a desirable pattern, which may, for example, take the form of a design, plan, map, or strategy. Spatial intelligence involves the ability to judge how best to direct one's actions toward a goal, while making the most of favorable conditions and avoiding or adapting to unfavorable conditions, as when, for instance, a surgeon in an operation must manage a hemorrhage or a pilot in a jet plane must cope with a storm.

The fact that President Bush successfully trained as a jet-fighter pilot and flew the F-102A Delta Dagger Interceptor for a period of several years without mishap, is testimony to his having spatial intelligence. The F-102A is a single-seat, single-engine jet fighter that Bush flew in the Texas Air National Guard. Almost fifty-seven feet in length with a wingspan of nearly thirty-six feet, "putting it in the sky," Bush recalled decades later, "required single-minded focus and attention."[97] Anyone who has sat in the cockpit of a fighter jet or has seen a film that shows the inside of a cockpit, knows the complexity of the instrument panel, the controls, and the firing mechanism of the guns. He or she quickly realizes that it takes a special kind of person to pilot such a war machine.

During the Democratic primaries prior to the '04 presidential election, the liberal media—aping the DNC's attempts to hurt the President's credibility—questioned the White House aggressively over several weeks regarding George W. Bush's service in the Texas Air National Guard. Their whole emphasis was on finding out if he had made up the time for a brief excused absence from the Guard—they knew that getting an excused absence was a common practice. Before the liberal media would believe

President Bush, they had to see his honorable discharge certificate, examine his service file, and hear from witnesses who came forward on their own and verified that Bush had, indeed, made up the time to complete his service requirement.

After it seemed that the liberal media had stopped attempts to blacken Bush's Guard record, CBS's *60 Minutes* claimed that it had memos critical of his National Guard service, written 32 years ago by one of his officers. Almost immediately, the memos were pronounced forgeries by experts. Also, two generals who commanded Bush publicly declared them fakes. Many in the media chastised CBS for not checking the facts before broadcasting a story that denigrated Bush's Guard service.

Doubtless, the fact that former president George H. W. Bush had served as a Navy fighter pilot in World War II influenced George W. Bush to want to learn to fly. So, when young Bush heard from friends that there were openings in the Texas Air National Guard, he joined—there were openings, he discovered, because most men were unwilling to devote almost two years for full-time duty that pilot training required.[98] Concerning the training, Bush later wrote, "The training was impressive. The need for precision and accuracy and exactness was drilled into us at every opportunity. We spent a lot of time responding to different situations, going through flight procedures time and time again."[99]

In the course of his training, Bush studied navigation, engineering, flight characteristics, formation flying, equipment, emergency procedures and ejections, radar, missiles, and instrument procedures. One of his instructors, Colonel Maury Udell, required him to locate the position of every switch and instrument in the cockpit while blindfolded.[100] He learned to fly in tight formation, three to five feet from another jet fighter at speeds that could reach 650 miles an hour—[101] someone capable of accomplishing such a feat is likely to be spatially-intelligent. By the time Bush passed the final check and earned his wings, half of the men who began training with him had washed out, attesting to the Guard's high standards.[102]

The narrow interest of the liberal media in George W. Bush's Guard service took no notice of the fact that flying is a hazardous occupation, especially for military personnel. When Bush served, the mission of the Air National Guard was to protect the American coast. "The duty was dangerous. The Texas Guard suffered a handful of pilot fatalities in the 1970s."[103] Several of Bush's fellow pilots had participated in a program called "Palace Alert," "which rotated Guard pilots into Vietnam to relieve active-duty pilots." Bush and a fellow pilot, Fred Bradley, wanted to participate in the program and so talked to Colonel Jerry Killian about doing so. They were told that the program was being phased out, that a few more pilots would go, but that Bush and Bradley had not logged enough flying hours to go with them.[104] It certainly was natural for these young men to want to see action, to put their training to the test—in Bush's case, to equal his father's exploits in World War II.

George W. Bush performed effectively in the Texas Air National Guard. Among the ways he displayed spatial intelligence while in training was in his exceptional ability to read pictorial presentations of the functional parts of the planes. When a trainee who found such materials confusing asked him how he managed to read such things, Bush answered that he had always been able to read charts.[105] This ability helped him to score high in academic areas of the training program. As Elizabeth Mitchell, in *W: Revenge of the Bush Dynasty*, writes, "George W. always demonstrated an ability to sift through data and consider it analytically."[106]

One might ask, "How did his spatial intelligence while in the Guard help him to develop attitudes and skills that enhanced his leadership abilities?" An answer is suggested in Bush's own words: "Cockpits of fighter jets are tiny and close, and they force you to learn economy of motion. They also force you to master yourself, mentally, physically, and emotionally. You have to stay calm and think logically."[107] These are characteristics that people have observed in George W. Bush. His management of space—confined areas and wide expanses—may account for his evident ability to adjust with ease to cramped spaces where he is surrounded by people whose company he enjoys, or to broad spaces when he addresses large audiences outdoors. In either situation, he projects a commanding presence that instills confidence in his listeners.

One might also ask, "What personal qualities are needed by military pilots to perform effectively, and are such qualities relevant to leadership?" A high-reliability field with a long history of emphasis on personnel selection is aviation—the high cost of training pilots and the price of poor performance are two good reasons for such an emphasis. Every effort is made "to ensure that the 'right stuff' is sitting on the flight deck. Consequently, the national air forces and the larger commercial airlines have devoted significant efforts and resources to identifying the personal qualities desired in pilots."[108] Researchers found that successful pilots have certain personal qualities, which influence their selection: "Influence/Leadership; Communication Skill; Organizing/Planning; Motivation/Energy; Analytical; Empathy; Emotional Maturity; Decision Making."[109] These are all important personal qualities for leaders, which George W. Bush likely displayed as a pilot, since he displays them now as a president. Colonel Ralph Anderson who trained with Bush, years later recalled: "He was a leader. He took things on and got them done."[110]

A myth that the Democrats interjected into the 2000 campaign—assisted by the megaphone of the liberal media—was that George W. Bush was not intelligent. They have said it in a hundred different ways, trying to convince the American public and reassure themselves. For example, the contest between Bush and Gore was characterized as "the scarecrow versus the tin man."[111] Of course, the journalist who invented those descriptions forgot that the scarecrow of Oz did have a brain, a brain good enough to make him chief executive of Emerald City after the departure of the phony wizard. A survey revealed that, between the start of the Democratic primary campaigns and the middle of March '04, the late-night comedy shows made fun of President Bush's intelligence 61 times, and Kerry's 0 times, even though Kerry had made a number of comical gaffes.[112] This myth has caused many Democrats to underestimate Bush, which, Karl Rove, his senior advisor, has said, "gives him an advantage." Mansfield makes the point, "Any other man introduced as a graduate of Yale and Harvard who made millions of dollars in business, who was a two-term state governor, and who became president of the United States would not be thought stupid, sight unseen."[113] Mansfield goes on to say that questioning Bush's intelligence appears "to deny the existence of various types of intelligence. Decades ago," he notes, "educators spoke in terms of one kind of intelligence: the literary, abstract-thought-oriented, philosophical variety. Now, research has shown what experience has long revealed: There are different types of intelligence."[114] We see that there is evidence that Bush has, at least, five types.

Prime Minister Blair has stood shoulder to shoulder with President

Bush in the war against terrorists. Blair has had many opportunities to observe Bush's intellectual capacities as, together, they have focused their attention on world crises. Blair has expressed disgust that anyone would question Bush's intellect. "It's all 'complete bull,' he has asserted, 'just nonsense. He is highly intelligent, and it's not clotted by so many nuances that the meaning is obscured.'"[115]

NOTES

1. Gardner, *Intelligence Reframed*, 41-43.
2. Howard Gardner, *Changing Minds: The Art and Science of Changing Our Own and Other People's Minds* (Boston: Harvard Business School Press, 2004), 31.
3. Gardner, *Intelligence Reframed*, 126.
4. Ibid.
5. Bush, *We Will Prevail*, 65.
6. Gardner, *Intelligence Reframed*, 126-127.
7. Ibid., 128.
8. Ibid.
9. Jay Nordlinger, "A Voice for Our Time," *National Review*, September 29, 2003, p. 37.
10. Kenneth T. Walsh, "On the Job," *U.S. News & World Report*, February 25/March 4, 2002, p. 72.
11. President's Speech on the U.S. Economy, Eisenhower Executive Office Building, Washington, D.C., C-SPAN, February 19, 2004.
12. Walsh, "On the Job," p. 72.
13. Bush, *We Will Prevail*, 241.
14. Ibid., 242-243.
15. Ibid., 244.
16. Kevin Whitelaw, "Washington Whispers," *U.S. News & World Report*, April 8, 2002, p. 2.
17. Greg Pierce, "Inside Politics," *Washington Times* National Weekly Edition, January 19-25, 2004, p. 20.
18. Ibid.
19. Ibid.
20. Karen Hughes, "Reflections," in George W. Bush, *A Charge to Keep* (New York: William Morrow, 1999), xiii.
21. Dennis Prager, "A Brief, Unforgettable Encounter with the President," *Washington Times* National Weekly Edition, February 9-15, 2004, p. 33.
22. Gardner, *Intelligence Reframed*, 43.
23. Ralph Reed, interview, *Rush Limbaugh*, KPNW, November 6, 2003.

24. Lisa Beamer, *Let's Roll: Ordinary People, Extraordinary Courage* (Wheaton: Tyndale House, 2002), 255.
25. Ibid., 256-257.
26. Hughes, "Reflections," xii.
27. Kathryn Dunn Tenpas and Stephen Hess, "The Contemporary Presidency: The Bush White House: First Appraisals," *Presidential Studies Quarterly*, September 2002, pp. 582-583.
28. Bush, *A Charge to Keep*, 103.
29. Cal Thomas, "Liberal Media Assault '04 Is Starting to Warm Up," *Washington Times* National Weekly Edition, January 12-18, 2004, p. 30.
30. Ibid.
31. Ibid.
32. Ibid.
33. Kenneth T. Walsh, "A Couple of Presidents in Primary Colors," *U.S. News & World Report*, June 21, 2004, p. 42.
34. Cook, "The Contemporary Presidency," p. 757.
35. Carl M. Cannon and Alexis Simendinger, "The Making of Team Bush," *National Journal*, September 22, 2001, p. 2918.
36. *ABC News*, KPNW, February 3, 2004.
37. Thomas, "Liberal Media Assault '04 . . .," p. 30.
38. *Book Events*, C-SPAN, September 13, 2003.
39. Evelyn Husband, *High Calling: The Courageous Life and Faith of Space Shuttle Columbia Commander Rick Husband* (Nashville: Thomas Nelson, 2003), 190-191.
40. Gardner, *Changing Minds*, 178.
41. Gardner, *Intelligence Reframed*, 43.
42. Ibid., 43, 128.
43. Ibid., 43.
44. Lane, *By All Means Communicate*, 13.
45. Jay Ambrose, "The Right Man at the Right Time," *Washington Times* National Weekly Edition, May 5-11, 2003, p. 31.
46. Ibid.
47. Kenneth T. Walsh, "W, as in War," *U.S. News & World Report*, February 25-March 4, 2002, p. 44.
48. Ibid.
49. Zell Miller, *A National Party No More: The Conscience of a Conservative Democrat* (Atlanta: Stroud & Hall, 2003), 234.
50. Fred Barnes, "Kerry Nation?," *Weekly Standard*, February 23, 2004, p. 10.
51. Jerry Falwell, interview, *Hannity and Colmes*, Fox News, February 25, 2004.
52. Jerry Falwell, "Falwell Confidential," February 25, 2004, www.falwell.com.
53. Bob Phillips, *Phillips' Book of Great Thoughts* (Wheaton: Tyndale House, 1993), 78.
54. Gardner, *Intelligence Reframed*, 130.
55. "Transcript of Bush's First News Conference," *New York Times*, November 5, 2004, p. A16.

56. Gardner, *Changing Minds*, 179.
57. Gardner, *Intelligence Reframed*, 128.
58. Ibid., 60.
59. *Bible*, Philippians 4:7.
60. Allan Nevins, "The Place of Franklin D. Roosevelt in History," in John A. Garraty, ed., *Historical Viewpoints: Notable Articles from American Heritage*, 6th ed. (New York: HarperCollins, 1991), 290.
61. Eleanor Roosevelt, *This I Remember* (New York: Harper & Row, 1949), 346.
62. David M. Abshire, "Wartime Faith of Washington, Lincoln and Roosevelt," *Vital Speeches of the Day*, June 15, 2003, p. 525.
63. Nevins, "The Place of Franklin D. Roosevelt in History," 297.
64. Ibid.
65. Samuel I. Rosenman, *The Public Papers and Addresses of Franklin D. Roosevelt*, vol. 1944-45 (New York: Harper & Brothers, 1950), 525.
66. Stephen Mansfield, *The Faith of George W. Bush* (New York: Tarcher/Penguin, 2003), 173.
67. Ibid., 173-174.
68. George W. Bush, "Inaugural Address," *Vital Speeches of the Day*, February 1, 2001, p. 227.
69. Terry Eastland, "Bush's Gospel," *Weekly Standard*, March 1, 2004, p. 18.
70. Mansfield, *The Faith of George W. Bush*, 173.
71. Eastland, "Bush's Gospel," p. 17.
72. Bush, *We Will Prevail*, 13.
73. Daniel Philpott, "The Challenge of September 11 to Secularism in International Relations," *World Politics*, October 2002, p. 91.
74. Mansfield, *The Faith of George W. Bush*, 134.
75. Ibid.
76. Tony Blair, Speech on War in Iraq and Terrorism, C-SPAN, March 5, 2004.
77. Philpott, "The Challenge of September 11 to Secularism . . .," p. 92.
78. Brian DeBose, "Kerry Says Bush Exaggerated Threat of Terrorism," *Washington Times* National Weekly Edition, February 2-8, 2004, p. 8.
79. "Remarks by the President at Whitehall Palace," Royal Banqueting House, London, England, November 19, 2003, www.whitehouse.gov.
80. Philpott, "The Challenge of September 11 to Secularism . . .," p. 92.
81. Eastland, "Bush's Gospel," p. 18.
82. Ibid.
83. Ibid.
84. Ibid.
85. Bush, *We Will Prevail*, 117-118.
86. Kouzes and Posner, *Credibility*, 218.
87. Ibid.
88. "Remarks by the President at the George C. Marshall ROTC Award Seminar on National Security," Virginia Military Institute, Lexington, Virginia, April 17, 2002, www.whitehouse.gov.

89. Bush, *We Will Prevail*, 5.
90. Ibid.
91. Ibid.
92. Ibid., 6.
93. Ibid.
94. Ibid., 7.
95. Bush, *A Charge to Keep*, 138.
96. Gardner, *Intelligence Reframed*, 42.
97. Bush, *A Charge to Keep*, 52.
98. Ibid., 51.
99. Ibid., 52.
100. Ibid., 52-53.
101. Kenneth T. Walsh and Dan Gilgoff, "From Boys to Men," *U.S. News & World Report*, May 3, 2004, p. 41.
102. Bush, *A Charge to Keep*, 52.
103. Walsh and Gilgoff, "From Boys to Men," p. 41.
104. Bush, *A Charge to Keep*, 54.
105. Elizabeth Mitchell, *W: Revenge of the Bush Dynasty* (New York: Hyperion, 2000), 122.
106. Ibid.
107. Bush, *A Charge to Keep*, 54.
108. Rhona Flin, "Selecting the Right Stuff," in Brent W. Roberts and Robert Hogan, eds., *Personality Psychology in the Workplace* (Washington, D.C.: American Psychological Association, 2002), 256.
109. Ibid.
110. Mitchell, *W: Revenge of the Bush Dynasty*, 122.
111. The Editors, "The Secret Skill of Leaders," *U.S. News & World Report*, January 14, 2002, p. 8.
112. *Special Report with Brit Hume*, Fox News, March 18, 2004.
113. Mansfield, *The Faith of George W. Bush*, 157.
114. Ibid.
115. Ibid.

Chapter 6
Style in Bush's Wartime Rhetoric

The true end of style is that the listener not only understand us, but that he may not be able to misunderstand us.
— Marcus Fabius Quintilian, *Institutes of Oratory*

Mark Twain is quoted as saying,

> In Paris they simply stared when I spoke to them in French; I never did succeed in making those idiots understand their own language.

Beneath Twain's humor lurks a key principle of communication—although Twain likely would have preferred we not find anything serious—which is: *meaning is in the mind of the receiver*. That is, the speaker connects with the listener when the listener can match meanings with the speaker's words for immediate understanding—as Quintilian would say, with no possibility of misunderstanding. This chapter contends that George W. Bush's style enables him to make this kind of contact with the minds of his hearers. He is clear and forceful in making himself understood. He speaks the average Americans' language in ways that maximize his persuasiveness as it encourages their responsiveness.

Stylistic Problems: Possible Answers

A positive appraisal of George W. Bush's style, of course, runs counter to the views of liberals. Although, he has essentially overcome the stylistic problems that marred his rhetoric before 9/11, the liberals continue to downgrade his style. They remember that in the 2000 presidential campaign and for a time afterward, he sometimes would mispronounce words, use words incorrectly, make syntactic errors, and violate grammatical rules. One source collected 47 of such instances—interestingly, although the list appeared in 2003, all of the instances date only from between January 2000 and August 2001.[1] Bush's tendency to misspeak during this period soon led liberals to equate verbal facility with IQ in *his* case, so that they could question both his style and intelligence. "If liberals truly believed verbal fluency were determinative of IQ," Ann Coulter queried, "why did they call Reagan dumb? The peculiar liberal obsession with verbal facility as a proxy for IQ seemed to recede a bit when the 'Great Communicator' was president."[2] Pointing up a typical liberal inconsistency, Coulter asserted, "Instead of hailing Reagan as the greatest genius ever to inhabit the White House, his very facility with words was derided as the vocational faculty of a hackneyed actor."[3]

While Bush's performance before and since becoming president attests to his sound intelligence—of a nature needed for wartime leadership—one does wonder what accounted for his early tendency to misspeak periodically when speaking publicly. A theory circulated by liberal writers was that Bush mispronounced words occasionally because he had dyslexia. For example, during a news conference during the 2000 presidential campaign, he mispronounced the word *subliminal* four times by adding a syllable to produce "subliminable."[4] However, some people who are not dyslexic may, on occasion, mispronounce a word, even one that comes from their professional vocabulary. Not long ago, the author heard a brilliant university president say "accredidation," instead of *accreditation*—apparently, he wanted to keep the university "accredided."

When Bush was on his last teleprompter practice for his "Address to a Joint Session of Congress and the American People" scheduled for delivery on September 20, 2001, he transposed a couple of words: instead of saying, "Office of Homeland Security," he said, "Homeland of Office Security."

Brought to his attention, he made the correction. People watching him practice said he was tired, which would have lowered his concentration;[5] plus, the new Cabinet title was just a phrase that stood for a concept yet to be fully developed. A speaker is more likely to make such a mistake when he or she focuses on the words, instead of on their meaning. Perhaps if he had focused more on the meaning of the words in his practice, he might have said, the "Homeland Security Office," which would have been a more acceptable mistake, had he made it in public.

Another problem that Bush displayed in his speaking during the 2000 presidential campaign was an occasional use of malapropisms, that is, using the wrong word due to its resemblance in sound to the correct one. On September 18, 2000, for example, Governor Bush made an appearance on *The Edge* with Paula Zahn and, in the course of the conversation with Zahn, said "A tax-cut is really one of the anecdotes to coming out of an economic illness."[6] Of course, Bush meant *antidotes*, a good word to use in this context.

Probably, this kind of error stemmed from insufficient practice in using terms needed for discussing certain topics during the presidential campaign. One might theorize that such terms as *subliminal*, *antidote*, and *anecdote* required more rehearsal—that is, opportunity to repeat them over and over—so that frequent repetition would strengthen their position in short-term memory and eventually transfer them to long-term memory.[7] Subsequent repetition doubtless enabled Bush to retain them in his vocabulary and use them correctly at will.

George W. Bush had to develop his vocabulary as he went from successful businessman to governor of Texas; and, certainly, he had to expand his vocabulary extensively when he became president of the most powerful nation in the world during wartime. He needed a vocabulary that would permit him to express fine points of meaning in answering challenging questions in press conferences and in interacting with accomplished world leaders.

The President has learned fast to speak the language of a national leader, who must be prepared to articulate facts and views on a wide array of topics, both domestic and foreign. On April 30, 2004, at the White House, President Bush and newly-elected Prime Minister Paul Martin of Canada held a joint press conference. At its close, Martin, in an admiring tone, suddenly exclaimed, "I've got to say that I *really do* like sharing a press conference with you. You answered those questions *perfectly*."[8]

Transformation: Bush Develops

There is reason to believe that prior to the terrorist attacks, Bush did not take his occasional lapses in grammar, syntax, and pronunciation seriously. In fact, when his critics referred to such mistakes to make fun of him, he generally joked about it. He might respond laughingly—using one of his invented terms—that his critics "misunderestimated" him.[9] After 9/11, he seemingly realized that how he said something affected some people's judgment of what he said.

Karen Hughes recounts in her candid memoir how, in September 2001, after President Bush had just delivered a "powerful" speech in Chicago, she had to tell him that he had mispronounced the same word three times. It made him temporarily unhappy to hear it. Hughes wrote, "I was reluctant to tell him. His statements had been so much more passionate, so much more convincing after September 11 that I realized in hindsight that he had been holding himself back during the early months of his presidency, perhaps," she thought, "worried about making a mistake." Then, less than a half hour after her disclosure, when they were on Air Force One, the President said to her, "You correct me whenever I screw up, always. I want you to." In the same context, Hughes noted that she "had promised to always be honest."[10]

After reviewing a collection of President Bush's post-9/11 speeches, Jay Nordlinger concluded, that most of Bush's speechwriters "would agree that Bush has grown in his ability to communicate, both in his prepared, professionalized speeches and in his unscripted remarks."[11] David Frum, former Bush speechwriter, draws an interesting comparison between President Kennedy and President Bush: "Both owed their connections with the public above all to the power of their words. John F. Kennedy's gorgeous speeches still resound forty years later; Bush's oratory in the ten days after the terrorist attacks transformed his leadership—and may perhaps last as long."[12]

"Nothing about the Bush presidency has been more surprising," wrote John Podhoretz, *New York Post* columnist and media fellow at the Hoover Institution, "than the brilliance, power, and intellectual seriousness of his speeches." Apparently drawing on inside information, he continued, "Bush is intimately involved in the crafting of his speeches, just as Clinton was. He just hasn't felt the need to let it be known how seriously he takes the task." After listening to his formal addresses on foreign policy, Podhoretz concluded, "Bush has emerged as a genuinely great speaker," who has delivered several "speeches that rank among the most powerful and important presidential addresses of the modern era." He expected historians, one day, to agree. "It pains me, a former speechwriter for Ronald Reagan, to say this," Podhoretz admitted, "but I believe Bush is the best presidential speaker since Franklin Delano Roosevelt."[13]

President Bush has also learned to speak persuasively in his press conferences, avoiding journalists' loaded or leading questions. On April 13, 2004, in a lengthy press conference, he answered the questions of 15 White House correspondents, nearly all of whom seemed bent on making it difficult for him to answer. Nevertheless, he remained calm, poised, and controlled in the face of unfriendly fire, speaking fluently, knowledgeably, and, at times, passionately—none of the speech problems that beset his style in previous years appeared, in spite of rude and cutting questions from the Washington press corps.

One might ask, "Is there any reason to believe that the Washington press corps tends to be partisan?" Ann Coulter seemed to answer such a question in stating: "In the 1992 presidential election, a mere 43 percent of Americans voted for Bill Clinton. That same year, 89 percent of Washington bureau chiefs and reporters voted for Clinton. Only 7 percent voted for Bush." She added, "A higher percentage of the Washington press corps voted for Clinton in 1992 than did this demographic category: Registered Democrats."[14]

Commenting on the April 13th press conference, the next day on *Special Report with Brit Hume*, Mort Kondracke, co-host of *The Beltway Boys*, described the correspondents' questioning with the words "contentious," "argumentative," "trying to embarrass the president." It appeared that most of the questions sounded as if they came out of the DNC's playbook. He and journalists Fred Barnes and Jeff Birnbaum thought, however, that the correspondents' unprofessional treatment of the President would gain him support[15]—this seemed likely, since Bush answered their questions quite effectively.

Even in press conferences when he has to answer questions inappropriately personal and intentionally barbed—as was the case in the April 13th press conference—President Bush does not retreat to a higher plane of status. Rather, he maintains a conversational tone and speaks from the heart to the correspondents as equals. He calls on a correspondent by name; he treats each one with respect and answers his or her question with deliberateness and careful thought. He certainly knows that any mistake will design the next day's headlines. And, in a conversational mode, he has to be careful not to say something that the Left can distort to promote its agenda. Bush can see that any mistake, no matter how trivial, feeds the liberals' fury.

But, the liberals have found it more difficult to describe Bush as being inarticulate and unintelligent since taking the lead in the war on terrorism. The complaints they raised against his leadership style lost a lot of traction soon after the collapse of the twin towers. "For those easily duped by media propaganda, there would be no more staggering surprise than George W. Bush's masterful response to a devastating terrorist attack seven months after he took office," Coulter wrote. "Never was the myth of a 'dumb' Republican shattered with such dispatch."[16] Or, as Gaddis described Bush's response to the 9/11 attacks: "one of the most surprising transformations of an underrated national leader since Prince Hal became Henry V." (That was in 1413.)

Suddenly, according to the elite media, President Bush "found his voice." Perhaps it was not so much that the President "found his voice," as it was that the attacks caused the media to really listen to what he said and not just to how he said it. In his *Newsweek* article of September 24, 2001, Howard Fineman suggested that one should not expect too much of Bush since "Dramatic acts and eloquent words are not his forte," but, he conceded, "his feet were on the ground, his bearings set: a late bloomer blossoming in the nick of time."[17] Apparently, this journalist did not see Bush's speech at Ground Zero delivered from a wrecked firetruck as "dramatic," or find his speech at the National Cathedral in remembrance of those who fell on 9/11 as "eloquent."

In contrast with Fineman's pronouncement, columnist Bob Herbert appeared willing to recognize Bush as a public speaker with some ability. Writing in the *New York Times* on September 24, 2001, Herbert called

Bush's "Presidential Address to a Joint Session of Congress," delivered four days before, "a near-perfect speech."[18] Certainly, it had moments that exemplified the grand style, to borrow a term from Cicero. We saw such a moment when he expressed the mood of the nation: "Tonight we are a country awakened to danger and called to defend freedom. Our grief has turned to anger, and anger to resolution. Whether we bring our enemies to justice, or bring justice to our enemies, justice will be done."[19]

This powerful speech revealed the identity of the enemy, showing that Bush's knowledge of global terrorists was up to speed. He said: "Americans have many questions tonight. Americans are asking: Who attacked our country? The evidence we have gathered all points to a collection of loosely affiliated terrorist organizations known as al Qaeda. They are the same murderers indicted for bombing American embassies in Tanzania and Kenya, and responsible for bombing the *USS Cole*."[20]

Then, the President made moral truth eloquent as he described the enemy's existential darkness: "They are the heirs of all the murderous ideologies of the 20th Century. By sacrificing human life to serve their radical visions—by abandoning every value except the will to power—they follow in the path of fascism, and Nazism, and totalitarianism. And," he assured his audience, "they will follow that path all the way, to where it ends: In history's unmarked grave of discarded lies."[21]

Understanding Americans' confusion and frustration in fighting an enemy that attacks under no flag, gives no quarter, uses suicide as a weapon, and seeks WMDs, President Bush said: "Americans are asking: How will we fight and win this war? We will direct every resource at our command—every means of diplomacy, every tool of intelligence, every instrument of law enforcement, every financial influence, and every necessary weapon of war—to the disruption and to the defeat of the global terror network."[22] Americans in that hour took the President at his word. And he has kept his word—to direct every resource at his command, including his speaking ability.

Through the delivery of public speeches, President Bush has informed and encouraged the nation on domestic and foreign-policy issues; he has worked to persuade Americans and allies to continue the fight against global terrorists in the face of suicide bombings in the world and clashes with Iraqi insurgents and Islamic extremists. By developing his conversational style he has enhanced his ability to inform and persuade his audiences to see his view of the issues.

The Hallmark: Conversational Style

The hallmark of George W. Bush's presidential rhetoric, as witnessed on most occasions, is his conversational style of speaking, which his predecessors during the past century have rarely matched in effectiveness. Robert MacNeil, former co-host of *MacNeil/Leher Report*, who produced the acclaimed PBS documentary *The Story of English*, was asked if he thought that voters were affected by Bush's use of language in the 2004 presidential campaign. He replied, "Yes, I think so. I think part of Mr. Bush's appeal is that he speaks a very relaxed and colloquial language . . . . It's folksy, down to earth . . . I think it's part of his political appeal."[23]

A past president whose style comes close to Bush's is Theodore Roosevelt. In fact, TR's "biographer Edmund Morris agrees that they're a lot alike: In a private White House staff lecture, Morris favorably compared Bush's traits, like 'energy and magnetism,' to the last youthful prez to open a new century."[24] He might also have compared GW's style to TR's. Here is an excerpt of TR's famous speech "The Strenuous Life," delivered close to the turn of the century:

> The twentieth century looms before us big with the fate of many nations. If we stand idly by, if we seek merely swollen, slothful ease, and ignoble peace, if we shrink from the hard contests where men must win at hazard of their lives and at the risk of all they hold dear, then the bolder and stronger peoples . . . will win for themselves the domination of the world.[25]

As noted in Chapter 3, "A persuasive speech has an oral quality that has the flavor of dialogue—for example, it avoids complex sentences and wording that obscures the meaning of ideas." A style having such a quality enables listeners to decode and interpret the speaker's language swiftly, so that they can immediately understand and respond. As this quality was evident in Theodore Roosevelt's speeches, it is evident in George W. Bush's speeches.

When one examines President Bush's speeches closely, it becomes clear that he prefers to address audiences in plain and simple language that creates instant comprehension for listeners. He, therefore, tends to use familiar, short, Anglo-Saxon words, that are likely to be in most people's vocabulary. Moreover, he avoids lengthy, complex sentences; he mainly uses straightforward sentences that produce ideas that are clear, simple, and to the point. It is easy to find examples of conversational style in Bush's rhetoric. For instance here is an excerpt from his speech to citizens and military personnel in North Carolina on March 15, 2002:

> Because of such soldiers, a vicious regime has been toppled in Afghanistan, and an entire people has been liberated from oppression. Because of American soldiers and our brave allies and friends who have fought beside them, the Taliban is out of business.
>
> At the beginning of this war, I made it very clear—as clear as a fellow from Texas could make it—either you're with us or you're against us. And if you harbor a terrorist, if you feed a terrorist, if you try to hide a terrorist, you are just as guilty as the murderers who killed innocent Americans on September the 11th. And thanks to the mighty United States military, the Taliban found out exactly what I meant.[26]

The Bush doctrine, reflected in the second paragraph above, typifies Bush's style of speaking in absolutes when he discusses the war on terrorism—morally, it is consistent with his Christian faith and its dictates of good versus evil; strategically, it realistically recognizes that the enemy thinks, plans, and acts according to absolutes; and politically, it gives a basis for definite goals that predict direct action, always appealing to Americans who expect leaders to act.

By expressing himself in clear, simple, and definite terms, as he does in this excerpt, Bush doubtless helped people for whom English was a second language to have a better understanding of his speeches. The fact that he is bilingual and governed a state with many immigrants, may have made him especially sensitive to the presence of immigrants in a typical mass audience in America.

The President's use of clear and simple language is so well known that it prompted David Letterman on his show to poke fun at Bush when he had used a "big word" in a speech. Letterman showed Bush using the word and then put it on the screen in large letters—**RAMIFICATIONS**—to help Americans learn a new word. The audience laughed. But Bush might have the last laugh, as his style continues to gain positive response.

One other president used plain, simple language with good effect, a fact which might surprise some Democrats—that president was Franklin D. Roosevelt. According to his biographer, Robert Jackson, FDR wanted his radio audience to feel that he was simply conversing with them as they sat by their fireside. To create this impression, "he eliminated all long, unfamiliar, foreign or technical words and brought the thought into simple, plain words, of Anglo-Saxon origin if possible. He knew the forcefulness of plain Bible English with the American people. He eliminated," Jackson recalled, "complicated and involved sentences and used short, simple and direct ones."[27]

In addition to similarities in these Presidents' use of clear and simple language, they are alike in one other regard in terms of style. President Bush does not, just as President Roosevelt did not, resort to vulgarities, profanity, or *ad hominem* attacks against political opponents. Jackson, speaking of FDR, wrote, "He knew that voters who listened to Presidents and would-be Presidents are self-respecting and quick to detect any condescension that seeks to prove by profanity and vulgarisms that the speaker is just a plain everyday fellow."[28] Unfortunately—as Senator Zell Miller has suggested in television appearances—Democratic-Party leaders practice an opposite style of refinement to that of FDR.

For example, in February 2004, Senator Kerry said of President Bush's leadership, "The arrogance, and the sheer sort of, almost stupidity of it, is stunning." Kerry has taunted many times: "We all saw George Bush play dress-up on an aircraft carrier." But, Kerry "set a new low for American presidential contests when he used the F-word in regards to Mr. Bush in an interview with *Rolling Stone* magazine. These low-level attacks could backfire. Americans hold the office of the presidency in high esteem." In 2003, Kerry joked that "General Boykin has confused the heck out of the White House on all this talk about the Almighty, when he talks about the Almighty, the president thinks he's talking about Cheney."[29] He received only polite laughter from a partisan audience in this attempt at humor, which, in the minds of some people, bordered on irreverence. A style that incorporates humor of this sort can offend as many people in the audience as it might entertain.

In seeking to make a speech relevant to a particular audience, the persuasive speaker makes every effort to adapt his or her style to the people expected to be present. One sees this adaptation in a speech that President Bush delivered on June 11, 2002 in Kansas City, Missouri at the opening of Oak Park High School. In the following, he seemed to alter his introduction with a spontaneous comment to the audience:

> I see a lot of you have brought your children; I want to thank you for that. And I want you, as moms and dads, and as grandparents, to make sure you tell your children that we fight not to seek revenge, but we do so because we seek justice; and the overriding ambition of this country is to achieve long-lasting peace.[30]

Toward the end of his speech, Bush appeared to discuss the issue of homeland security in language that would appeal to youth as well as adults. He told the audience:

> It may seem kind of easy, but here's the problem. There's a hundred different agencies involved with Homeland Security. It means there's a lot of people in the Congress and in the Senate who have got jurisdiction over those agencies. In other words, that's what they call *turf*. And people like to defend their turf. And so, all of a sudden, when you're saying, well, you know, Mr. Chairman, we're going to have to take this away from you and put it in a single agency, you don't get to fund it anymore, it kind of makes the chairman nervous.
>
> So . . . I need the help of the American people to remind the turf fighters not to be nervous, because we're talking about doing what's right for America.[31]

One would not expect to hear former Presidents George H. W. Bush or Bill Clinton refer to members of Congress and the Senate as "turf fighters," but the metaphor, not especially negative, was sufficiently colorful to stick in the listeners' minds, so that they might remember to contact their representatives and senators, as Bush suggested.

Distinct Styles: Bush and Kerry

During the presidential campaign between President Bush and presumptive Democratic nominee John Kerry, writers in the media compared the style of the two men. Rarely on the mark, their comparisons showed their political perspective more than an objective analysis of the two political leaders' rhetoric. However, a comparison of styles here provides an opportunity to identify certain characteristics of the Bush style.

George W. Bush and John F. Kerry have very different public-speaking styles. Journalists in the elite press would agree, since they favor Kerry's style over Bush's. In *Time*, Joe Klein wrote, "The contrast between complex-sentence Kerry and simple-sentence Bush could not be clearer."[32] In *Time*'s next issue, Klein again emphasized the notion that Bush's style lacked complexity. "Clearly," he said, "the President and Karl Rove believe that Americans want a strong, God-fearing, plainspoken leader who doesn't burden them with complexities." Then with unshaded dislike for Bush, Klein stated, "He is not a simpleton. He just plays one—wittingly, it seems—on TV."[33] Aside from the fact that his pronouncement is sweeping and unsupported, it suggested that millions of Americans, including a great number of bright people who have stated otherwise, were simpletons to be fooled by President Bush.

By advancing essentially the same theme, liberal writers promoted Kerry's presidential aspirations. Angie Cannon in *U.S. News* quoted Rutgers political scientist Ross Baker as saying: "Kerry has a thoughtful approach, but thoughtfulness is not necessarily a strong quality to have in a presidential campaign. Subtlety flies out the window and is replaced with hard-edged clichés, which the president happens to be very good at."[34]

In this remark, Baker lauds Kerry's thoughtfulness and, by implication, his subtlety that he apparently found in his speeches. He suggests in this comparison that Bush is neither thoughtful nor subtle, but, instead, clichéd in his style, which the unthinking electorate prefers. However, Bush does not have a style characterized by clichés (that is, expressions that have become trite), unless one finds his traditional Christian phrases objectionable, as many liberals do. He and his speechwriters used a vocabulary adaptable to the realities of the 21st century—war with global terrorism and ways of dealing with domestic and international crises, such as the U.S. spy-plane standoff on China's Hainan Island.

Writing in *Newsweek*, Howard Fineman and Tamara Lipper commented, "This is a president who often would rather preach than answer questions—or ask them."[35] Assuming that they are serious, it might be noted that, while President Bush may refer to God in his speeches, he does not "preach." And in meetings, he makes every effort to answer all questions, as he did when he met with members of the so-called 9/11 Commission on April 29, who afterward gave him high marks for his candid answers; he also answers correspondents' questions as completely as possible, even when they are impertinent.

Then there is Evan Thomas writing in *Newsweek*, who mined Bob Woodward's *Plan of Attack* for any hint of negative nuance against Bush. He said, "In Woodward's portrait, President Bush is single-minded, and possibly simple-minded, in his resolve. He seems to have relied more on divine guidance than the considered opinions of top advisors."[36] Yet, Woodward's book, on balance, portrays a strong leader in George W. Bush. "We're urging people to buy the book," announced the White House Communications Director, Dan Bartlett. "What this book does is show a president who was asking the right questions and showing prudence as well as resolve during very difficult times. This book undermines a lot of critics' charges."[37]

Liberal journalists tried to portray Bush's style as simple, because he used fewer complex sentences than Kerry did; and they sought to present Kerry's style as complex, because he used fewer simple sentences than Bush did. But, a more important distinction between the two styles is that Bush's speeches are essentially *rhetorical*, prepared to be heard; whereas Kerry's speeches are essentially *essayistic*, written, it seems, with readers in mind rather than listeners. Essays tend to use a great many complex sentences, as one sees in Kerry's speeches.

Speech theorists teach that short, simply-structured sentences are preferred to long, complex-structured sentences in speeches. Speech professors Douglas Ehninger and Wayne Brockreide, in their classic *Decision by Debate*, advise speakers: "For maximum intelligibility, a sentence should not only be as short as practicable, but the thought should move forward naturally and easily, without awkward interruptions and without distracting excursions into related ideas."[38] They also note that sentences in effective speeches are "direct and simply structured. They render the speaker's meaning instantly and unmistakably clear. Moreover, the precision of expression adds weight to the ideas."[39] Their model for such sentence structure is President Franklin D. Roosevelt.[40]

Good speechwriters and effective speakers understand that shorter, simpler sentences should predominate in a speech. They seek to enable listeners to grasp the meaning of statements quickly and correctly for optimum persuasive impact. They make complex sentences—especially useful in supplying details—as short and precisely worded as possible, realizing that "long sentences, even when skillfully handled, put a strain on the attention and memory."[41] They work to avoid—as Ehninger and Brockreide stress—"unnecessary wordiness" and "ambiguous statements."[42]

President Bush understands and applies these principles. Karen Hughes, in her book *Ten Minutes from Normal*, tells how he corrects and alters the first draft of a speech, including the striking out of excess words. "I used to tease him that he edits out most all of the adjectives."[43] He requests drafts of a speech weeks or months early and then, using a black Sharpie pen, indicates desired changes to clarify key points.[44] Bush strives to make his statements concise, so that ideas stand out. He knows a short sentence does not have to "shortchange" ideas—a few words can capsulize significant meanings.

For example, on March 19, 2004, at the White House, with members of the Diplomatic Corps and ambassadors representing 84 countries in attendance, addressing the nation, President Bush compressed important ideas into relatively few words. Here are some sentences selected: "The war on terror is not a figure of speech." "There can be no separate peace with the terrorist enemy." "The only certain way to protect our people is by early, united, and decisive action." "Our coalition is taking urgent action to stop the transfer of deadly weapons and materials." "The people of Afghanistan are a world away from the nightmare of the Taliban."[45]

Then, on November 6, 2003, the President delivered a speech at the 20th Anniversary of the National Endowment for Democracy U.S. Chamber of Commerce. His speech shows how careful sentence structure and word selection enhance his style, as the following paragraph with complex sentences evinces:

> Other men, and groups of men, have gained influence in the Middle East and beyond through an ideology of theocratic terror. Behind their language of religion is the ambition for absolute political power. Ruling cabals like the Taliban show their version of religious piety in public whippings of women, ruthless suppression of any difference or dissent, and support for terrorists who arm and train to murder the innocent. The Taliban promised religious purity and national pride. Instead, by systematically destroying a proud and working society, they left behind suffering and starvation.[46]

One can see in Bush's complex sentences clearly-stated ideas, unencumbered by ambiguity and wordiness. On reading the paragraph, one senses its energy and conviction, strengthened by a balance between generalization and specificity, and between factual information and emotional appeal. All it needed was a strong, forceful delivery, which Bush gave it.

In comparing Bush's style with Kerry's when it came to unscripted situations such as interacting with audience members or participating in interviews, Bush expressed himself more clearly, directly, and conversationally. In July 2002, a reporter asked him about Osama bin Laden's status. "He may be alive," the President said. "If he is, we'll get him. If he's not, we got him." *National Review* editor Jay Nordlinger noted, "Speechwriters could labor for weeks and not come up with anything better."[47] Doubtless, Bush's directness prompted Nordlinger to observe: "When he is most purely himself, he is blunt, unfussy, a little salty—Trumanesque."[48]

In Kerry's case the problem is not that his style is too thoughtful, complex, and subtle to be persuasive, the problem is that his style lacks clarity of expression and position. Americans see evidence of Kerry's clarity deficit in his continual need to explain what he meant in a statement or where he stands on an issue. We see his clarity deficit pointed up in an interview he granted White House correspondent Kenneth Walsh of *U.S. News*. On the subject of "tough decisions," Walsh elicited a response from Kerry as follows: "There's a complexity in some of these choices that people need to acknowledge. If everything is so simple, and you've learned everything when you're 21 years old, you might as well shut your mind and stop learning. I think it's important to grow and express that growth as you go along."[49] (One can guess whose style Kerry might see as complex and whose style he might see as simple.)

The author asked several people to read Kerry's interview response concerning "tough decisions" and all were mystified as to its meaning. The three sentences do not provide a clear chain of thought for continuity. Also, the relationship between the ideas in the clauses of the second sentence is unclear. It does not help that two clauses in this sentence say essentially the same thing—that someone has stopped learning. The problem is twofold: word selection and sentence structure, which together produce a murky statement.

Even leading Democrats, worried about the lack of clarity in Kerry's campaign rhetoric, offered advice: Mario Cuomo, former New York Governor was quoted as saying, "[Kerry must] stop talking in sentences with three commas in them. . ." However, his style suffered from more than excessive commas. Joseph Biden, Senator for Delaware, was quoted as remarking, "I don't think John [Kerry] should go back and try to explain accurate statements that are unexplainable."[50] How does one judge the accuracy of statements that cannot be explained?

Kerry, on July 16, 2003, delivered a major address to the New York City firefighters in the Bronx. Early in his speech he made this statement:

> We should not just ask how to respond but how to prevent. And police are not just among the first responders, they are the first preventers.
>
> We need to make certain they have the training and resources to protect their communities and their country. They need fundamental training in who the terrorists are, where they come from, how they think and how police need to think to deal with them. The police officers of America should go through exercises in how terrorists work. This is how the Israelis do it and now we must too. It requires technical assistance, knowledge, veterans and trainers. It doesn't require many millions of dollars—it just requires dedication, imagination, and recognition of the paramount importance of state and local police in the protection of the country.[51]

These two paragraphs above were selected, because they contained Kerry's proposal to improve police officers' training for dealing with terrorists. In the first paragraph, Kerry seemed to advocate a more prominent role for police in dealing with terrorism. But, at the same time, he set up a false distinction between the terms *respond* and *prevent*—he suggested that response did not include preventing attacks as well as dealing with their aftermath, which likely would have caused some confusion for listeners. Contrary to what Kerry implied, however, the main thrust of first responders has been prevention—they receive intelligence about a possible threat and act to protect the target identified.

One would expect the second paragraph to be clearer, since it focused on his proposal. But, it also lacked clarity, due to the overuse of general language that needed concrete wording for support. Kerry's use of abstract terms, without explanation, such as "fundamental," "technical," "knowledge," "veterans," and "recognition" must have dulled listeners' understanding of what he meant. He was not too complex or subtle, he was vague. The most definite idea he offered was that U.S. police should imitate Israeli training for fighting terrorism. However, Israeli training is geared to fighting terrorist groups that have their own agenda, methods and goals. Much of what Kerry seemed to be saying about what the police should know sounded like he was confusing the police with the C.I.A. and F.B.I. Kerry's proposal offered no tangible improvement on the functioning of the Department of Homeland Security, which, minutes earlier, he dismissed as "a bureaucracy in Washington."

A major difference between Bush's and Kerry's style is that the President's speeches tend to create interested listeners and the Senator's speeches tend to produce boredom in listeners. During the presidential campaign, one could easily see these reactions in the candidates' audiences, as one observed them on television. Evan Thomas and fellow reporters at *Newsweek* were given exclusive access to Kerry's campaign, which, after the election, culminated in their book *Election 2004*. Their compilation of observations included critical appraisals of Kerry's rhetorical style. They wrote that just days before the November 2 election, in Reno, Nevada, the Senator

> launched into a long and rambling speech, one of his most soporific in weeks. A simple line in his prepared text on the need to fix Social Security became a five minute explanation of how the system got broken. He gave the same prolix treatment to health care, with a strange overreaching assertion that the Bush health-care plan was "killing millions of Americans." A 25-minute speech went on for close to an hour.[52]

Another big difference between the Bush style and the Kerry style is that the President speaks decisively regarding positions (determined, firm, able to decide); whereas the Senator speaks indecisively regarding positions (hesitant, vacillating, unable to decide). Former General Electric Chairman Jack Welch, in April 2005 on MSNBC's *Hardball*, speaking of the 2004 election, said, "George Bush, . . . you know where he stood . . . He tells you what he thinks. He says it. And he acts on it."

In March and April of 2004, President Bush's resolve in staying the course in Iraq was tested. Spain's newly-elected leadership retreated from Iraq in compliance with terrorist demands, and insurgents and foreign terrorists attacked American troops in three Iraqi cities with a high loss of life. Speaking to the nation on March 19, 2004, the President stated, "We will never turn over Iraq to terrorists who intend our own destruction. We will not fail the Iraqi people, who have placed their trust in us. Whatever it takes, we will fight and work to assure the success of freedom in Iraq."[53]

When Americans compare Senator Kerry's voting record in the U.S. Senate with his campaign positions on the stump, they see evidence of indecisiveness. On October 11, 2002, he voted in the Senate for authorization to use force in Iraq. Then, on September 2, 2003, in Mount Pleasant, South Carolina, he claimed he voted "to threaten" use of force in Iraq and described himself as "an anti-war candidate." On October 25, 2001, he voted for the Patriot Act. But then, on December 1, 2003, at Iowa State University, Iowa City, he attacked the Patriot Act and said it should be replaced with "a new law that protects our people and our liberties at the same time." He did not offer specifics as to what form such a law would take. On June 10, 1998, Kerry voted against eliminating the marriage penalty for married taxpayers with combined incomes of less than $50,000 per year. Then, on October 23, 2003, on Fox News' *Special*

Report, he said that he would fight to keep tax relief for married couples.[54] Such reversals showed serious vacillation to many people. Speaking on Kerry's electability, Governor Howard Dean asserted, "He appears to change his mind so often . . . . It appears that his word is no good."[55]

Leadership that is decisive in style is especially crucial in wartime. A leader who makes a decision and then moves to the opposite extreme is likely to be uncertain in determining the right policies and unconfident in responding to the attacks of enemies. "Seeing seven sides to an issue is useful in the study of metaphysics," observed Tony Blankley. "But men of action—and world events always have required American presidents to be men of action—must be capable of decisive action."[56]

The Grand Style: Practical Eloquence

When asked about Bush's style of speaking, a college professor who teaches business said, "There's an unpredictable quality in his style, which likely is worrisome to his handlers. When he receives a tough question from a reporter, there's an exquisite agony as you wait for him to respond—and to the reporter's surprise, it's often an effective response." She concluded, "He's in sync with the way people talk—not always polished, but the result of careful thought."

President Bush's conversational style, as the business professor noted, is "not always polished"—if it were, it would not be conversational style. However, he can give polished speeches that exemplify, in many respects, the grand or elevated style of persuasive public speaking. Formal occasions create opportunities to deliver such speeches, as when he addresses the United Nations General Assembly, a Joint Session of Congress, the nation on the State of the Union, or large formal gatherings in foreign countries.

On these occasions, Bush often demonstrates an ability to speak with eloquence. A modern definition of *eloquence* is a "speech or writing that is vivid, forceful, fluent, graceful, and persuasive."[57] In other words, eloquence has, as its practical end, the influence of people's behavior by use of impressive language, effectively presented. An anonymous source tells us, "The finest eloquence is that which gets things done; the worst is that which delays them."

When President Bush presents a speech with a formal or elevated style, the occasion, audience, and purpose require it. He can move easily and smoothly between a conversational mode and a more formal style, something that even some famous speakers were unable to do. Queen Victoria is said to have asked Prime Minister William Gladstone "not to speak to her as if he were addressing a public audience."[58] George Stephanopoulos, former Clinton staffer, briefly compared Bush's speeches to those of Clinton in *Newsweek*, August 2000: "George W. Bush's formal speeches mark a return to a crisper, more self-consciously eloquent style, rather than Clinton's stream-of-consciousness style of persuasion."[59]

United Nations Speech

George W. Bush delivered one of his most important formal persuasive speeches to the United Nations General Assembly on November 10, 2001. The body that he addressed—a 20th century entity that had long since lost its teeth and the memory of its original purpose—substituted talk for action. Its members had become accustomed to listening to world leaders speak in generalities, diplomatically refraining from exerting the pressure of persuasion. But, Bush's style of address broke with this tradition as, with clarity, directness, and eloquence, he challenged governments to confront global terrorism, arguing that it posed a worldwide threat that demanded immediate action.

In words plain and forthright rather than subtle and suggestive—as many diplomats present would have preferred—Bush stated his new doctrine that was "binding on every nation." He declared, "We have a responsibility to deny any sanctuary, safe haven, or transit to terrorists."[60] According to this doctrine, "there is no such thing as a good terrorist."[61] He thus repudiated the practice in the U.N. of condemning some terrorist groups such as al Qaeda, while excusing such groups as Hamas and Hezbollah, whose terrorism some members saw as efforts to free Palestine. His words took on an ominous tone when he asserted, "Any government that rejects this principle, trying to pick and choose its terrorist friends, will know the consequences."[62]

Toward the end of his speech, Bush became more pointed in his statements that the U.N. as an institution should take up the fight against the terrorists. "And, finally," he said, "this struggle is a defining moment for the United Nations, itself. And the world needs its principled leadership."[63] He warned, "The only alternative to victory is a nightmare world where every city is a potential killing field."[64] Three years later, after terrorist attacks in many countries, including Muslim, Bush's words proved prophetic.

Although President Bush's U.N. speech contained important foreign-policy pronouncements and displayed an arresting, provocative style, it did not receive the press coverage or plaudits of citizens that it rightfully deserved. On the other hand, his second "State of the Union Address" elicited positive reactions from Americans and aroused considerable interest in the press around the world.

State of the Union Address

President Bush's "State of the Union Address" on January 29, 2002, sought to convey with conviction three key ideas—or, as Bush described them, "three great goals for America: We will win this war; we'll protect our homeland; and we will revive our economy."[65] Not surprisingly, he devoted most of his speech to the war on terrorism. He began with this emphasis by giving a succinct summary of accomplishments, made impressive stylistically by using active verbs and only three conjunctions ("and") as follows:

> We last met in an hour of shock and suffering. In four short months, our nation has comforted the victims, begun to rebuild New York and the Pentagon, rallied a great coalition, captured, arrested, and rid the world of thousands of terrorists, destroyed Afghanistan's terrorist training camps, saved a people from starvation, and freed a country from brutal oppression. (Applause.)[66]

We see the President's hand in this paragraph. He said to one speechwriter, for example, "that page is way too passive; I'm not bobbing along like some cork; I want active verbs."[67]

Throughout this address, Bush phrased simple and complex sentences—as in the paragraph quoted above—simply and clearly, likely enabling listeners to follow his statements with ease as he moved from one idea to the next. In effect, his style created a sense of movement for listeners that would keep their energy fresh and their interest high. We can see this clear movement of ideas in these statements:

> Our discoveries in Afghanistan confirmed our worst fears, and showed us the true scope of the task ahead. We have seen the depth of our enemies' hatred in videos, where they laugh about the loss of innocent life. And the depth of their hatred is equaled by the madness of the destruction they design. We have found diagrams of American nuclear plants and public water facilities, detailed instructions for making chemical weapons, surveillance maps of American cities, and thorough descriptions of landmarks in America and throughout the world.
>
> What we have found in Afghanistan confirms that, far from ending there, our war against terror is only beginning. Most of the 19 men who hijacked planes on September the 11th were trained in Afghanistan's camps, and so were tens of thousands of others. Thousands of dangerous killers, schooled in the methods of murder, often supported by outlaw regimes, are now spread throughout the world like ticking time bombs, set to go off without warning.[68]

When President Bush presented these and other sentences in his speech, a pleasant rhythm came through in his delivery, which helped to convey meanings and emotions. Both Aristotle and Cicero considered rhythm an important attribute of rhetorical style. Various elements, along with his delivery, produced the rhythm in Bush's speech, including variation in sentence length; distribution of accented syllables (only a few in succession); natural pauses that emphasized key phrases (for example, after "our worst fears," and after "outlaw regimes"); and use of periodic sentences in which the main statement remained uncompleted until the end or near the end of the sentence (for example, "*Thousands of dangerous killers*, schooled in the methods of murder, often supported by outlaw regimes, *are now spread throughout the world* like ticking time bombs, set to go off without warning"). Periodic sentences are more typical of a formal or elevated style.

Cicero taught that figures of speech also influenced rhythm. And, in addition, they endow the spoken word with beauty and distinction. Perhaps more than any other stylistic device, figures contribute to the eloquence of an address by creating vividness of expression. Bush's second "State of the Union Address" has an abundance of figures of various kinds.

One of the rarer figures of speech is *apostrophe*, which is displayed as the speaker turns away from the audience to address one person. The President mentioned that Michael Spann, a CIA officer and Marine had recently been killed in Afghanistan, and that his widow, Shannon Spann, was "with us tonight." Then, addressing her, he said, "Shannon, I assure you and all who have lost a loved one that our cause is just, and our country will never forget the debt we owe Michael and all who gave their lives for freedom."[69]

Another figure found in Bush's address was *simile*. At one point, while speaking about terrorists trained in Afghanistan who were in many parts of the world, he said, they were "like ticking time bombs, set to go off without warning."[70] This comparison created an image that made the terrorist threat seem more real.

Bush used *metaphor* to produce striking images for the audience. In referring to terrorists, he said, "These enemies view the entire world as a battlefield."[71] Probably, there were people present, especially Democrats, who considered this metaphor an exaggeration. (Of course, subsequent terrorist attacks in many countries demonstrated otherwise.)

One of Bush's favorite figures is *personification*. He likes to apply human traits to the country, such as "character" and charge the enemy with thinking Americans are weak, fearful, and selfish. He told his audience: "I've been humbled and privileged to see the true character of this country in a time of testing." Then minutes later, he asserted, "yet after America was attacked, it was as if our entire country looked into a mirror and saw our better selves."[72]

A figure strongly identified with the style of Bush's formal, elevated speeches is *antithesis*. The contrast it sets up can, in a few words, endow a statement with force, emotional appeal, or ironic humor. For instance, "Terrorists who once occupied Afghanistan now occupy cells at Guantanamo Bay."[73] Or, "We began to think less of the goods we can accumulate, and more about the good we can do."[74]

The speaker always enhances eloquence in using the figure *anaphora*. Bush achieved this by the repetition of a phrase at the beginning of a clause in successive statements. In addressing the economy, he stated:

"Good jobs also depend on reliable and affordable energy . . . ." "Good jobs depend on expanded trade . . . ." "Good jobs depend on sound tax policy . . . ."[75] This kind of parallel structure can be persuasive as it reinforces retention of ideas.

Like figures of speech, *alliteration* influenced Bush's rhythm and also added beauty and distinction to his style. Alliteration repeats the same initial sound in two or more words in a phrase. Here are some examples: "a sustained strategy of homeland security," "to fight freedom's fight," "a decisive decade in the history of liberty," "patient and persistent in the pursuit of two great objectives."

One additional stylistic feature of Bush's "State of the Union Address" created a strong identification with his listeners: *personal pronouns*. A count of his personal pronouns revealed a total of 236, which, impressively, included the usage of *our* 72 times and *we* 80 times. His "usage of personal pronouns creates an 'imagined community' in which the president and his listeners coexist on a level plane."[76]

The media coverage missed much of what should have been seen as important ideas in this speech because of their obsession with three words: "axis of evil." William Schneider, writing in *National Journal* about Bush's "State of the Union Address," said, "Even his threat to Iran, Iraq, and North Korea—the rougue states he branded an 'axis of evil'—was unspecified."[77] Schneider then quoted Bush as to what he did specify regarding the "axis of evil," except that he left out Bush's two most important statements, which were: "We will develop and deploy effective missile defenses to protect America and our allies from sudden attack. (Applause.) And all nations should know: America will do what is necessary to insure our nation's security."[78] Schneider conceded that a Gallup poll found that 64 percent of people who had viewed the President's address believed that his proposals for dealing with terrorism could prove "very effective." And 73 percent of viewers believed that his economic program would get the nation out of recession.[79]

Whitehall Palace Speech

President Bush's speech of November 19, 2003 at Whitehall Palace in London, will doubtless stand as one of his finest presidential addresses. In keeping with the formality of the occasion, he delivered a speech that, in

Ciceronian terms, approached the grand style, as shown in the dignity and eloquence of its language. By his style, Bush made historical facts, tragic events, and policy principles clear, interesting, and memorable. His vividly-phrased statements caused the audience to give attention to material that might otherwise have been perceived as dry and dull. He was careful not to dwell too long on any one idea, but, through concise and direct language, kept the speech moving along to new ideas. Not surprisingly, Bush endowed his key points with his most striking and colorful phrasing.

For example, wanting to reinforce the shared vision and common values of Great Britain and America, the President said, "more than an alliance of security and commerce, the British and American peoples have an alliance of values. And, today, this old and tested alliance is very strong." (Applause.)[80] And, becoming more personal, he emphasized the friendship between Prime Minister Tony Blair and himself by simply referring to their respective origins: "And whether one learns these ideals in County Durham or in West Texas, they instill mutual respect and they inspire common purpose."[81] Then, connecting values with foreign policy—and, incidentally, expressing some personal philosophy—he declared, "The deepest beliefs of our nations set the direction of our foreign policy. We value our own civil rights, so we stand for the civil rights of others. We affirm the God-given dignity of every person, so we are moved to action by poverty and oppression and famine and disease."[82]

President Bush next recalled President Woodrow Wilson's belief in the League of Nations that ultimately, failed in its goals. His language became more emotionally charged when he stated, "At Wilson's high point of idealism, however, Europe was one short generation from Munich and Auschwitz and the Blitz. Looking back, we see the reasons why. The League of Nations, lacking both credibility and will, collapsed at the first challenge of the dictators. Free nations failed to recognize, much less confront, the aggressive evil in plain sight."[83] He then drew a crucial lesson from history: "Through world war and cold war, we learned that idealism, if it is to do any good in this world, requires common purpose and national strength, moral courage and patience in difficult tasks."[84] Bush listed all of the cities that had experienced terrorist attacks, beginning with New York. Afterward, with strong words of warning that risked critics' charges of exaggeration, he asserted, "These terrorists target the innocent, and they kill by the thousands. And they would, if they gain the weapons they seek, kill by the millions and not be finished."[85]

Having created a context conducive to acceptance of his foreign policy principles, the President indicated that free nations' peace and security rested on three pillars: "First, international organizations must be equal to the challenges facing the world, from lifting up failing states to opposing proliferation."[86] What he only suggested in first referring to the League of Nations, he now asserted, "America and Great Britain have done, and will do, all in their power to prevent the United Nations from solemnly choosing its own irrelevance and inviting the fate of the League of Nations."[87]

"The second pillar of peace and security in our world," Bush stated, "is the willingness of free nations, when the last resort arrives, to restrain aggression and evil by force."[88] He followed with four sentences that, in clear, crisp language, tactfully put into perspective for anti-war protesters the difference between judging by motives and judging by motives and duty. He said, "There are principled objections to the use of force in every generation, and I credit the good motives behind these views. Those in authority, however, are not judged only by good motivations. The people have given us the duty to defend them. And that duty sometimes requires the violent restraint of violent men. In some cases, the measured use of force is all that protects us from a chaotic world ruled by force."[89] One could imagine that Bush's statement might have been inspired by St. Thomas Aquinas' famous line: "For a war to be just, three things are necessary—public authority, just cause, right motive." Consistent with the grand style, Bush asked a rhetorical question: "And who will say that Iraq was better off when Saddam Hussein was strutting and killing, or that the world was safer when he held power?"[90]

Bush presented his third pillar as "our commitment to the global expansion of democracy, and the hope and progress it brings, as the alternative to instability and to hatred and terror."[91] Capsulizing the goal of his foreign policy, the President made clear: "We cannot rely exclusively on military power to assure our long-term security. *Lasting peace is gained as justice and democracy advance.*"[92] He explained, "In democratic societies, men and women do not swear allegiance to malcontents and murderers; they turn their hearts and labor to building better lives."[93] Bush conceded,

"In the West, there's been a certain skepticism about the capacity or even the desire of Middle Eastern peoples for self-government." He responded by pointing out that "more than half of the world's Muslims are today contributing citizens in democratic societies."[94] He also had a message for terrorists whose "strategy" is "cruelty": "We did not charge hundreds of miles into the heart of Iraq and pay a bitter cost of casualties and liberate 25 million people, only to retreat before a band of thugs and assassins." (Applause.)[95]

Typically, the Bush style incorporates lighter material in the speech to save the audience from being overwhelmed by wartime concerns and potentially-worrisome statements. Bush adhered to this practice in his conclusion as he recalled that Americans were stationed in Britain during World War II: "the English people did get used to Americans. They welcomed soldiers and fliers into their villages and homes, and took to calling them 'our boys.' About 70,000 of those boys did their part to affirm our special relationship. They returned home with English brides."[96] We see in this formal speech George W. Bush's ability to adapt his style to the audience—in this case, a staid British audience that appreciated the dignity, reserve, and eloquence of the speech's style. Bush's humor elicited laughter nine times, and his statements caused the audience to applaud 14 times. Bush's language both clarified and vivified his grand strategy for waging war against terrorism—he thus met the requirement for style laid down by the Roman teacher Quintilian: "True beauty is never divorced from utility."

Second Inaugural Address

On January 20, 2005, after taking the 39-word oath of office, George W. Bush delivered his 21-minute "Second Inaugural Address" at the West Front of the U.S. Capitol for America's 55th inauguration ceremony. He spoke to thousands of people who had gathered in snowy weather to hear him; and he addressed the millions in mass audiences at home and abroad who received his speech via television.

Elevated in style, as the occasion required, Bush's speech was eloquent in expression and pointed in meaning in articulating his vision of how he would keep the oath he had taken to keep America secure. Statements in his speech often reflected the themes of war against global terrorism—although he did not use the words *terrorism* or *terrorist*, but instead spoke of "tyranny" and "tyrants," so that he could broaden the application of his remarks.

In his introduction, he reminded Americans of the nature of an enemy that must arouse a sensible fear. He asserted, "We have seen our vulnerability—and we have seen its deepest source. For as long as whole regions of the world simmer in resentment and tyranny—prone to ideologies that feed hatred and excuse murder—violence will gather, and multiply in destructive power, and cross the most defended borders, and raise a mortal threat." Just prior to this statement, Bush had declared, "For a half century, America defended our own freedom by standing watch on distant borders. After the shipwreck of communism came years of relative quiet, years of repose, years of sabbatical—and then there came a day of fire."[97] With these words, Bush warned Americans against complacency, after years of "relative quiet" that has followed the 9/11 attacks. Failing to see the connection between these two paragraphs, many journalists suggested that Bush said this to take a veiled swipe at President Clinton by implying that he had been asleep and derelict in his duty during years between communism's fall and terrorism's rise.

Using language clear and compelling, Bush found "only one force of history that can break the reign of hatred and resentment, and expose the pretensions of tyrants, and . . . that is the force of human freedom." His language appealing to people's rationality, he continued, "We are led, by events and common sense, to one conclusion: The survival of liberty in our land increasingly depends on the success of liberty in other lands. The best hope for peace in our world is the expansion of freedom in all the world."[98] Unencumbered by vagueness and qualification—the window dressing that hides the truth behind many political leaders' views—Bush linked three imperatives: survival of America, liberty in other lands, and world peace. Then building on religious belief that all human beings everywhere "bear the image of the Maker of Heaven and earth," he came to his boldest pronouncement: "So it is the policy of the United States to seek and support the growth of democratic movements and institutions in every nation and culture, with the ultimate goal of ending tyranny in our world."[99] Herein he voiced the two great foreign policy themes of his presidency: freedom and democracy.

The President's pronouncement "of ending tyranny in the world," prompted some critics to accuse him of being too aggressive or, as one *U.S. News* reporter put it, "unexpectedly provocative." Kenneth Walsh, in a *U.S. News* article on Bush's inaugural remarks, wrote: "It was a day for the true believers—the social conservatives, Christian activists, foreign-policy hawks, and of course, George W. Bush himself."[100] Taken as a whole, Bush did not, as Walsh and others seemed to imply, deliver a sword-rattling speech that only certain groups would appreciate. Doubtless, many of the record 62 million Americans who voted for President Bush found his speech relevant, for it dealt with the security of their country in wartime and the peace of the world. It is surprising that informed citizens would find the themes of his address unexpected, since they echoed ideas—naturally in different form—found in Bush's previous speeches. Moreover, they were consistent with the Bush Doctrine concerning terrorists and those countries that harbor or help them.

So as to preclude any misunderstanding about what he advocated when he spoke of "ending tyranny," Bush stated, "This is not primarily the task of arms . . ." Then, his style taking a philosophical bent, he explained, "Freedom, by its nature must be chosen, and defended by citizens, and sustained by the rule of law and the protection of minorities. And when the soul of a nation finally speaks, the institutions that arise may reflect customs and traditions very different from our own."[101] Adopting more emphatic language, Bush added, "America will not impose our style of government on the unwilling. Our goal instead is to help others find their own voice, attain their own freedom, and make their own way."[102] Thus, the President made it clear that America was ready to support nations to achieve democracy, which included helping "leaders of governments with long habits of control."[103]

At one point in his speech, Bush departed from inaugural tradition and addressed his remarks "anew to the peoples of the world":

> All who live in tyranny and hopelessness can know: the United States will not ignore your oppression, or excuse your oppressors. When you stand for your liberty, we will stand with you.
>
> Democratic reformers facing repression, prison, or exile can know: America sees you for who you are: the future leaders of your free country.[104]

These lines might well show the influence of Natan Sharansky's book *The Case for Democracy: The Power of Freedom to Overcome Tyranny and Terror*. Soon after the book's publication, Sharansky told Rush Limbaugh in an interview that President Bush called him to say that he had read his book and that he wanted to see him. "We had a meeting [in the Oval Office]. It was really surprising to see how strongly the President felt about the points in the book." Sharansky, who spent nine years of torture in the Soviet Gulag, said that in the days of his dissent, President Reagan's policies and words were "our major hope, because he was the one who understood that you cannot separate security from the idea of a free society . . . He linked these two questions. And that's exactly . . . what President Bush does today."[105] It seems clear that the President, in addressing his remarks to people in the world, intended to send a message of hope to dissidents and those suffering under dictatorial regimes. Concerning these people, Bush declared, "America will not pretend that jailed dissidents prefer their chains, or that women welcome humiliation and servitude, or that any human being aspires to live at the mercy of bullies."[106]

After briefly speaking "anew to the peoples of the world," Bush, using parallel phrasing, addressed his remarks "anew to my fellow citizens." He began with words of tribute: "From all of you, I have asked patience in the hard task of securing America, which you have granted in good measure. Our country has accepted obligations that are difficult to fulfill, and would be dishonorable to abandon." Then, becoming specific in the moral emphasis of his thought, he appealed to Americans' national pride in saying, "Yet because we acted in the great liberating tradition of this nation, tens of millions have achieved their freedom."[107] He did not name the liberated countries of Afghanistan and Iraq, perhaps because he thought by not mentioning them he would arouse less adverse political feeling that would undercut unity.

Bush certainly wanted all of his listeners with him, as he moved next to what he must have known was the most eloquent passage in his speech: "By our efforts, we have lit a fire as well—a fire in the minds of men. It warms those who feel its power, it burns those who fight its progress, and one day this untamed fire of freedom will reach the darkest corners of our world."[108] The striking phrase "fire in the minds of men" comes from Feodor Dostoyevsky's novel *The Possessed,* which focused on a town impressed by new revolutionary ideas. Writing in *U.S. News*, Michael Barone observed, "Bush is routinely . . . castigated by political opponents as a reactionary. But in his second inaugural he revealed himself to be a revolutionary."[109] In the sense that he works to bring about new, major or fundamental changes to improve governmental policies and practices, Bush *is* a revolutionary.

Probably, George W. Bush's "Inaugural Address" set forth the most ambitious goals for Americans and America of any past president of modern times. His revolutionary ideas not only infuse his foreign policy, they also infuse his domestic agenda. "In America's ideal of freedom," Bush told his inaugural audiences, "citizens find the dignity and security of economic independence, instead of laboring on the edge of subsistence. This is the broader definition of liberty that motivated the Homestead Act, the Social Security Act, and the G.I. Bill of Rights." Then, in more stately terms, he added, "And now we will extend this vision by reforming great institutions to serve the needs of our time. To give every American a stake in the promise and future of our country, we will bring the highest standards to our schools, and build an ownership society."[110] Two weeks later, he would provide details of proposed programs in his "State of the Union Address."

President Bush's "Second Inaugural" gave listeners a bold, uncompromising vision of a better tomorrow for the nation and the world. His style reflected his energy, faith, confidence, and forward-looking leadership. Each of these characterizes lines from a graceful closing:

> We go forward with complete confidence in the eventual triumph of freedom. Not because history runs on the wheels of inevitability; it is human choices that move events. Not because we consider ourselves a chosen nation; God moves and chooses as He wills. We have confidence because freedom is the permanent hope of mankind, the hunger in dark places, the longing of the soul."[111]

Contrary to some critics' predictions, President George W. Bush's "Second Inaugural Address" will long be remembered. Historians will return to it again and again in search of insights into the nature of the man, his foreign policy, and the role he took in world peace. Historians will come to see that Bush, more than any other world leader of his time, was an internationalist, who set big goals and measured results in global dimensions.

NOTES

1. Michael Silverstein, *Talking Politics: The Substance of Style from Abe to "W"* (Chicago: Prickly Paradigm Press, 2003), 91-112.
2. Coulter, *Slander*, 182.
3. Ibid., 182-183.
4. Hughes, *Ten Minutes from Normal*, 161.
5. Ibid., 260.
6. Silverstein, *Talking Politics*, 111.
7. Darley et al., *Psychology*, 239.
8. President's White House Press Conference, Fox News, April 30, 2004.
9. David Frum, *The Right Man: An Inside Account of the Bush White House* (New York: Random House Trade Paperbacks, 2003), 5.
10. Hughes, *Ten Minutes from Normal*, 264.
11. Nordlinger, "A Voice for Our Time," p. 37.
12. Frum, *The Right Man*, 125.
13. John Podhoretz, *Bush Country: How Dubya Became a Great President While Driving Liberals Insane* (New York: St. Martin's Press, 2004), 8-9.
14. Coulter, *Slander*, 71.
15. *Special Report with Brit Hume*, Fox News, April 14, 2004.
16. Coulter, *Slander*, 184.
17. Howard Fineman, "A President Finds His True Voice," *Newsweek*, September 24, 2001, p. 50.
18. Bob Herbert, "In America: Leading America Beyond Fear," *New York Times*, September 24, 2001, p. A31.
19. Bush, *We Will Prevail*, 12.
20. Ibid., 12-13.
21. Ibid., 14.
22. Ibid.
23. Jeff Stoffer, "English, American Style," *American Legion Magazine*, January, 2005, p. 19.
24. Paul Bedard, "George 'McKinley' Trades Up to a 'Theodore' Bush," *U.S. News & World Report*, January 14, 2002, p. 4.
25. Copeland, *The World's Great Speeches*, 346.
26. Bush, *We Will Prevail*, 136.
27. Jackson, *That Man*, 159-160.
28. Ibid., 160.

29. "Kerry's Mouth," *Washington Times* National Weekly Edition, March 8-14, 2004, p. 36.
30. "Remarks by the President at the Opening of Oak Park High School," Kansas City, Missouri, June 11, 2002, www.whitehouse.gov.
31. Ibid.
32. Joe Klein, "A Solemn Unifier for the Democrats," *Time*, April 26, 2004, p. 61.
33. Joe Klein, "Does Bush Really Get Us?" *Time*, May 3, 2004, p. 23.
34. Angie Cannon, "Kerry Draws a Line in the Terrorism War," *U.S. News & World Report*, May 3, 2004, p. 42.
35. Howard Fineman and Tamera Lipper, "The Gospel According to George," *Newsweek*, April 26, 2004, p. 20.
36. Evan Thomas, "I Haven't Suffered Doubt," *Newsweek*, April 26, 2004, p. 23.
37. Andrew Ferguson, "Bob Woodward's Washington," *Weekly Standard*, May 3, 2004, p. 23.
38. Ehninger and Brockreide, *Decision by Debate*, 274.
39. Ibid., 275.
40. Ibid.
41. Ibid., 274.
42. Ibid., 276.
43. Hughes, *Ten Minutes from Normal*, 147.
44. Fleischer, *Taking Heat*, 33.
45. George W. Bush, "Overcoming Terrorism Together," *Vital Speeches of the Day*, March 15, 2004, p. 323.
46. George W. Bush, "Freedom in Iraq and Middle East," *Vital Speeches of the Day*, December 1, 2003, p. 100.
47. Nordlinger, "A Voice for Our Time," p. 35.
48. Ibid.
49. Kenneth T. Walsh, "A Frank Conversation with a Candidate," *U.S. News & World Report*, May 3, 2004, p. 36.
50. Rush Limbaugh, "Stupid Quotes," *The Limbaugh Letter*, October 2004, p. 17.
51. John Kerry, "The Preparedness Gap," *Vital Speeches of the Day*, August 1, 2003, p. 619.
52. Thomas, *Election 2004*, 172.
53. Bush, "Overcoming Terrorism Together," p. 324.
54. "The Race Is On," *Rising Tide*, Spring 2004, p. 29.
55. Ibid.
56. Tony Blankley, "The Struggle to Explain John Kerry," *Washington Times* National Weekly Edition, May 3-9, 2004, p. 30.
57. Neufeldt, *Webster's New World Dictionary*, 441.
58. Jackson, *That Man*, 159.
59. George Stephanopoulos, "Clinton's Long Shadow," *Newsweek*, August 21, 2000, p. 35.
60. "President's Speech to the United Nations General Assembly," United Nations Headquarters, New York, New York, November 10, 2001, www.whitehouse.gov.

61. Ibid.
62. Ibid.
63. Ibid.
64. Ibid.
65. "President's State of the Union Address," The United States Capitol, Washington, D.C., January 29, 2002, www.whitehouse.gov.
66. Ibid.
67. Hughes, *Ten Minutes from Normal*, 147.
68. "President's State of the Union Address," January 29, 2002.
69. Ibid.
70. Ibid.
71. Ibid.
72. Ibid.
73. Ibid.
74. Ibid.
75. Ibid.
76. Ryan L. Teten, "Evolution of the Modern Rhetorical Presidency: Presidential Presentation and Development of the State of the Union Address," *Presidential Studies Quarterly*, June 2003, p. 339.
77. William Schneider, "Long on Character, Short on Details," *National Journal*, February 2, 2002, p. 350.
78. "President's State of the Union Address," January 29, 2002.
79. Schneider, "Long on Character, Short on Details," p. 350.
80. "Remarks by the President at Whitehall Palace," November 19, 2003.
81. Ibid.
82. Ibid.
83. Ibid.
84. Ibid.
85. Ibid.
86. Ibid.
87. Ibid.
88. Ibid.
89. Ibid.
90. Ibid.
91. Ibid.
92. Ibid. Italics mine.
93. Ibid.
94. Ibid.
95. Ibid.
96. Ibid.
97. George W. Bush, "Second Inaugural Address," *Vital Speeches of the Day*, February 1, 2005, p. 226.
98. Ibid.

99. Ibid.
100. Kenneth T. Walsh, "A Clarion Call to End Tyranny and Spread Freedom Worldwide," *U.S. News & World Report*, January 31/February 7, 2005, p. 14.
101. Bush, "Second Inaugural Address," pp. 226-227.
102. Ibid., p. 227.
103. Ibid.
104. Ibid.
105. Rush Limbaugh, "My Conversation with Natan Sharansky," *The Limbaugh Letter*, January 2005, p. 6.
106. Bush, "Second Inaugural Address," p. 227.
107. Ibid.
108. Ibid.
109. Michael Barone, "Revolutionary President," *U.S. News & World Report*, January 31/February 7, 2005, p. 16.
110. Bush, "Second Inaugural Address," pp. 227-228.
111. Ibid., p. 228.

Chapter 7
Political Humor Is No Laughing Matter

Humor is a serious thing. I like to think of it as one of our greatest and earliest national resources which must be preserved at all costs.
— James Thurber, CBS-TV, March 4, 1956

In a culture that has a great capacity for entertainment and appreciates those who can make people laugh, it is not surprising that Americans like politicians who can be funny, including candidates for the highest office. Of course, it is obvious in watching politicians try to be funny, that very few have a gift for comedy. But, they make the effort, because it is clear that, today, people expect their political leaders to have the ability to make them laugh—to interject humor into their speeches effectively.

Even after unfunny politicians receive expert coaching and material from comedy writers, they often fail to get laughs—perhaps deep down they lack a sense of humor. Classic examples in recent history include Michael Dukakis, Al Gore, Phil Gramm, Steve Forbes, and Gray Davis, "who crashed," according to Joshua Green, a senior editor for *Atlantic Monthly*, "at least in part because voters deemed them too dull, stiff, or creepy."[1] It seems that, as a general rule, humor does not come naturally for politicians. Ben Karlin, an executive producer of Jon Stewart's *The Daily Show* believes, "They're trained to exhibit a certain range of behaviors:

serious, compassionate, practical. Comedy isn't one of them."[2]

The late-night shows provide opportunities for presidential candidates to show a warm, approachable, witty side in an effort to raise their likeability rating. Writing about John Kerry, Green said, "Whether Kerry can pull it off remains to be seen. Last November he made a disastrous appearance on *The Tonight Show*, where he was the butt of jokes by a sock puppet named Triumph the Insult Comic Dog." Finding Kerry "humor-impaired," Green noted, "Though he has had material provided to him by a former writer for the comedian Bill Maher, and now draws on a phalanx of sitcom writers, little evidence of their handiwork has manifested itself."[3]

In contrast to the great majority of political leaders—including most of our past presidents—George W. Bush has a natural talent for humor, which he has assiduously developed over most of his life. If Kerry's inability to use humor makes him Michael Dukakis's heir apparent, as Green suggests,[4] then Bush's ability to use humor makes him Ronald Reagan's heir apparent.

President Bush's conversational style of speaking allows for interjection of humorous comments, both planned and spontaneous. He can also use dry and subtle humor when called for on formal occasions. And adding to his advantage over less-witty opponents is his ability to make people laugh with a variety of kinds of humor. Humor emerges in his speeches and interactions with audiences as a natural expression of his personality.

Humor: An Expression of Bush's Personality

Throughout his life, George W. Bush has called on humor to amuse others and deal with problems. Probably, his sense of humor was cultivated early in childhood when he discovered that he could use it to cheer people up and make them laugh. When he was seven years old, he saw a need for this talent in his own family. At age seven, he lost his sister to leukemia, which cast a pervasive depression over George W.'s once-happy home. "The mood in the home had an unusual effect on little George W. He began to feel that it was his job to cheer his parents up. He started telling stories and jokes, anything to see a smile again on his mother's grieving face."[5] Years later, Barbara Bush wrote in her memoirs that one day she overheard George W. tell a neighbor child that he was not able to play because his mother needed him. "That started my cure," she wrote. "I realized I was too much of a burden for a little seven-year-old boy to carry."[6]

Barbara Bush's story provides an important insight into George W. Bush's personality. His biographer points out, "Even at seven years of age, he felt he had the power to make those around him feel differently. Call it charm or personality, wit or a winsome manner, he believed he had a force within him that could lift spirits and restore."[7] As he grew up in Midland, Texas, attended public school, became active in sports, this quality continued to manifest itself in his relationships. Probably most people who knew him then would have found him likeable and funny, although not many would have thought him spiritual or ambitious.

In his formative years, humor served George W. well. A joke, a quip, or an anecdote could help someone to forget his or her troubles; it could help him to create a bridge between himself and another person; and it could rescue him from boredom, which seems to have colored his moods rather often. But, perhaps humor had still another function for him—he could use humor to change the atmosphere in a situation in which he felt uncomfortable or out of place.

Bush's humor matured somewhat during his years at Yale. While it may be true, as some have said, that he devoted much of his time to having a good time, he attended classes and learned much that prepared him for later responsibilities. On one occasion, while discussing the conclusion of a speech with Karen Hughes, she asked him where he had learned his speech theory and he replied, "The History of American Oratory, at Yale."[8]

Although George W. had become popular within his own circle of friends at Yale, his discovery of "snobs" and "intellectual arrogance" at the Ivy League institution, probably diminished his sense of humor by his graduation in 1968. One incident especially shaped his feelings about Yale for decades, and that was a conversation with William Sloane Coffin, a liberal activist and the campus chaplain. It occurred just after George W.'s father had lost a bid for a Senate seat in a race against the incumbent Democrat. Still saddened by the election outcome, George W. saw the chaplain on campus one day and introduced himself. The chaplain, responsible for comforting and guiding the spiritual development of students, responded, "Yeah, I know your father, and your father lost to a better man." These words hurt Bush deeply. Speaking about the incident later, he said, "Texas people are more polite. I don't think a Texan would do that to a son."[9]

Back in Texas, he recovered his sense of humor in a freer environment that, unfortunately, produced a lifestyle that included aimless parties and drinking. Doubtless, this period intensified his self-deprecating humor, since he could plainly see that he was headed nowhere and in a hurry to get there. So, he decided to join the Texas Air National Guard. During his jet-fighter training between November 1968 and June 1970, he had to keep his humor on hold, except during raucous parties at the officers' bar. After training, he devoted one weekend a month to Guard duty and worked at various jobs. Perhaps realizing he needed more discipline in his life, and additional knowledge—though still lacking a game plan for his life—he headed for Harvard where he would receive an advanced degree in Business. He recalled, Harvard "gave me the tools and the vocabulary of the business world. It taught me the principles of capital, how it accumulated, risked, spent, and managed."[10] The experience also must have taught him to make humor more purposeful and strategic in making contacts in the Texas petroleum industry, where he made a lot of money, and lost a lot of money.

In 1977, George W. Bush, the successful businessman, met and married Laura Welch. Laura Bush certainly had a settling influence on her husband—one can only guess that this included encouragement for him to control better his attempts at humor. Stephen Mansfield writes, "Perhaps Laura's greatest influence on him, though, was in drawing him to the Methodist church."[11] Although he became a faithful member of the church, his participation was more out of a sense of duty than a heart-felt commitment. Hoping to see George W. deepened spiritually, Laura took him to a James Dobson seminar. It was a good try, but it did not work. George W. left his seat and sat next to a friend. The inspirational effect was not as intended. He was inspired to share some humorous quips. He whispered, "What kind of pants did the Levites wear?"[12]

His eventual spiritual conversion in the Methodist church, through the ministry of evangelist Arthur Blessitt and later by talks with evangelist Billy Graham, gave him a higher purpose for his life and work.[13] His personality started to come into line with a man no longer adrift. He soon quit drinking, making his decision in the middle of a daily three-mile run. In his autobiography, Bush wrote, "Drinking . . . magnified aspects of my personality that probably don't need to be larger than they already are—made me more funny, more charming (I thought), more irrepressible. Also, according to my wife, somewhat boring and repetitive." He added as one who has come to an important realization: "What may have been funny in moderation was not so funny in exaggeration."[14] Influenced by his faith, his marriage to Laura, and his family, George W. Bush faced the necessity of redirecting his life toward something worthwhile, something that would make a difference for other people. That "something" proved to be political leadership, first as a two-term governor of Texas and then as president of the United States—both offices he won against all odds by fighting hard for what he believed with all of his abilities, including his ability to make people laugh as he spoke to them.

Humor: Bush's Rhetorical Advantage

George W. Bush learned early in life that humor can help people to face and deal with their troubles and concerns—that humor has value in dispelling gloom and inertia. Of course, every humorist discovers—as Bush has—that attempts to make people laugh may have an opposite effect. But, overall, Bush's batting average in the humor game has earned him high points. His use of humor in his speeches is one reason why people like him—it has entertained them and raised their spirits when national crises have threatened their morale and their confidence in the future. Romain Gary, the novelist, said it well: "Humor is an affirmation of dignity, a declaration of man's superiority to all that befalls him."[15] And, another reason why humor enhances his likeability is because through his humor, he opens himself to people, which conveys a genuineness that helps them to feel they can know and trust him.

Impression of Spontaneity

In his speeches, President Bush introduces humor in various forms, and almost always unexpectedly from an audience perspective. At times, he seems to interrupt himself to say something funny that has just occurred to him—much like someone does in a conversation with a friend. Speaking to high-school students, for example, he said, "You've been learning this by studying your history—at least *some* of you by studying your history." (Laughter.)[16]

Again, the impression of spontaneity occurs when Bush uses a humorous aside, which he did in his speech to the Newspaper Association of America Annual Convention on April 21, 2004 in Washington, D.C. At one point, he was expressing his belief that Muslims or Arabs can develop a democracy. "I remind you," he said, "some people thought the Japanese could never self-govern or be free." And, "as I said in my press conference the other day, I had the honor of sitting down to dinner with . . . Prime Minister Koizumi. And we were talking about North Korea, which I'll get to here in a second." Then, putting "North Korea" on hold a couple of minutes, he shared this anecdote: "He's a great guy, by the way. Elvis Presley is one of his favorites. (Laughter.) His favorite movie was Gary Cooper in *High Noon*. One time he walked up to me and said, 'You like Cooper.' (Laughter.) 'I'm like Cooper?' He said, 'Yes.' (Laughter.) I finally figured out what he meant." (Laughter.)[17]

President Bush addressed a friendlier audience than the newspaper editors when he spoke to members and friends of the American Israel Public Affairs Committee (AIPAC) on May 18, 2004 in Washington, D.C. After he was introduced, he expressed his appreciation for the warm welcome he had received. He said, "Thank you all very much. Finally, AIPAC elected a President I can kiss." (Laughter and applause.)[18] Bush then kissed the President on her cheek. This opening line sounded spontaneous, and did not follow the pattern of his usual opening statement. Still in his introduction, two more funny lines sounded spontaneous. He noted, "I'm told there are over 850 students here from 50 states." Then he seemed to depart from his prepared remarks when he added, "Make sure the Texas students behave well." (Laughter.) "Your mothers are watching." (Laughter.)[19]

Quick Witty Quips

Among the forms of rhetorical humor most admired by speech theorists and probably many people in audiences is the classic quip. In use, it is a quick-thinking, witty reply or remark, which usually is brief and prickly.

We see this kind of humor in action in the introduction to Bush's Newspaper Association speech of April 21st. As was his custom, the President expressed his appreciation for the invitation to speak, in this case, to people who had not always written nice things about him. In this polite context, his quip seemed unexpected, which doubtless added to the humor. He said, "Thanks for letting me come. Tom, thank you for your invitation. Dean, thank you for having me here. Members of the politburo—(laughter.) I mean, my fellow Americans." (Laughter and applause.) After stating his proposal, he told the audience, "And then I'll be glad to—I'll be glad to duck some questions." (Laughter.) "Just like my mother told me to do." (Laughter.)[20]

George W. Bush got a lot of humor out of speech references to his mother, a famous person in her own right. In December 2001, he led a Town Hall meeting at the Orange County Convention Center in Orlando, Florida. Children as well as adults asked the President questions. One teenager said that his parents believed that a family was strong if its members ate together. He asked, "Is it something that you did when you were a kid and that you and Mrs. Bush believe in?" The President's reply got him his biggest laugh: "I did eat with my family, so long as my mother wasn't cooking."[21]

On the same occasion that he addressed the Newspaper Association audience, President Bush, following his speech, answered questions. Burl Osborne, publisher and editor of the *Dallas Morning News*, asked him questions supplied by the audience. In the course of answering one of the questions, Bush stressed that he intended to make sure that certain world leaders spoke plainly to the Iranians regarding nuclear weapons. As he finished, Osborne said: "Just for the record, I've always understood you clearly." (Laughter.) To which Bush quipped, "Then why don't you write that way?" (Laughter.) Osborne responded: "Touché, touché." (Laughter and applause.) Bush added: "I've known him a long time." (Laughter.)[22] The audience, of course, was aware of the fact that the Dallas newsman had not always written positively about President Bush when he served as governor of Texas. As usual, G. K. Chesterton is on the mark when he says, "Wit is a sword; it is meant to make people feel the point as well as see it."

Speaking at Whitehall Palace in London in November 2003, President

Bush showed his ability to quip wittily but dryly. Stressing the importance of keeping the United Nations from becoming irrelevant like the old League of Nations became, Bush referred to Wilson, who fought for a viable international body. In this context, Bush noted, "President [Woodrow] Wilson [in 1918] had come to Europe with his 14 Points for Peace. Many complimented him on his vision; yet some were dubious. Take, for example, the Prime Minister of France. He complained that God, Himself, had only 10 commandments." (Laughter.) "Sounds familiar." (Laughter.)[23]

In a speech on June 16, 2004 at MacDill Air Force Base, President Bush spoke to military personnel at the Base and to troops stationed around the world. He talked about terrorist attacks in Iraq and about constructive developments in Iraqi society that showed new-found freedom of speech. He said, "I saw the other day, they even have talk radio. I don't know if they've contacted Rush [Limbaugh] yet." (Laughter.)[24]

Humor Against Opponents

President Bush, in a campaign speech made in early 2004, unleashed his humor against his political opponents. Bill Sammon, in *The Washington Times*, wrote that Bush "couched his attacks on Sen. John Kerry, his likely Democratic opponent, in humor whenever possible, believing voters will respond better to levity, campaign strategists say."[25] On February 23rd, President Bush, in a speech to the Republican Governors Association, began to use humor against Kerry's candidacy. Talking about Democrats who campaigned for their Party's nomination, he said, "They're for tax cuts and against them; they're for NAFTA and against NAFTA; they're for the Patriot Act and against the Patriot Act; they're in favor of liberating Iraq, and opposed to it. And," he added, "that's just one senator from Massachusetts."[26] The governors rewarded Bush with uproarious laughter.

Speaking at a Bush/Cheney rally in Orlando, Florida on March 20, 2004, President Bush once more directed his humor against Senator Kerry. Early in the speech, he declared,

> The presidential primary contest is over. I finally got an opponent. (Laughter.) He's following an interesting strategy. The other day, here in Florida, he claimed some important endorsements from overseas. He won't tell us the names of the foreign admirers. That's

> okay—either way, I'm not worried, because I'm going to keep my campaign right here in America. (Laughter, applause, and hollers.)[27]

Bush next turned to the theme of Kerry's flip-flopping on positions, saying,

> He's an experienced senator, and he's built up quite a record. In fact, Senator Kerry's been in Washington long enough to take both sides on just about every issue . . . . (Laughter.) My opponent clearly feels strongly about each of these issues. (Laughter.) So strongly that one position—is never just enough. (Laughter and applause.) He demonstrated that technique the other day. Someone asked Senator Kerry why he voted against the $87 billion dollar funding bill to help our troops in Iraq. Here's what he said, "I actually did vote for the $87 billion, before I voted against it." (Laughter.) End of quote. It sure clears things up, doesn't it. (Laughter.)[28]

Speaking to a large, enthusiastic audience at a Bush-Cheney campaign event in Reno, Nevada on June 18, 2004, President Bush again made humorous references to Kerry's flip-flops. He began by citing several instances where the Senator voted on an issue in Congress and then took an opposite position in his campaign. "His position on these issues reminds me of a saying we have in Texas about the weather," Bush said. 'If you don't like it, just wait a few minutes and it will change.'" (Laughter and applause.) "We had another example recently," he added. "Last December, I had the honor of signing the healthy forest act . . . . As we were talking and debating in Washington, my opponent opposed the law, saying we were taking a chainsaw to public forests. Well, now he's packing his bags, and he's getting ready to head out west. And he says he now likes parts of the law. He says he wants there to be a strong logging industry. You know something, it's not only the wildfires that shift with the wind." (Laughter and applause.)[29]

Bush used humor to take issue with Kerry's positions, rather than to disparage Kerry's character, personality, or appearance—the favorite foci of liberals. In terms of technique, he turned Kerry's statements against him or showed reversals on positions he had taken, and then allowed the audience to laugh at the perceived incongruence, a basic ingredient of humor.

Kerry continued to supply Republicans with humorous material through his comments as when, for instance, he appeared on *Meet the Press* on April 18, 2004. Host Tim Russert asked Kerry about a newspaper's review of travel records that showed only in one case was he and a world leader in the same town at the same time. Russert raised the subject to give Kerry a chance to explain how he got world leaders' endorsements. "Mr. Kerry laughed and provided a few hints about where he might have met with these foreign endorsers." He explained, "What I said is true. I stand by my statement. I mean you can go to New York City and you can be in a restaurant and you can meet a foreign leader. There are plenty of places to meet people without traveling abroad."[30]

His silly answer strained credulity and inspired various jokes at his expense as when, for example, Representative Mario Diaz-Balart of Florida remarked: "I just wanted to make sure Senator Kerry understands that just because you go into an International House of Pancakes does not mean you are meeting with foreign leaders—unless of course you are referring to their Belgian waffles, stuffed French toast, or German pancakes."[31]

After Senator Kerry in the presidential campaign bragged that his side had better hair than their opponents, President Bush, at Ty Cobb Field in Lakeland, Florida, on October 23, commented,

> I'm proud of my running mate, Dick Cheney. He's doing a great job. (Applause.) I see some others out here who are follically challenged. (Laughter.) See, I admit he doesn't have the waviest hair in the race. (Laughter.) You'll be pleased to hear I didn't pick him for his hairdo. (Laughter.) I picked him because he can get the job done . . . . (Applause.)

Kerry's Humor Counterattack

The Kerry campaign countered, saying that they could be just as funny as Republicans. To prove it, Kerry, after having surgery on his right shoulder, in early April 2004, deadpanned to a campaign audience, "I've been having problems with the right wing lately."[32] Speaking in behalf of the Kerry campaign, Kathy Roeder commented, "I really like that one." In her opinion, "If you're always talking about really serious stuff, humor is a good way for the candidate to break things up and put some of their personality into the campaign."[33]

According to *Newsweek's* Evan Thomas et al., in *Election 2004*, Senator Kerry told an audience in Spring Green, Wisconsin, that "he knew how hard it was to find the right financial options because he had two children and three stepchildren." Knowing that the Senator is married to a billionaire, the audience "laughed audibly at him."[34] Sometimes Kerry is funniest when he is not trying to be funny.

Hoping for a humorous response, Kerry, in a campaign ad, "portrayed Mr. Bush as a schoolboy flunking math because he couldn't balance the federal budget."[35] Then on May 22, when Bush suffered "minor abrasions and scratches" after an accident on his mountain bike near the end of a 17-mile ride, "Kerry told reporters in front of cameras, 'Did the training wheels fall off?' Mr. [Matt] Drudge reported on his web site."[36]

In portraying President Bush as an inept child in an attempt at humor, Kerry belittled his opponent; he portrayed him as a child, apparently, to make himself appear bigger, superior. One wonders, too, if Kerry sees a child flunking math or falling off his bicycle as inherently funny. Even some Democrats said that Kerry's campaign had "a humor deficit."[37]

As Roeder declared, humor provides a way for the candidate to put some of his personality into the campaign. However, that is not all, humor also contributes something of his character. Kerry's humor tended to be more *ad hominem* in emphasis in that it focused on Bush the man; whereas Bush's humor tended to focus on Kerry's statements and voting record, questioning his judgment and consistency. Sammon quoted Democratic strategist Patrick Caddell as saying that "the Bush campaign 'should go even further' in its use of humor against Mr. Kerry."[38] But, George W. Bush seemed to reject such advice, as he stuck to his own brand of humor, often evoking laughter in respect to subjects other than political opponents.

Humor for U.S. Enemies

The President turned some of his best humor on enemy leaders, which showed how he used humor as a weapon against America's enemies. Here are a couple of examples, with understatement in play: Bush in Boston on October 4, 2002, delivered a speech at the Victory 2002 Reception in which he said, "We still got this coalition of freedom-loving nations we're working together with. And we're hunting them down; the other day, one of them popped up, popped his head up, named bin al-Shibh. He's no longer a problem." (Laughter.)[39] Then, in Roswell, New Mexico on January 22, 2004, speaking at the Roswell Convention & Civic Center, Bush told his enthusiastic audience, "Of the 55 top leaders of the [Iraqi] regime, 45 have been captured or killed; the other 10 have got to be nervous." (Laughter.)[40]

Responses to Protesters

When confronting hecklers or protesters, Bush characteristically responds with humor and without showing signs of irritation nonverbally. On October 23, 2003, in Canberra, Australia, for instance, when a woman in the Green Party heckled him during his speech to the Parliament on terrorism, he smiled and called, "I like free speech!"[41] The audience laughed and applauded.

In London at Whitehall Palace, President Bush addressed a large audience on November 19, 2003. Commenting on a gathering of protesters outside Whitehall, he joked, "It was pointed out to me that the last noted American to visit London stayed in a glass box dangling over the Thames," he said, making reference to David Blaine's performance stunt. "A few might have been happy to provide similar arrangements for me." (Laughter.) And then, gently turning the tables on the protesters, Bush noted, "They now have that right in Baghdad as well." (Laughter and applause.)[42]

Enhancement of Arguments

Anyone who has tried to be funny in a speech knows how hard it is to get a laugh—a real guffaw—from the audience. "Dying is easy," the actor-comedian George Burns once remarked, "comedy is hard." Humor is elusive; sometimes it works when it should not, and sometimes it does not work when it should. It works more often than not for Bush. He often gets his audiences to laugh, partly because his timing is instinctively good. As a general rule, Bush's humor enhances his post-9/11 speeches. A speech theorist has written: "humor can create a community through stimulating a uniform response, it can reflect well on the character of the speaker, and it can serve to emphasize or make memorable features of the speaker's argument, so long as its use is decorous."[43]

Audiences appear to respond uniformly to Bush's humor, indicative of a community spirit; moreover, his humor encourages listeners to harbor good feelings about his character; when it comes to using humor to emphasize aspects of his argument, he, like most persuasive speakers, is less consistent—in the following two examples from the same 2002 speech in Kansas City, Missouri, Bush is ineffective in the first and effective in the second (but gets laughs with both):

First Example

> This is an unusual kind of war . . . . Sometimes there will be moments of high drama and, of course, good reporters will be going—all kinds of hyperventilating about this action or that action. (Laughter.) And sometimes you won't see a thing.[44]

Second Example

> Right now, there are over one hundred agencies responsible for a part of homeland security—one hundred different entities at the federal level. I'm a person who believes in accountability. One reason I believe in accountability is because I understand who the American people are going to hold accountable if something happens. (Laughter.) Me. (Laughter.)[45]

Humor that Humanizes

"For politicians to succeed, humor must also be carefully calibrated to humanize them," observed *Atlantic* editor Joshua Green. The most important kind of humor to do this, he thought, was that which poked fun at oneself.[46] A political leader for whom this form of humor came naturally was Ronald Reagan. For example, at the Republican National Convention in Houston on August 17, 1992, Ronald Reagan spoke, and treated the audience to a taste of vintage Reagan by making fun of his age. In the introduction of his speech, he said, "Tonight is a very special night for me. Of course, at my age, every night's a special night." (Laughter.)[47]

Then later in the speech he remarked, "This fellow they've nominated [Bill Clinton] claims he's the new Thomas Jefferson. Well, let me tell you something—I knew Thomas Jefferson." (Laughter and applause.) "He was a friend of mine." (Laughter and applause.) "And, governor, you're no Thomas Jefferson." (Applause.)[48]

In contrast to Reagan, few political leaders have the desire or the ability to focus humor on themselves. In fact, "some of the most talented politicians—most famously, the Clintons—bridle at being the target of their own jokes, to the frustration of [Mark] Katz and the assortment of other comedy writers who supply them."[49]

Self-deprecating humor characterizes someone who can laugh at himself, without feeling insecure or embarrassed. This is an apt description of George W. Bush, who, over the years, has often made people laugh with self-deprecating humor. He has, as Reagan did, a natural talent for such humor. One might think that this conclusion was beyond dispute. But, no, Kenneth Walsh, in *U.S. News*, June 2004, quoted Democratic pollster Geoff Garin as saying, "Bush . . . lacks the self-deprecating wit and the 'sense of humility' that Reagan showed."[50] Apparently, some critics feared that Bush's self-deprecating humor would increase his likeability among voters as they believed it did for Reagan, and so tried to say he lacked it.

Like Reagan, Bush can find humor in opponents' varied forms of attack. After his post-9/11 leadership and his approval of $40 billion for New York's recovery, he was pleased with the reception he received from New Yorkers, who had gone for Al Gore by 1.6 million votes. Following a visit to Lower Manhattan, he quipped in an aside: "I was surprised to see that New Yorkers could wave with all five fingers."[51]

Bush had a field day with self-deprecating humor in his speech at the White House Correspondents Dinner on May 1, 2004. In the opening lines of his introduction, he said:

> I was going to start off tonight telling some self-deprecating jokes. (Laughter.) But then, I couldn't think of any mistakes I had made to be self-deprecating about. (Laughter and applause.)
>
> In my press conference, John Dickerson of *Time* magazine—(applause)—asked the question about what I considered my biggest

> mistake. It's an excellent question that totally stumped me. (Laughter.) I guess looking at it practically, my biggest mistake was calling on John. (Laughter and applause.) Or take that one about Cheney and me answering questions together [in a meeting with the 9/11 Commission]. That was a toughie. (Laughter.) So from now on, Dick and I will be holding joint press conferences. (Laughter and applause.)
>
> We could do it that way, or we could do it this way: You could ask the question, then I could tell Bob Woodward—(laughter)—and he could tell you. (Laughter.)
>
> I thought about giving an economics speech tonight. It really gets me when the critics say I haven't done enough for the economy. I mean, look what I've done for the book publishing industry. (Laughter and applause.) You've heard some of the titles: *Big Lies*; *The Lies of George W. Bush*; *The Lies and the Lying Liars Who Tell Them*. (Laughter.) I'd like to tell you I've read each of these books, but that would be a lie. (Laughter and applause.)[52]

These self-deprecating jokes provoked laughter, but, at the same time, carried an underlying message. By exaggerating the challenge and difficulty of two questions put to him at a recent press conference, Bush implied that they lacked seriousness and moment, while he showed a good-natured attitude toward the questioners. Bush next referred to Woodward's new book that drew heavily on an interview he had granted the author. Here he implied that the book presented a positive view of his administration rather than a negative one as the liberal media had predicted prior to its publication. And, finally, his joke about the economy allowed him to imply that he had done a lot for the economy; it also allowed him to take a humorous swipe at books that had accused him of lying; in effect, he was saying they were beneath his notice and not to be taken seriously.

Bush used self-deprecating humor with a subtle persuasive element before. For example, at the annual Al Smith dinner in New York in October 2000, Bush, standing next to Al Gore, soon after their presidential debates, said, "And I see Bill Buckley's here tonight, a fellow Yale man. We go way back, and have a lot in common. Bill wrote a book at Yale. I read one. He founded the Conservative Party. I started a few parties myself. Bill won every debate he ever had—and, well, I know how that feels."[53] The dinner guests laughed heartily.

President Bush even managed to bring humor into his 2004 "Acceptance Speech" in New York City. He received one of his biggest laughs when he said, "Even when we don't agree, at least you know what I believe and where I stand. (Applause.) You may have noticed I have a few flaws, too. People sometimes have to correct my English. (Laughter.) I knew I had a problem when Arnold Schwarzenegger started doing it." (Laughter and applause.)[54]

In a time of war, Americans may especially appreciate a little humor in a political leader's speech that gives them pause to smile or laugh. Humor breaks the tension that anxieties about the future bring and paves the way for a fresh perception of the speaker's message. George W. Bush—by personality and practice—has the ability to use humor to lighten the mood and build his listeners' energy, as when discussing the war against terrorism. His varied forms of humor are functional—they serve his purpose in that they are relevant to the points he seeks to make in his speeches. We see, then, there is a logic that guides his humor—a logic that determines how best to help listeners perceive the hard facts and serious issues. Since humor comes naturally to George W., he did not have to strain to give listeners comic relief, whether in his wartime rhetoric or in his campaign speaking.

NOTES

1. Joshua Green, "Funny Business," *Atlantic Monthly*, May 2004, p. 37.
2. Ibid.
3. Ibid., p. 38.
4. Ibid.
5. Mansfield, *The Faith of George W. Bush*, 33.
6. Barbara Bush, *Barbara Bush: A Memoir* (New York: St. Martin's Paperbacks, 1995), 50.
7. Mansfield, *The Faith of George W. Bush*, 33.
8. Hughes, *Ten Minutes from Normal*, 147.
9. Mansfield, *The Faith of George W. Bush*, 49.
10. Bush, *A Charge to Keep*, 60.
11. Mansfield, *The Faith of George W. Bush*, 53.
12. Ibid., 60

13. Ibid., 63-69.
14. Bush, *A Charge to Keep*, 135.
15. Romain Gary, *Promise at Dawn* (New York: Harper & Brothers, 1961), 136.
16. "Remarks by the President on the 'Lessons of Liberty' Initiative," Thomas Wootton High School, Rockville, Maryland, October 30, 2001, www.whitehouse.gov.
17. "Remarks by the President at the Newspaper Association of America Annual Convention," Omni Shoreham Hotel, Washington, D.C., April 21, 2004, www.whitehouse.gov.
18. "Remarks by the President to the American Israel Public Affairs Committee," Washington Convention Center, Washington, D.C., May 18, 2004, www.whitehouse.gov.
19. Ibid.
20. "Remarks by the President at the Newspaper Association of America Annual Convention," April 21, 2004.
21. Frum, *The Right Man*, 217.
22. "Remarks by the President at the Newspaper Association of America Annual Convention," April 21, 2004.
23. "Remarks by the President at Whitehall Palace," November 19, 2003.
24. President's Speech at MacDill Air Force Base, Florida, C-SPAN, June 16, 2004.
25. Bill Sammon, "Humor Provides Relief in Political Campaign, to a Point," *Washington Times* National Weekly Edition, April 19-25, 2004, p. 23.
26. Republican Governors' Association, C-SPAN, February 23, 2004.
27. President's Speech, Bush/Cheney Campaign Rally, Orlando, Florida, Fox News, March 20, 2004.
28. Ibid.
29. President's Speech, Bush/Cheney Campaign Event, Reno, Nevada, C-SPAN, June 18, 2004.
30. Charles Hurt, "Kerry Interview Butt of GOP Jokes," *Washington Times* National Weekly Edition, April 26-May 2, 2004, p. 10.
31. Ibid.
32. Sammon, "Humor Provides Relief in Political Campaign, to a Point," p. 23.
33. Ibid.
34. Matthew Continatti, "The Making of the President, 2004," *Weekly Standard*, January 24, 2005, p. 29.
35. Sammon, "Humor Provides Relief in Political Campaign, to a Point," p. 23.
36. "Kerry Pokes Fun at Bush After Bicycle Accident," *Washington Times* National Weekly Edition, May 31-June 6, 2004, p. 10.
37. Sammon, "Humor Provides Relief in Political Campaign, to a Point," p. 23.
38. Ibid.
39. "Remarks by the President to Massachusetts Victory 2002 Reception," Boston, Massachusetts, October 4, 2002, www.whitehouse.gov.
40. President's Speech at Roswell Convention & Civic Center, Roswell, New Mexico, C-SPAN, January 22, 2004.

41. President's Speech to the Australian Parliament, Canberra, Fox News, October 23, 2003.
42. "Remarks by the President at Whitehall Palace," November 19, 2003.
43. Thomas O. Sloane, "Humor," in Thomas O. Sloane, ed., *Encyclopedia of Rhetoric* (Oxford: Oxford University Press, 2001), 359.
44. "Remarks by the President at the Opening of Oak Park High School," June 11, 2002.
45. Ibid.
46. Green, "Funny Business," p. 37.
47. *Coverage of the Death of Reagan*, Fox News, June 6, 2004; Ronald Reagan, "America's Best Days Are Yet to Come," *Vital Speeches of the Day*, September 15, 1992, pp. 715-716.
48. Ibid.
49. Green, "Funny Business," p. 38.
50. Walsh, "A Couple of Presidents in Primary Colors," p. 42.
51. Cannon and Simendinger, "The Making of Team Bush," p. 2918.
52. "Remarks by the President at the 2004 White House Correspondents' Dinner," Washington Hilton, Washington, D.C., May 1, 2004, www.whitehouse.gov.
53. Frum, *The Right Man*, 77.
54. *Republican National Convention*, Fox News, President's "Acceptance Speech," Madison Square Garden, New York City, September 2, 2004.

Chapter 8
The Themes of Value in Bush's Rhetoric

Man's capacity for justice makes democracy possible, but man's inclination to injustice makes democracy necessary.
— Reinhold Niebuhr, *The Children of Light and the Children of Darkness*

While one can argue that great events can make great leaders, one can also argue that great leaders can make great events. George W. Bush belongs more to the latter group than to the former. He is an activist leader who makes things happen. Speaking to a large audience in York, Pennsylvania in July 2004, President Bush declared, "It is the President's job to confront problems and not to pass them along to future generations."[1] His approach is to lead by confronting problems and persuading people to believe in their ability to solve them. He would subscribe to the principle: "Leaders take actions and create conditions that strengthen their constituents' self-esteem and internal sense of effectiveness."[2] He incorporates value themes in his rhetoric to strengthen Americans' belief in themselves and in the nation's efforts to increase their security against both domestic and foreign threats to their welfare.

When Bush came to the White House, the recession he had warned about in the campaign had hit hard with a massive loss of jobs; the stock market was in decline, reducing the wealth of people and pension funds; and a series of corporate scandals revealed large-scale corruption that cost stockholders millions of dollars and undermined investors' confidence. And, if this were not enough, eight months into his presidency, the homeland was attacked by terrorists—only this time it was not six lives lost as when the World Trade Center was bombed in 1993, no, this time the terrorists destroyed 3,000 lives and the World Trade Center itself.

President Bush responded to these and other crises with bold leadership that produced plans and policies, the details of which he set forth in his speeches and public remarks. Those who listened closely to his major addresses or, perhaps, read them, knew what he believed and where he stood on the key domestic and foreign policy issues. As David Frum, Bush's former speechwriter, colorfully puts it, "Like Babe Ruth pointing to the stands before hitting his home run, Bush clearly indicates in advance exactly what he will do."[3] In his 2000 "Acceptance Speech," Bush spoke similarly himself: "When I act, you will know my reasons; when I speak you will know my heart."[4] Certainly, President George W. Bush's audiences heard what was on his heart as when, in his speeches, he drew on the ideas of compassionate conservatism.

Compassionate Conservatism in Bush's Rhetoric

George W. Bush described his efforts to meld a compassionate approach to people's social problems with a conservative understanding of individual responsibility and the backing of government resources as "compassionate conservatism." He adopted this concept during his first term as governor of Texas (1995-1999). And, when he ran for a second term, he emphasized the theme of compassioned conservatism in his campaign speeches. He had developed a personal commitment to its ideals, having seen it successfully applied in his state in the form of social programs, such as Teen Challenge, a national drug treatment program, founded by pastor David Wilkerson; and Prison Fellowship, a program of Christian teaching for convict rehabilitation, founded by Christian writer Chuck Colson.

In his speeches, Governor Bush made a case for leaders in government to deal aggressively with the growing social problems in society and the attendant erosion of traditional values. In the words of Marvin Olasky, journalism professor at the University of Texas at Austin, Bush "described how a minimizing of personal responsibility had pushed America toward a spiritual and moral crisis, with the familiar symptoms of broken or never-formed families, teen drug abuse and pregnancy, crime, civic disengagement, and disenchantment with public life." Olasky added, "In short, he was laying out the history of our nation's long descent from true compassion to the liberal variety. Sadly, the press rarely picked up on his history telling, which ran counter to the conventional wisdom."[5]

Olasky was one of the men who influenced George W. Bush's thinking about compassionate conservatism and what came to be known years later in the Bush administration as "faith-based initiatives." Olasky first met Bush in 1993, and a year later he published *The Tragedy of American Compassion*, which showed the failure of present-day welfare and the importance of faith in social programs. Another person who influenced Bush was Myron Magnet, whose book, *The Dream and the Nightmare*, looked at 1960s America and found a serious cultural mistake in the view that society was made up of "victims."[6]

George W. Bush, apparently, saw compassionate conservatism as a kind of firebreak against cultural decline. He, therefore, promoted it in his speeches and sermons. Moreover, it offered a new outlook on government's role in making a difference for Americans who needed a helping hand. Probably, the first time the term was connected with Bush nationally occurred in August 1997 on CNN. A journalist on that network reported that Governor Bush had gained "legislative approval for a series of tax, welfare and educational reforms he calls compassionate conservatism in the face of a Democrat-controlled state house."[7] When the 1998 election was over, the press reported that George W. Bush had received seven out of ten votes to award him a second term as governor of Texas. The press credited his victory to a pleasant personality, rather than to the rhetorical emphasis he had given to cultural decline and his efforts as Governor to reach out to needy groups.[8]

But, in remarks made in November 1998, Governor Bush conceded that compassionate conservatism had provoked criticism. Sounding perplexed, he said, "I know this approach has been criticized. But why? Is compassion beneath us? Is mercy below us? Should our party be led by someone who boasts of a hard heart? . . . It is conservative to cut taxes. It is compassionate to help people save and give and build."[9]

Marvin Olasky, in his book *Compassionate Conservatism* (2000), suggested a reason for the criticism of which Bush spoke. He wrote, "Compassionate conservatism is neither an easy slogan nor one immune from vehement attack. It is a full-fledged program with a carefully considered philosophy."[10] Olasky implied that some people may have found the concept difficult to grasp and so criticized it unfairly. In this connection, he observed that the term "compassionate conservatism" had undergone a "decade-long development" that "politicians and journalists did not know or understand . . ."[11] Certainly, over this period, the term acquired connotations that people in both major parties would have found objectionable, especially without the benefit of careful explanation. For example, early in the race for the 2000 Republican presidential nomination, "former Tennessee governor Lamar Alexander called the term 'weasel words'—clever but meaningless."[12]

During his campaign for president, George W. Bush's speeches sought to persuade conservatives of different camps to perceive him as economically conservative, but socially committed to government programs that redeem lives. For example, in a speech in Indianapolis on July 22, 1999, he emphasized this balance between conservatism and compassion: "I am an economic conservative. I believe we should cut taxes to stimulate economic growth. Yet I know that economic growth is not the solution to every problem. A rising tide lifts many boats—but not all. Many prosper in a bull market—but not everyone."[13] Later in the speech, he declared, "A president can speak without apology for the values that defeat violence and help overcome poverty. A president can speak for abstinence and accountability and the power of faith."[14] With these principles stated, Bush acknowledged that past presidents' wars on poverty had failed and that a "bold new approach" was needed. Then, using a simile from the Old Testament (Exodus 5:7), he asserted, "It is not enough for conservatives like me to praise these [private and faith-based] efforts. It is not enough to call for volunteerism. Without more support and resources—both private and public—we are asking them to make bricks without straw."[15] Concluding his speech, he said, "In this campaign I bring a message to my own party. We must apply our conservative and free market ideas to the job of helping real human beings—because any ideology, no matter how right in theory, is sterile and empty without that goal."[16]

In the course of the presidential campaign, Al Gore spoke disparagingly of Bush's compassionate approach to societal problems, saying what the governor advocated amounted to "crumbs of compassion."[17] Speaking in July 1999, Bush responded: "Some Washington politicians call these efforts 'crumbs of compassion.' These aren't 'crumbs' to people whose lives are changed, they are the hope of renewal and salvation. These are not the 'crumbs of compassion,' they are the bread of life."[18] George W. Bush's strong rebuttal shows the high regard in which he held the philosophy of compassionate conservatism, which at times he seemed to express in words of personal faith.

George W. Bush's presidential speeches continued to emphasize the values, proposals, and positions that flowed out of compassionate conservatism. But, "compassionate conservatism," observed David Frum, Bush's former White House speechwriter, did not give the President the "big organizing idea" that Dwight D. Eisenhower had in "Peace and prosperity," Richard Nixon had in "Law and order," and Ronald Reagan had in "Government is the problem."[19] Doubtless, these presidents' slogans connected with people's emotions about the times in which they lived. Moreover, most people would have found them immediately comprehensible, without much explanation.

Understandably, Frum, in helping to write speeches for President Bush, likely wanted a key phrase that would draw together the President's views, proposals, and policies and resonate with the American people. Instead, he concluded, compassionate conservatism was not "a big idea at all, but a whole agglomeration of little ideas—government funding for religious organizations, school testing, a higher minimum wage, tax credits for young children—wrapped together to look like a big idea."[20]

In truth, compassionate conservatism *was* a big idea in the sense that it was important and capable of subsuming diverse policies and positions, without their becoming, as Frum suggested, "agglomerated." It had the potential of integrating all of Bush's domestic and foreign policy proposals and decisions; for it offered a broad philosophical basis that the Bush Administration could apply to a wide variety of adverse conditions that groups of people faced and from which they needed rescue. It was a values-driven approach that, in the words of George W. Bush, "cares about people, and makes a concrete effort to help them bring lasting change into their lives."[21]

However, one could argue that the term "compassionate conservatism," with all it implied, was too complex a concept for typical audiences to easily understand. In many situations, the term would require careful definition. It referred, after all, to a far-reaching social-political philosophy to which Bush had devoted a whole speech in July 1999. Interestingly, in that speech, he did not use the term "compassionate conservatism," instead, he simply said "compassionate" (or "compassion") or "conservative." And in subsequent speeches—especially after the attacks of 9/11—he tended to say "compassionate" or "compassion" when speaking of the philosophical basis for his agenda, often in a phrase with the word *nation*, *acts*, *country*, *government*, or *America*.

For example, in a speech in Kalamazoo, Michigan on March 27, 2001, President Bush said, "I trust the people of this country. I not only trust them to spend their own money more wisely than the federal government will spend it, but I trust the people to provide a compassionate tomorrow for our fellow citizens."[22] Then after September 11th, the President adapted his compassionate philosophy to a wartime posture. In a speech at the Massachusetts Victory 2002 Reception, in Boston on October 4, he said, "You see, it's the millions of acts of kindness and compassion that really define the true character of our country and will enable us to defy the killers by making this country a more compassionate and decent place." With a continuing emphasis on culture change, he explained, "These acts of kindness don't have to be huge, they've just got to be significant enough to change America one person at a time."[23] And in Washington, D.C. on July 21, 2004, President Bush told a large audience at the President's Dinner: "I've seen the spirit of service and compassion renewed in our country."[24]

George W. Bush's advocacy of the ideals of compassionate conservatism as governor and president has done much to reshape the Republican Party and redefine its platform. Moreover, those ideals created a common ground for different groups of conservatives and so helped to strengthen the unity of conservatives—those who wanted the government to leave them alone and those who wanted Washington to strive for national greatness. As

Michael Barone, in his January 2002 article in *U.S. News*, commented: "Bush's strong support of tax cuts and his solid conservative positions on cultural issues in 2001 appealed to leave-us-alone conservatives; his steely and morally clarified prosecution of the war since September 11 has appealed to the national-greatness conservatives." Barone also noted, "His faith-based initiative and his friendly attitudes toward Latinos were part of a 'compassionate conservatism' based on a duty to help the less fortunate."[25] While some conservatives were critical of certain of Bush's domestic-policy decisions, most seemed to appreciate his emphasis on individual choice and accountability, and his leadership in protecting traditional marriage and banning partial-birth abortion. Also, his unapologetic statements of faith struck a responsive chord in many Christian evangelicals. President Bush "has gathered the various strains of conservatism," Barone wrote, "and personifies the Republican Party today . . . more than anyone since his strategist Karl Rove's exemplar, William McKinley."[26]

President Bush once more sounded the theme of unity as he addressed the national Urban League Conference in Detroit, Michigan on July 23, 2004, which proved to be one of his best presidential campaign speeches. In this speech, he emphasized his expansion of minority entrepreneurship and home ownership in terms relevant to African Americans. Realistically beaming his message more to conservatives and moderates in the audience, he outlined his domestic and foreign policy achievements. He declared, "Progress for all citizens, including African Americans, depends on the spirit of compassion for others . . . . And we'll have the traditional programs of help, the safety nets. They're there . . . . But I strongly believe," he insisted, "the federal government must welcome programs of faith into the compassionate delivery of help to those who hurt." (Applause.) And with obvious reference to Afghanistan and Iraq, Bush asserted, "Our foreign policy is tough and it's compassionate . . . . We liberated over 50 million people who were brutalized by tyrants. We're proud to lead the armies of liberation." He summed up the ways he had acted on his agenda by saying, "Ours is a solid record of accomplishment. And that's why I've come to talk about compassionate conservatism and what I envision for the future. I'm here for another reason. I'm here to ask you for your vote." (Applause.)[27]

One might wonder why, in this speech, President Bush once again used the term "compassionate conservatism," after having omitted it in many previous speeches. A possible answer: He was extending an invitation to African Americans to join the Republican Party and become participants in its compassionate philosophy that he was careful to explain. In closing, he said, "You see, I believe in my heart that the Republican Party, the party of Lincoln and Frederick Douglass, is not complete without the perspective and support and contribution of African Americans." (Applause.)[28]

The term *compassion* remains an important term in the Bush lexicon. As President, he sees Americans' kindness and generosity in coming to people's aid in the aftermath of disasters. In his 2005 "State of the Union Address," Bush asserted, "Because one of the deepest values of our country is compassion, we must never turn away from any citizen who feels isolated from the opportunities of America. Our government will continue to support faith-based and community groups that bring hope to harsh places."[29] He thus wisely freed the term from politics by elevating it from a policy to a value that motivates us to act in helping others. Moreover, he exemplified compassion by referring to his faith-based initiatives that he set up against considerable opposition, and which, he made clear, he continued to support.

Faith and Religion in George W. Bush's Speeches

In George W.'s rhetoric, the theme of compassionate conservatism found much of its purpose and authority in another dominant theme—the Christian faith. Many of Bush's speeches and public statements suggest that his compassionate approach to government and world affairs provide a way of putting Christian principles into action to improve lives. For example, in July 2003, he visited an AIDS clinic in Uganda that had a successful program in reducing HIV cases through government and religious-group cooperation. Sounding as much like a preacher as a president, he gave a brief talk to the clinic's staff, saying, "I believe God has called us into action. We have a responsibility to help a neighbor in need, a brother and sister in crisis."[30] And Bush acted on his words—he requested from Congress fifteen billion dollars more over a five year period to fight AIDS in Africa.

Because faith is a motivating force in George W. Bush's life, it is not surprising that it finds its way into his speeches. His religious references never sound forced or insincere—they never have the flavor of pretense or contrivance, designed to create a false impression. Rather, his comments about faith and religion come from the heart; they are not slick statements from a political playbook. In the course of a September 2003 interview with Brit Hume of Fox News, President Bush said, "Well, I pray daily, and I pray in all kinds of places. I mean, I pray in bed, I pray in the Oval Office. I pray a lot . . .as the Spirit moves me. And faith is an integral part of my life."[31]

Invariably, interviewers have questioned Bush about his faith. During one such interview in June 2003 with Peggy Noonan for *Ladies' Home Journal*, he responded to some people's concerns about his faith: "You shouldn't fear a religious person. The Bible talks about love and compassion . . . . That's really behind my passion on the AIDS policy, for example."[32] Noonan, speechwriter for George H.W. Bush in the 1988 presidential campaign, in the Foreword to *We Will Prevail*, wrote, "Bush is unafraid of sounding like what he is, a Christian reborn in faith who sees the world through a prism of belief. Life is not accident; it has meaning and governance." She also noted: "Bush is a pray-er. He has told me he is grateful to be the focus of the prayers of others, and that he feels those prayers."[33] He comes from a family background of Christian believers, who regularly spent time in prayer.

For instance, according to one source, George W.'s grandparents, Prescott and Dorothy Bush, made it a rule to pray and read Scripture each morning before Prescott went off to the U.S. Senate.[34] More senators should adopt such a practice.

George W. continued to express his Christian beliefs in his speeches, even though media pundits and political opponents derided him for those beliefs. In many cases, their derision became outright attack, revealing deep-seated anger and hatred. Referring to the Democrats' 2004 campaign tactics, Tony Blankley, in his insightful commentary "United by a Common Hatred," asserted, "They repeated endlessly their contempt for Mr. Bush's Christian faith—which apparently induces contempt and hatred among the Democratic Party faithful."[35] (See Appendix B for Blankley's complete article.)

In a brief critique of Bob Woodward's appearance on CBS's *60 Minutes* to push a new book, Rush Limbaugh, in a *Wall Street Journal* op-ed, wrote that "Mr. Woodward said that . . . God talks to President Bush and President Bush listens; and President Bush is an idiot who distains the truly smart people of the world." Concerning Woodward's observations about Bush's "personal relationship with God, etc.," Limbaugh responded, "Remember this from JFK's inaugural address? 'In the long history of the world, only a few generations have been granted the role of defending freedom in its hour of maximum danger . . . . The energy, the faith, the devotion which we bring to this endeavor will light our country and all who serve it—and the glow from the fire can truly light the world.' It sure sounds to me like Mr. Bush is a man of his time and that his critics have lost their anchor."[36]

Liberal journalists could more easily attack George W.'s statements of faith than the Democratic Party officialdom could. Politicians had to be careful to avoid the appearance of disrespect toward religion, whereas journalists could, with impunity, charge Bush with playing politics with his faith. In her *New York Times* column in December 1999, Maureen Dowd, attempting to sound witty in disparaging George W.'s expressions of faith, wrote: "George W. Bush finally scored some debate points on Monday night by supporting the holy trinity of ethanol, Jesus, and soft money." She continued, "When you take something deeply personal and parade it for political gain, you are guilty either of cynicism or exhibitionism . . . . Genuinely religious people are humbled by religion and guided by it on the inside. They don't need to wear Jesus on the outside as a designer label."[37]

In her remarks, Dowd made the assumption that a politician who shares something "deeply personal" wants to "parade it for political gain" and is, therefore, a cynic or an exhibitionist. Of course, all politicians, including presidential candidates, share things that some people might consider "deeply personal." Such disclosures may help or hurt the candidate's credibility, depending on how listeners' view them. Some Americans thought President Bill Clinton revealed too much in a show on MTV when he told the audience what type of underwear he wore, "boxers or briefs." George W. Bush would certainly have known that his declarations of faith could just as easily diminish as enhance "political gain"—he could be sure that he would not endear himself among liberals.

But, his subsequent speeches and public statements showed that he expressed his faith naturally and openly, *as a source of important ideas and principles.*

According to Dowd, "[g]enuinely religious people" keep their religion inside for personal guidance and have no need of an outside demonstration of religion. But, in point of fact, a genuinely-religious person tends to be highly motivated to share his religion with others, so that they may experience the peace and understanding that he has found in that religion. Moreover, deeply religious people tend to have a desire to act on their beliefs—such as Mother Teresa did—to put into practice what their religion teaches. Without these "outside" signs of a spiritual revelation, could we identify those genuinely religious people? And when Dowd implied that Bush's religion was not genuine because he wore "Jesus on the outside," she overlooked Jesus' words in the Gospel of Mark: "For whoever is ashamed of Me and My words in this adulterous and sinful generation, the Son of Man will also be ashamed of him when He comes in the glory of His Father with the holy angels" (8:38).

But, how did the attacks on George W. Bush compare with similar attacks on other presidents? History reveals that no U.S. president in the last century had to endure the kind of malevolent attacks that George W. Bush has. The Bush haters on the Left targeted President Bush almost as soon as he took office; their attacks against him became increasingly virulent and vile, even as he devoted himself to making the nation more secure in the war on terrorism. As the 2004 election drew nearer, the Left indulged in "flights of paranoia, far-out analogies, conspiracy theories, and wild charges devoid of evidence," wrote Fred Barnes in *The Weekly Standard.*[38] They had one common objective—to besmirch President Bush's character, believability, and personal values.

Throughout this propaganda barrage, George W. remained calm, patient, and in control of his feelings, focused on the tasks and goals of his high office; he restrained from responding to the abuse with abuse of his own. A good test of the depth of a person's Christian experience is how he or she responds to others' abusive attacks, especially when they have no basis in truth. In fact, he did not dignify such attacks with statements of defense. One might imagine though that on occasion, during his daily devotions, he may have felt the need of rereading Christ's words as recorded in Matthew's Gospel: "But I say to you, love your enemies, and pray for those who persecute you" (5:44). Bush's "enemies" (self-declared) were quick to condemn him for bringing Scripture and spirituality into his speeches. When these elements drew wrathful jabs from the Left, perhaps he turned to the same passage and read: "Blessed are you when men cast insults at you, and persecute you, and say all kinds of evil against you falsely, on account of me" (5:11).

President George W. Bush expressed his faith in his speeches, primarily, in one of three ways: First, he expressed the belief that God would bless America in the current struggle and strengthen Americans to meet the uncertainty of the future with courage. For example, in his "Presidential Address to the Nation" on September 11, 2001, Bush drew on his faith to offer comfort and hope from a divine source of power. "Tonight I ask for your prayers for all those who grieve, for the children whose worlds have been shattered, for all whose sense of safety and security has been threatened," he said. "And I pray they will be comforted by a power greater than any of us, spoken [of] through the ages in Psalm 23: 'Even though I walk through the valley of the shadow of death, I fear no evil, for You are with me.'"[39]

And then, nine days later, his "Address to a Joint Session of Congress" concluded:

> The course of this conflict is not known, yet its outcome is certain. Freedom and fear, justice and cruelty, have always been at war, and we know that God is not neutral between them.
>
> Fellow citizens, we will meet violence with patient justice—assured of the rightness of our cause, and confident of the victories to come. In all that lies before us, may God grant us wisdom, and may He watch over the United States of America.[40]

George W. Bush's speeches contained other examples of this particular expression of faith as he dealt with serious challenges in the years following.

In his speeches from January 2003 onward, he, secondly, expressed his faith by asserting that freedom and liberty were ordained by God for all human beings. He brought this concept into his rhetoric in his "State of the Union Address" on January 28, 2003 when he stated: "Americans are a free people, who know that freedom is the right of every person and the future of every nation. The liberty we prize is not America's gift to the world, it is God's gift to humanity."[41]

By stressing this concept that he obviously felt deeply about, he made known that he did not believe that liberty was something that one government bestowed upon another—it was not an American export. Rather, liberty originated with God. Moreover, he seemed to imply that God wanted people to be free, and that America could serve His purpose by spreading liberty to countries that desperately needed it.

President Bush expanded this thought in a speech on September 11, 2002 at Ellis Island, New York, New York. Speaking to mark the observance of the September 11th attacks, he remarked, "Our deepest national conviction is that every life is precious, because every life is the gift of a Creator who intended us to live in liberty and equality. More than anything else, this separates us from the enemy we fight." Several minutes later, he picked up the thread of this thought again and, with persuasive appeal, told the audience: "Be confident. Our country is strong. And our cause is even larger than our country. Ours is the cause of human dignity; freedom guided by conscience and guarded by peace. This ideal of America is the hope of all mankind. That hope drew millions to this harbor." Then with a Scriptural allusion to the Gospel of John 1:5, he added, "That hope still lights our way. And the light shines in the darkness. And the darkness will not overcome it."[42]

In time, President Bush's rhetoric connected the historical origin of freedom with divine origin. Addressing the 2004 National Urban League conference, he declared, "We're standing true to this great American ideal that freedom is the almighty God's gift to each man and woman in this world." Such statements elicited anger and denunciations from Bush's Leftward opponents, who did not seem to know that it was a reworking of the second paragraph of the Declaration of Independence. They might better have attacked this document's principal author, Thomas Jefferson, who, in 1774, said: "The God who gave us life, gave us liberty at the same time: the hand of force may destroy, but cannot disjoin them . . . . Well aware that Almighty God has created the mind free."[43]

A third way that George W. expressed his faith was in stating the Biblical injunction to practice the Golden Rule in the treatment of others.

On March 6, 1999, at the Second Baptist Church in Houston, Texas, Governor Bush preached a sermon entitled "Faith Can Change Lives." At one point in his message, he remarked, "Our society has plenty of *advisors*. What we need are *doers*, like the people in this church who are following the apostle Paul's admonition to 'serve one another in the spirit of love.'"[44] He made it plain that this was more likely to happen in a culture where people understand that "we're responsible for loving our neighbors as we'd like to be loved ourselves . . ."[45]

George W. Bush took his interpretation of the Golden Rule to the Oval Office where he often repeated the idea in his speeches—sometimes rather unexpectedly from the point of view of the audience. For example, in March 2001, talking about the economy in Michigan, President Bush declared:

> We'll debate budgets and line-items and all that, but one thing that can't be debated is the true strength of our country lies in the hearts and souls of citizens who hear the universal call to love a neighbor just like they would like to be loved themselves.[46]

After combat operations began in Afghanistan, President Bush applied the Golden Rule to the war. He delivered a speech at Southern Maine Technical College on January 25, 2002 in which he said, "Our job is not only to win the war overseas, our job is not only to protect the homeland, to make sure we can live peacefully; our job is to fight evil on a daily basis, by loving a neighbor just like you'd like to be loved yourself."[47]

After significant progress in the war on terrorism in Afghanistan and Iraq and in homeland security and job creation in America, President Bush, campaigning for reelection, once again expressed his faith in terms of the Golden Rule. Speaking in Niceville, Florida at Okaloosa-Walton College on August 10, 2004, he suggested that in practicing the Golden Rule, people showed "the heart and soul" of America. "Think about it—," he said, "this is a country that has got people from all walks of life willing to love a neighbor just like they'd like to be loved themselves." Then, relating the Golden Rule to culture change, he declared, "The ability to change our country one heart and one soul at a time is real because there are people who are willing to love a neighbor." Because, he understood this source of compassion, he told the audience, was one reason why he was running again for president. For, "part of the job of a President is to rally that compassion and call upon people to serve."[48]

President Bush did more than merely talk about the need for "people to serve." In his 2002 "State of the Union Address," he announced the creation of the USA Freedom Corps to help Americans get involved in some kind of service as volunteers. His speech offered an invitation to all Americans "to join the new USA Freedom Corps. The Freedom Corps will focus on three areas of need: responding in case of crisis at home; rebuilding our communities; and extending American compassion throughout the world." Bush also pointed out, "One purpose of the USA Freedom Corps will be homeland security. America needs retired doctors and nurses who can be mobilized in major emergencies; volunteers to help police and fire departments; transportation and utility workers well-trained in spotting danger."[49] George W., then, once more acted on his words—he put action behind the values he voiced.

Even though President Bush has shown over four years that his faith manifests itself in his speeches as an expression of concern for others' welfare, he continues to experience attacks for his references to God. Some of the attacks originate with the professional antireligion litigators, who seek to expunge religious symbolism—especially Christian—from the public square. Speaking of these attacks in December 2004, Michael Gerson, Bush's head speechwriter, said that the attempts to remove religious symbolism from the public square would "flatten political rhetoric and make it less moving and interesting." In fact, he noted, it would undermine "one of the main sources of social justice in our history. Without an appeal to justice rooted in faith, there would be no abolition movement or civil rights movement or pro-life movement."[50] Gerson's words made it clear that George W. would keep God in his speeches. In a January 2005 interview with editors and reporters of *The Washington Times*, George W. said, "I don't see how you can be president—at least from my perspective, how you can be president, without a relationship with the Lord."[51]

Optimism and Resolution in Bush's Rhetoric

In the aftermath of 9/11, President Bush's rhetoric expressed optimism and resolution that pointed the nation to values that would enhance morale in response to the attacks. He helped the American people to see basic human values that stood out amidst the death and devastation from the 9/11 attacks, which the terrorists could not destroy but only reinforce, because, as he reminded his hearers, love is stronger than hate.

Always the optimistic leader, Bush consistently spoke with the conviction that opportunities could rise above crises and moral good above evil with God's help. In so doing, he instilled confidence in Americans as they adopted his faith in the country's ability to win the war against terrorism. He had come to the presidency with an optimistic belief in the character of his countrymen and in the nation's capacity for positive culture change. The actions of Americans in the wake of 9/11, confirmed his high opinion.

Three days after the attacks, at the National Cathedral for a national day of prayer and remembrance, President Bush said, "It is said that adversity introduces us to ourselves. This is true of a nation as well. In this trial, we have been reminded, and the world has seen, that our fellow Americans are generous and kind, resourceful and brave." He then backed up his words, with examples: "We see our national character in rescuers working past exhaustion; in long lines of blood donors; in thousands of citizens who have asked to work and serve in any way possible." His examples became more poignant, as he said: "And we have seen our national character in eloquent acts of sacrifice. Inside the World Trade Center, one man who could have saved himself stayed until the end at the side of his quadriplegic friend. A beloved priest died giving the last rites to a firefighter."[52]

Bush sounded the same theme, but emphasized the values that Americans showed the rest of the world when, in a speech in Rockville, Maryland in October 2001, he declared:

> We have a renewed appreciation of the character of America. We are a generous people, a thoughtful people who hurt, and share the sadness when people lose their lives or when people are hurt. We've helped each other in every way we know, in donations, in acts of kindness, in public memorials, in private prayer. We have shown in difficult times that we're not just a world power, that we're a good and kind and courageous people.[53]

And, the President wanted to make clear that Americans are not only the kind of people who come to the aid of hurting fellow Americans, they also come to the aid of hurting people in foreign lands. He had in mind the Afghan people who were oppressed by the Taliban, when, in his next statement in this speech, he asserted, "As we pursue the enemy in Afghanistan, we feed the innocents. As we try to bring justice to those who harmed us, we find those who need help."[54]

When President Bush addressed the nation on November 8, 2001 from Atlanta, Georgia, he specified some of the basic values that, he believed, Americans appeared to prize more, following the 9/11 attacks. He told the country:

> And something even more profound is happening across our country. The enormity of this tragedy has caused many Americans to focus on the things that have not changed—the things that matter most in life: *Our faith, our love for family and friends, our commitment to our country and to our freedoms and to our principles.*[55]

In his optimistic vision of a nation changed by war, Bush saw a new comprehension of the brave sacrifice that some people make for the welfare of others. He stressed this change in his remarks to personnel of the New York Police Department in New York City in February 2002. Using words that carried strong emotional appeal—especially for listeners who lost fellow officers at the World Trade Center—Bush observed:

> We're understanding more about ourselves as a result of what went on. We understand heroism. We understand now what it means to recite a prayer, tell your wife, "I love you," on the phone, and drive a plane into the ground to save others' lives. We're beginning to understand more about sacrifice, personal responsibility.[56]

The President then brought his message closer to home, saying, "See, I believe out of this terrible evil can come some great good. I believe there's a better understanding of the sacrifice the police and firefighters make.

And that's good for America. I believe there is a different culture evolving . . ."[57]

Late in February 2002, Bush visited the Osan Air Base in Seoul, Republic of Korea and spoke to the U.S. military there. In the course of his remarks, he once more reminded his audience of the heroic actions of the passengers of Flight 93 on 9/11, who overpowered terrorists to dive the plane into the ground. "There's a new way of thinking in America," he said. "It was defined by the actions of Flight 93, when several people aboard an airplane got the word that that airplane might be headed to the Capitol, or the White House—but certainly headed to hurt [fellow Americans]. They were on the telephone with their loved ones," he explained. "They told them they loved them. They said a prayer. And then they said: 'Let's roll.'" Bush next told his listeners: "There is a new spirit of sacrifice in America that understands that we must, in life, serve something greater than ourselves."[58] Bush continued to tell the story of Flight 93 in his speeches, since it illustrated the highest value—self-sacrifice.

When President Bush addressed the German Bundestag in Berlin, Germany on May 23, 2002, he again expressed his optimism that good could come from evil. He did this by quoting a famous German martyr, who personified self-sacrifice in fighting the evil of his day:

> One of the greatest Germans of the 20th century was Pastor Dietrich Bonhoeffer, who left the security of America to stand against Nazi rule. In a dark hour, he gave witness to the Gospel of life, and paid the cost of his discipleship, being put to death only days before his camp was liberated.
>
> "I believe," said Bonhoeffer, "that God can and wants to create good out of everything, even evil."[59]

Thus, Bonhoeffer's words brought divine authority to one of Bush's favorite themes, which he then applied to European history in the following statement:

> That belief [of Bonhoeffer's] is proven in the history of Europe since that day—in the reconciliation and renewal that have transformed this continent. In America, very recently, we have

> also seen the horror of evil and the power of good. In the tests of our time, we are affirming our deepest values and our closest friendships.[60]

Doubtless, Bush was reminding his listeners of America's role in the restoration of Germany after World War II to maximize the audience relevance of his speech.

In effect, Bush founded his optimism on the premise that good is stronger than evil. Following the 9/11 attacks, he saw evidence of that throughout America in helping acts that demonstrated basic human values. As a man of faith, Bush understood that the Author of goodness was also the Author of peace. It, then, was not surprising that he broadened his theme to include world peace. Speaking at a ceremony honoring Port Authority heroes at Port Elizabeth, New Jersey in June 2002, the President said, "I think out of evil done to America, the evil so many saw firsthand and had to live with, will come incredible good. I believe there will be peace in the world if America continues to lead and remain strong. And," he added, "I believe here at home, thanks to the loving hearts of thousands of our fellow citizens, America can not only be a safer place, but a better place."[61]

George W. Bush's speeches not only revealed an optimistic leader who promoted altruistic values, they showed a resolute leader who fostered values of resilience in response to terrorist attacks on the homeland and resistance to fear and intimidation in the face of continuing threat of violence. This wartime president encouraged Americans to stand resolved and make the most of their "life, liberty, and the pursuit of happiness."

Just six days after he visited Ground Zero, President Bush, to a Joint Session of Congress, gave one of his most eloquent and forceful speeches. Toward his conclusion, he asserted, "We have suffered great loss. And in our grief and anger we have found our mission and our moment. Freedom and fear are at war . . . . We will not tire, we will not falter, and we will not fail." Then, his tone softening, Bush said, "It is my hope that in the months and years ahead, life will return almost to normal. We'll go back to our lives and routines, and that is good. Even grief recedes with time and grace. But our resolve must not pass."[62]

In a speech to military personnel at Travis Air Force Base in October

2001, expressing his resolution metaphorically, the President communicated a warning to terrorists, who likely were listening somewhere: "People have struck us. They've tested our mettle and tested our character. But they are going to find that this nation understands we've reached a pivotal moment in history," he emphasized, "where we will plant our flag on the ground—a flag that stands for freedom—and say to anybody who wants to harm us or our friends and allies, you will pay a serious price, because we're a nation that is strong and resolved and united."[63]

A fourth-grade girl wrote President Bush a letter shortly after the 9/11 attacks. He quoted one of her statements in his address to the nation from Atlanta, Georgia on November 8, 2001, "that seemed to say it all: 'I don't know how to feel, sad, mad, angry. It has been different lately. I know the people in New York are scared because of the World Trade Center and all, but if we're scared, we are giving the terrorists all the power.'"[64] Building on the key point the girl had made in her letter, Bush declared, "In the face of this great tragedy, Americans are refusing to give terrorists the power. Our people have responded with courage and compassion, calm and reason, resolve and fierce determination. We have refused to live in a state of panic—or a state of denial." Bush went on to say proudly, "People are going about their daily lives, working and shopping and playing, worshiping at churches and synagogues and mosques, going to movies and baseball games. Life in America is going forward—and as the fourth-grader who wrote me knew, that is the ultimate repudiation of terrorism."[65]

Such statements as this by President Bush apparently caused Professor Steven Goldzwig of Marquette University, Milwaukee, to say that in his response to the 9/11 crisis, Bush's "value message" was mixed. One method Bush recommended for helping America "get back to normal" was for each American to resume his or her role as a consumer as an antidote to the damage done by September 11 and a flagging economy. While his recent calls for self-sacrifice through a two-year pledge of public service (utilizing the existing Peace Corp and Americorp) are in line with republican virtues, the former call seemed geared toward "individualism" and free enterprise. Thus, selfish motives seem destined to compete with the selfless in the new world order of civil religion.[66]

An examination of hundreds of President Bush's speeches did not reveal appeals to Americans to become more active consumers in order to help the economy and, as Goldzwig put it, "get back to normal." Rather, as excerpts from Bush's speeches clearly show, he stressed the importance of Americans remaining resolved and carrying on with their lives, not allowing the terrorists to intimidate them—as they succeeded in doing in Spain after terrorist attacks there in 2004. As noted earlier in this section, Bush observed that Americans were "going about their daily lives," which certainly did involve consumption. However, instead of consumption, the President, from the time he entered office, emphasized tax cuts to improve the economy. Also, one would think that any proper "method" that improved the economy and, therefore, created jobs for the unemployed, so that they could care for their families would qualify as a "value message" and not, in any sense, be "selfish," as Goldzwig asserted.

As George W. Bush spoke in a variety of situations throughout 2003 and 2004, a value theme that he retained in his rhetoric was his resolution to protect America by winning the war against terrorism. In fact, he seemed to intensify this message in his presidential campaign against Senator John Kerry. Addressing the American Israel Public Affairs Committee on May 18, 2004, President Bush concluded his speech: "We are living through historic times. We are called to do important work in the world. We will stand together against bigotry in every land and in every language. We will answer violent men with patient, determined justice." Then, with his eye seemingly on the future of the Middle East, he continued, "We will expand human freedom and the peace that freedom brings. And by our resolve, and by our courage, we *will* prevail." (Applause.)[67] Bush's words and delivery communicated the confidence that he would lead the nation in a second term.

At the Marriott Wardman Park in Washington, D.C., May 5, 2004, President Bush, speaking to 1,500 people attending the Presidential Gala—a fund-raising event for the Republican Party—said, "There's going to be many turns in this campaign, but this will remain constant: I will offer a positive, optimistic and hopeful vision to the American people. I have a plan to win the War on Terror and to spread peace and freedom throughout the world."[68] The optimism and resolution Bush thus expressed in defeating terrorism was well received by the audience and, according to polls taken in the last months of the campaign, the majority of the electorate.

However, to a vocal and significantly-large minority, such value themes in Bush's speeches were a source of fear, which manifested itself in deep-seated hatred for the President. The Italian poet Giovanni Casti (1724-1803) wisely observed: "Short is the road that leads from fear to hate." These words especially ring true when the road taken is rough and requires courage at each step forward; the fearful naturally look backward to the ruins of false security, hoping against hope that they can be rebuilt without sacrifice.

NOTES

1. President's Speech, Bush/Cheney Campaign Rally, York, Pennsylvania, C-SPAN, July 9, 2004.
2. Kouzes and Posner, *Credibility*, 164.
3. Frum, *The Right Man*, 281-282.
4. Bush, "Compassionate Conservatism," p. 645.
5. Marvin Olasky, *Compassionate Conservatism: What It Is, What It Does, and How It Can Transform America* (New York: Free Press, 2000), 11.
6. David Aikman, *A Man of Faith: The Spiritual Journey of George W. Bush* (Nashville: W Publishing Group, 2004), 101.
7. Olasky, *Compassionate Conservatism*, 11.
8. Ibid., 12.
9. Ibid., 13.
10. Ibid., 1.
11. Ibid., 12.
12. Ibid.
13. George W. Bush, "The Duty of Hope," in Marvin Olasky, *Compassionate Conservatism: What It Is, What It Does, and How It Can Transform America* (New York: Free Press, 2000), 216.
14. Ibid., 218.
15. Ibid., 221.
16. Ibid., 225.
17. Olasky, *Compassionate Conservatism*, 12.
18. Bush, "The Duty of Hope," 224.
19. Frum, *The Right Man*, 274.
20. Ibid.
21. George W. Bush, "Foreword" in Marvin Olasky, *Compassionate Conservatism: What It Is, What It Does, and How It Can Transform America* (New York: Free Press, 2000), xi.

22. "Remarks by the President to Southwest Michigan First Coalition/Kalamazoo Chamber of Commerce Joint Event on the Economy," Western Michigan University, Kalamazoo, Michigan, March 27, 2001, www.whitehouse.gov.
23. "Remarks by the President to Massachusetts Victory 2002 Reception," October 4, 2002.
24. "President's Remarks at the 2004 President's Dinner," Washington Convention Center, Washington, D.C., July 21, 2004, www.whitehouse.gov.
25. Michael Barone, "Trading Places," *U.S. News & World Report,* January 14, 2002, p. 28.
26. Ibid.
27. "Remarks by the President to the 2004 National Urban League Conference," Detroit Marriot Renaissance Hotel, Detroit, Michigan, July 23, 2004, www.whitehouse.gov.
28. Ibid.
29. George W. Bush, "State of the Union," *Vital Speeches of the Day,* February 15, 2005, p. 261.
30. Aikman, *A Man of Faith,* 170.
31. Ibid., 157.
32. Peggy Noonan, "Be Proud of What We Stand For," *Ladies' Home Journal,* October 2003, p. 134.
33. Peggy Noonan, "Foreword" in George W. Bush, *We Will Prevail: President George W. Bush on War, Terrorism, and Freedom*/Selected and Edited by National Review (New York: Continuum, 2003), xvi.
34. Doug Wead, *George Bush: Man of Integrity* (Eugene, OR: Harvest House Publishers, 1988), 53.
35. Tony Blankley, "United by a Common Hatred," *Washington Times* National Weekly Edition, August 2-8, 2004, p. 30.
36. Rush Limbaugh, "Woodward at War," *Wall Street Journal,* April 21, 2004, p. A18.
37. Maureen Dowd, "Playing the Jesus Card," *New York Times,* December 15, 1999, p. 23 (late ed.).
38. Fred Barnes, "The Democrats and the Loony Left," *Weekly Standard,* August 2, 2004, p. 10.
39. "Presidential Address to the Nation," The United States Capitol, Washington, D.C., September 11, 2001, www.whitehouse.gov.
40. "Presidential Address to a Joint Session of Congress," The United States Capitol, Washington, D.C., September 20, 2001, www.whitehouse.gov.
41. "President's State of the Union Address," The United States Capitol, Washington, D.C., January 28, 2003, www.whitehouse.gov.
42. "Presidential Address to the Nation Marking the Observance of the September 11th Attacks," Ellis Island, New York, New York, September 11, 2002, www.whitehouse.gov.
43. Thomas Jefferson, "A Summary View of the Rights of British America," in Adrienne Koch and William Peden, eds., *The Life and Selected Writings of Thomas Jefferson* (New York: Random House, 1944), 311.

44. George W. Bush, "Faith Can Change Lives," sermon delivered at Second Baptist Church, Houston, Texas, March 6, 1999 in David Aikman, *A Man of Faith: The Spiritual Journey of George W. Bush* (Nashville: W Publishing Group, 2004), 209.
45. Ibid., 210.
46. "Remarks by the President to Southwest Michigan First Coalition/Kalamazoo Chamber of Commerce Joint Event on the Economy," March 27, 2001.
47. Bush, *We Will Prevail*, 105.
48. "President's Remarks at Ask President Bush Event," Okaloosa-Walton College, Niceville, Florida, August 10, 2004, www.whitehouse.gov.
49. "President Delivers State of the Union Address," The United States Capitol, Washington, D.C., January 29, 2002, www.whitehouse.gov.
50. Joseph Bottum, "Merry Christmas," *Weekly Standard*, December 27, 2004, p. 7.
51. James G. Lakely, "America Is a Remarkable Place When It Comes to Religion and Faith," *Washington Times* National Weekly Edition, January 17-23, 2005, p. 22.
52. "Remarks by the President at National Day of Prayer and Remembrance Ceremony," The National Cathedral, Washington, D.C., September 14, 2001, www.whitehouse.gov.
53. "Remarks by the President on the 'Lessons of Liberty' Initiative," Thomas Wootton High School, Rockville, Maryland, October 30, 2001, www.whitehouse.gov.
54. Ibid.
55. Bush, *We Will Prevail*, 64. Italics mine.
56. Ibid., 117.
57. Ibid.
58. Ibid., 126.
59. Ibid., 157.
60. Ibid.
61. "Remarks by the President at Ceremony Honoring Port Authority Heroes," Port Elizabeth, New Jersey, June 24, 2002, www.whitehouse.gov.
62. "Presidential Address to a Joint Session of Congress," The United States Capitol, Washington, D.C., September 20, 2001, www.whitehouse.gov.
63. Bush, *We Will Prevail*, 48.
64. "President Discusses War on Terrorism in Address to the Nation," World Congress Center, Atlanta, Georgia, November 8, 2001, www.whitehouse.gov.
65. Ibid.
66. Steven R. Goldzwig, "Official and Unofficial Civil Religious Discourse," *Journal of Communication and Religion,* March 2002, p. 112.
67. "Remarks by the President to the American Israel Public Affairs Committee," May 18, 2004.
68. "Presidential Gala Sets Record," *Rising Tide*, Summer 2004, p. 5.

Chapter 9
Bush's Delivery: Seeing and Hearing Is Believing

The challenge of statesmanship is to have the vision to dream of a better, safer world and the courage, persistence and patience to turn that dream into a reality.
— Ronald Reagan, A Speech in 1985

The previous chapters strongly suggest that much of the language in George W. Bush's speeches originates with him. This is especially the case when it comes to the value themes that are so pronounced in his rhetoric. The man's style seems stamped on every line he speaks—not always smooth, but sincere, not always oratorical, but conversational. He demonstrates credibility, rather than strategy in that he will persist in pursuing a course of action that sometimes upsets even his most ardent supporters. This disregard for political expediency is highly revealing—it shows a man who does what he believes is right, after first seeking the counsel of some of the best minds in government. One is reminded of that great line that the talented comedian Flip Wilson left us: "What you see is what you get!"

When George W. Bush takes his place on the platform to deliver a speech, he, like any public speaker, is on his own. He is beyond the reach of speechwriters, advisors, and family members. It is up to him to transform a gathering of people into an occasion that listeners will find meaningful and memorable. To be persuasive—the whole point of his presence—the words, inert on paper, must be called to life through symbolic sight and sound. The audience, in turn, will match every word, every phrase with the person and leader President Bush presents through his delivery.

The response Bush receives when delivering a speech is a good indication of how much the audience believes in him and his message. And, typically, audiences respond throughout his speeches very enthusiastically. For example, the introduction to his address to the American Israel Public Affairs Committee in May 2004, aroused listeners to laughter six times. And the audience interrupted his remarks 67 times with applause; in fact, he became a little hoarse after raising his voice a number of times to speak above the applause. While, of course, some response might be an expression of courtesy for the President of the United States; yet, the people in his audiences show, nonverbally, a genuine liking for George W. as a person and leader, which seems to translate into trust.

The people who have attended a campaign rally to hear George W. Bush speak, tend to go away with positive impressions of the man, as conveyed by his delivery, or what one attendee called "Bush's charismatic forcefulness." When a young attorney in a leading Texas law firm was asked about Bush's persuasive public speaking, he replied:

> During George W. Bush's second gubernatorial run, I heard him speak in Dallas twice. He spoke once before a large audience and once in a much smaller group and made both settings feel personal. Like his predecessors, his verbal miscues have provided fodder for late night talk show hosts, but his slip-ups are produced by the very approach to public speaking that made his speeches feel personal—a willingness to go unscripted. He spoke without being tied to a lectern or sounding rehearsed; he spoke with an animation responsive to those around him. I felt like he wasn't so much reading speeches at me as talking to me. He created a connection through which he could share not only the topics of his speeches, but also the passion he felt for those topics. What's more, he created a connection through which I could join with him. In doing so,

he inspired me and many others in attendance. Bush could have stuck to a sterile script, but rather than focus on perfect delivery, he risked a few blunders and concentrated on communicating.

Meaningful Moves on the Platform

As the young Texas attorney suggested, George W. Bush exhibits a certain spontaneity as he adapts his speech to the audience, verbally and nonverbally. For instance, in his Urban League speech in July 2004, he noted that the Republican Party had a lot of work to do to gain African Americans' support. Then, spotting Jesse Jackson in the audience nodding in agreement, Bush, with a smile and a friendly hand gesture in his direction, said, "You didn't need to nod your head that hard, Jesse." (Laughter.)[1] In such situations, Bush speaks extemporaneously, from notes, rather than a complete text.[2] His movements on the platform often seem guided by his emotions.

George W. puts his heart into whatever he undertakes, which includes the delivery of a speech and the interaction with listeners afterward. Karen Hughes, his former Communications Director, recalled, "I learned how fully George W. Bush threw himself into everything—laughing, working or exercising; everything was all out, never halfway."[3] She described how exhausted he was after giving a speech and then greeting hundreds of people who came to hear him.[4] One can see that when he speaks, he expends a lot of energy—he shows his concentration and what he thinks and feels about the ideas in his message. While he may use humor in a speech, he never forgets the nation is at war.

Recently, a journalist remarked, "It is often said that the attacks of 9/11 made a wartime President of George W. Bush."[5] Yes, he speaks as a wartime president, who saw Ground Zero firsthand only three days after the attacks. He saw six square blocks of rubble and debris, where once stood two tall, gleaming towers that dominated the city's skyline. He viewed the scene of ultimate disaster where lingering smoke and fire could not dampen the smell of death, the death of more than 3,000 souls who gave life and purpose to the towers. The hours he spent at that site of mass murder forever changed him, as it must change any real leader, and the change is evident in his nonverbal communication as he speaks about the war against terrorists and the security of America.

Whether by daily intelligence reports, speeches, or meetings with people who have reason to remember 9/11, President Bush opens himself to constant reminders of Ground Zero. He was talking and shaking hands with people after speaking at a campaign event in Lebanon, Ohio, when he shook hands with Lynn Faulkner and his 15-year-old daughter, Ashley; he was about to move past them when someone in the crowd directed attention to Ashley, saying, "This girl lost her mom in the World Trade Center on 9/11." The President stopped and asked her, "How are you doing?" She answered, "I'm okay," her eyes filling with tears. Bush then gave the girl a warm hug. Holding Ashley in his arms, he said, "I can see you have a father who loves you very much." The exchange occurred so fast that nobody in the national press corps saw it. However, the father described the President's kindness toward his daughter to a local reporter and mentioned that she showed more emotion in that brief encounter than she had in two and a half years. Later, Ashley explained, "The way he was holding me, it felt like he was trying to protect me. I thought, Here is the most powerful guy in the world, and he wants to make sure I'm safe."[6]

Bush's nonverbal communication, as well as his verbal, conveys to many people the same sense of strength that Ashley experienced—his visual cues create an impression of self-assurance, purposefulness, and believability. "More than any recent President, we know who he is," said political science professor Martha Joynt Kumar, an authority on presidential communication at Towson University in Maryland. "He's comfortable with himself; he's willing to take risks; he has a sense of his moral compass. People may not like it, but they know what he stands for."[7] Even a less critical observer might draw similar conclusions, based on Bush's facial expressions, the look in his eyes, his demeanor, gestures, and the way he walks and carries himself.

George W. Bush's visual cues generally augment and strengthen his verbal communication and, therefore, enhance his delivery. He links his words with facial expressions that provide the listeners with cues that show them how he feels about what he is saying. In the course of a speech, the audience expects a speaker to display a variety of emotions through facial expressions. A person watching Bush deliver an address on television could turn off the sound and, on the basis of facial expressions only, see his face change from sorrow as he speaks of the loss of life caused by a terrorist bomb, to appreciation as he refers to the decency and skill of our military, to pleasure as he recounts the story of a child's letter containing words of courage.

During his 2004 "Acceptance Speech" on September 2nd at the Republican National Convention in New York City, President Bush gave his remarks a lot of facial expression. His face reflected the feelings that his words stirred in him. In his introduction, he expressed his gratitude for the support of Vice President Dick Cheney and his wife Laura Bush, accompanying his words with a slight shake of the head and a smile that signified wonderment at having such good fortune. He smiled broadly at some points of his address when listeners applauded a statement—it seemed that he was showing his pleasure that it had registered so well with them. For example, his face lit up with a big smile when his statement that terrorists "should be afraid because freedom is on the march" elicited sustained applause. References to Saddam Hussein brought a steely-eyed expression to Bush's face that communicated his strong conviction that America and the world were better off with the tyrant in jail. Bush's face took on a look of incredulity when quoting Senator Kerry's words that participants at a Hollywood gala who indulged in crude behavior represented "the heart and soul of America." When he spoke of his meetings with the families of fallen heroes in the war against terrorists, his eyes teared up, and he showed a look of humble amazement when he said that, in spite of their grief, they told me that "I'm in their prayers."[8] This "Acceptance Speech" ranks as one of his best speeches, partly because of his delivery, including his visual cues. He was interrupted 108 times by applause, bringing audience members to their feet many times.

Following the first presidential debate on September 30th, some journalists and the DNC criticized President Bush for facial expressions that they insisted conveyed irritation when Senator Kerry spoke. Such expressions, however, would be better described as frustration and incredulity in response to Kerry's outlandish charges. The journalists also complimented Kerry on his facial control when Bush spoke; but, they neglected to mention that when Kerry spoke, the same control was evident—his face and vocal tone remained essentially expressionless. Wayne Fields, Washington University English professor and author of *Union of*

Words: A History of Presidential Eloquence, watched the debate and concluded, "They both started strong. Both with confidence and strength. Body language and timing suggested they're confident." He continued, "Kerry is more controlled, but I'm not sure that's a disadvantage for the president. He runs on emotion. That has been his strength in all of this."[9] Probably, most Americans want to know how a debater feels on hearing an opponent say something absurd. But his cues must be subtle and spontaneous, as Bush's generally appeared to be.

An ancient Chinese proverb declares: "To see a person's face is better than to hear of his reputation." The wise person who coined that saying likely thought of the face's capacity to inspire trust or raise doubt in the mind of the observer. The eyes contribute most significantly to such impressions. Comments from people who have sat and listened to George W. speak say that they had the feeling that he made eye contact with them—that he did not look through them, but at them, "with interest and respect," as one person put it. In many of his speeches, Bush shows his awareness of individuals in the audience as when, for example, he recognizes someone with a smile, a wave of the hand, and, sometimes, one of his short, soft chuckles.

Gaius Petronius (d. AD 66), who wrote the first Roman novel, observed, "From a man's face, I can read his character; if I can see him walk, I know his thoughts." Certainly, body language is highly revealing, including the way a man walks. George W. has a brisk, deliberate step and a long stride for his height. The American people witnessed these characteristics when, shortly after the 9/11 attacks, he strode from his helicopter across the wide expanse of lawn toward the White House. His head up and shoulders back, he kept a steady, but unhurried pace. He told his Secret Service that he would walk by himself, so that he could show the people that he was not afraid and that they should not be afraid—this was a courageous act, since nobody knew where or when the enemy might strike again.

When Bush first entered the presidency, he had what Peggy Noonan called "a businessman's slouch, a regular guy's posture."[10] Although his staff had encouraged him to stand straight, he had been slow to take their advice. In June 2001, Noonan interviewed George W. in the Oval Office and wrote about the meeting. She said that he asked her if she had any advice for him and she replied, "Yes." She told him, "You mean to be the leader of a great nation, the United States; you will be its president and you must stand tall." He confided that his staff had given him the same advice. Noonan urged the President to listen to them. "And he did," she noted.[11] His upright posture as he walks on to the platform and stands before the audience has become a part of his public persona.

When Americans see President Bush on television walking with a world leader at his Crawford, Texas ranch, they might notice that he does have a distinctive walk, especially dressed in jeans. It is the kind of walk that a man might develop as he strides through the wide-open spaces of West Texas. His critics have described how he walks on to the platform to speak as a "John Wayne swagger," whereas his supporters would agree with a fellow Texan who said, "He has the walk and look of an outdoorsman who has tough miles to go." In his 2004 "Acceptance Speech," President Bush showed that he took criticism about how he walked good-naturedly and as a source of humor. He told the audience at Madison Square Garden that people had pointed out his flaws. "Some folks," he said, "look at me and see a certain swagger that in Texas is called walking." (Laughter.)[12]

When President Bush delivers a more formal address where the occasion requires an elevated style, he uses few hand gestures. At such times, his hands tend to rest on the lectern, called into action only infrequently. For example, during the delivery of his 2004 "Acceptance Speech," in one of his few gestures, he brought his left hand up to his heart as he said, "I ask you to stand with me." This gesture—as with most of his gestures—proved symbolically significant, since it was well-timed, appropriate, and visually effective. It may be a truism to say that hand gestures should decrease with the formality of the speech.

Bush increases his hand gestures somewhat in situations that call for greater informality where a conversational mode of address is appropriate. For example, a Bush/Cheney campaign rally found him more relaxed and more physically active in delivery—this was evident in the rally held at Poplar Bluff, Missouri on September 6, 2004. The President began his speech by expressing his appreciation for the invitation to speak that contained 10,000 signatures. Looking out over the huge outdoor crowd, he remarked that there appeared to be more than 10,000 present. When he was well into his speech, a light rain began that seemingly had no effect on his energy or the crowd's enthusiasm. Without the protection of a jacket, the rain soon left his shirt quite wet. Except for wiping water once from the back of his neck, he showed no reaction to the rain, nor did the people sitting on the platform behind him. He kept his hand gestures low, close to the lectern, with the exception of a favorite gesture where he brought both hands to his chest, palms in, as when he spoke of Iraq embracing freedom. He leaned one elbow on the lectern as he often did, which conveyed a relaxed, informal approach to the audience. Uncharacteristically, he used a visual aid—he held up in each hand a thick volume of the tax code that represented, he said, "more than a million words of complicated rules." He made it plain that he wanted to see the code simplified, which, he noted, "weighs *heavily* on our economy."[13] After his speech, in spite of the rain, he spent considerable time, shaking hands with people on the platform and in the crowd and posing with individuals for pictures. His nonverbal communication suggested that the rain had not dampened his enjoyment of interacting with the folks of Poplar Bluff.

Bush Sounds Off on the Platform

In preparing a speech for delivery to a particular audience, President Bush must not only decide on the best choice of words, he must also decide on the right sounds to go with them. Like putting music to lyrics, he needs to select the appropriate tone for the words and decide: How soft or loud? How slow or fast? When to pause? What inflection to give phrases? What words to emphasize? Such considerations depend greatly on the needs of listeners and his purpose in talking to them.

Occasionally, journalists try their hand at appraising President Bush's rhetoric, including his vocal delivery, usually with more confusion than clarity, more criticism than creativity. For example, take Alexis Simendinger's July 2002 article "No Bully in the Pulpit," in which she criticized the President's corporate ethics speech. First, objecting to the President's selection of the audience and the place where he spoke, she fumed, "All modern presidents understand that bully pulpit atmospherics count, but this time Bush staged his speech in front of the wrong crowd—and traveled to their territory to do it. Wall Street pooh-bahs? To borrow a phrase: It should have been the victims, stupid."[14] The logic here is skewed. What would be the purpose of the focus she suggests? Speaking just to the "victims" of corporate scandals, of course, would create a media event where Bush could attack corporations and turn public opinion against them. But, had he done so, he would have adopted a typical liberal approach—blame the many because of the bad behavior of the few. Taking such a stance would have meant undermining investor confidence, retarding the recovery of the stock market, and hurting the economy—with the result that more people would have become victims.

Simendinger also objected to the place where Bush had decided to speak—Wall Street. However, by speaking in "their territory," Bush communicated nonverbally that he was addressing an entire institution as well as a room full of individuals; that presidential power extended to Wall Street; and that this effort signaled that corporate ethics was a high priority. Moreover, going to Wall Street likely increased the press coverage of his speech.

Talking about the President's delivery, Simendinger opined, "Bush missed another ingredient: discernible outrage. He talked tough, but his flat, clipped sentences lacked the umbrage his aides had privately described to reporters as evidence of Bush's exasperation with a few corrupt souls among the corporate class . . . . Bush's bully pulpit needed a bully."[15] But, Bush's purpose was not to bully (to hurt, frighten, or tyrannize those who are weaker), but, rather, to persuade influential men and women to give their support in creating a more ethical business environment. This writer heard the speech and thought it did not sound clipped or flat in tone. His delivery communicated his confidence that the audience would do the right thing. Hindsight shows that in content and delivery, President Bush's speech and subsequent actions of his administration—working through Congress and the courts—brought about constructive change in corporate business practices.

In nearly all of Bush's speeches, when he makes a statement that he feels deeply about, his voice will sometimes drop to a lower pitch and take on a rough, husky quality, which, at first, sounds like the onset of hoarseness; however, this quality soon disappears after a couple of lines. People listening closely might have heard this vocal quality when, in his 2004 "Acceptance Speech," he asserted, "Because the union of a man and woman claims an honored place in our society, I support the protection of marriage against activist judges." Also, during the speech, he displayed this vocal quality when he stated, "I believe that America is called to lead the cause of freedom in a new century."[16] Undoubtedly, this change in vocal quality occurs naturally without design, and, if anything, adds interest and emphasis to what Bush says in his delivery.

George W. Bush "sounds like an American man from Texas," observed Peggy Noonan.[17] Certainly, the pronunciation of his words reflects his background in Texas, but the way he pronounces his words also shows his years in the Northeast, especially his time at Harvard. For instance, he uses a broad "a" in pronouncing the word "rather." His Texas accent becomes stronger as he speaks with greater feeling in a conversational mode. His Texas origin was quite evident, for example, when he spoke at a Bush/Cheney rally in Poplar Bluff, Missouri in September 2004. This is not unusual. The movie actor Sean Connery will sometimes slip briefly into the accent of his Scottish background when the script calls for a high level of emotion.

During the elections of 2000 and 2004, George W.'s delivery made his speeches easy to follow and understand, which gave him an advantage over his opponents. He enunciated his words clearly, and distinctly. And, he displayed the ability to keep his delivery focused on word groups that contained a whole idea or parts of an idea, based on their logical connection. Separated by natural pauses, these units of thought were relatively short. This technique in Bush's delivery should have increased listeners' comprehension of his message. Al Gore in the 2000 presidential campaign found this a difficult skill to master. Bush also outdid Gore, and later John Kerry, with his ability to emphasize key words, so that listeners knew how they should interpret the feelings and attitudes behind his statements. Bush's 2004 "Acceptance Speech" supplied the following example:

> I *faced* the kind of decision that comes only to the *Oval* Office. A decision no President would *ask* for, but *must* be prepared to make. Do I forget the lessons of *September 11th* and take the word of a *madman*, or do I take *action* to *defend* our country? Faced with that *choice*, I will **DEFEND AMERICA EVERY TIME!**[18]

The foregoing example shows that President Bush used light and strong word stress—the latter in the last four words, which brought him sustained applause. A number of the applause lines in his speeches end with strong word stress. This vocal characteristic, along with variations in pitch, volume, and rate, create vocal variety that enhances his delivery as it builds audience attention. In sharp contrast with President Bush, Senator Kerry lacked vocal variety in the delivery of his speeches during the 2004 presidential campaign, which was a major reason why both Republicans and Democrats perceived him as a boring speaker. Interestingly, vocal variety enhances a public speaker's credibility and persuasiveness as, for example, through pitch variation, noted in Chapter 3.

Visual Impact of Bush's Platform

Since the rise of television news coverage of U.S. Presidents' public appearances and speeches, it has become necessary—if not crucial—for the President to give attention to the visual context of his speech. The President must rely on the guidance and work of staff professionals to create platform backdrops and control visual elements in the physical surroundings of the place where the President will speak—the staff professionals strive to produce visual effects that nonverbally reinforce the topic of the President's speech as he delivers it.

The aides of President Ronald Reagan, for instance, gave careful attention to staging his public appearances for maximum visual impact. During Reagan's reelection campaign in 1984, opposing Walter Mondale, his appearances were "choreographed down to the smallest detail." His aides sought to exclude any unwanted image that would "interfere with whatever message they want[ed] sent to the voters via television's campaign coverage that night."[19] One reporter at the time concluded that such media staging and event planning was the main reason for Reagan's big lead in the polls.[20] But, that view discounted President Reagan's effectiveness as a campaign orator, whose character, ideas, and style connected with the American people.

Doubtless, some critics of President Bush would say the same about the success of his campaign in 2004. Yet, a great visual background only works when there is a great candidate in the foreground, such as George W. Bush. His delivery, in bodily action and voice, brings meaning to the design of the setting where he speaks. Karl Rove, Bush's senior political advisor, would possibly say that George W. completes a winning picture. Rove told an interviewer:

> There is reason why that old saw, a picture is worth a thousand words, how we look, how we sound and how we project is important. So winning the picture is important and having a president with the right kind of people to drive and hone the emphasis of the message, to be seen in a positive, warm and strong way.[21]

So that Bush's staff achieve the desired visual impact as the President delivers his speech, the background behind him is carefully designed to take into account the "tight" shots of television cameras. Often the liberal news teams keep cameras close, so as to exclude views of large audiences responding enthusiastically. To gain the most benefit from the "tight" shots, a slim lectern (or podium) was developed—named "Falcon"—to allow viewers to see more of the backdrop that enhances the President's delivery.[22] Moreover, the slimmer lectern makes Bush's body language more visible to viewers.

Probably more than any previous administration, the Bush White House devotes professional planning to the creation of physical arrangements and platform backdrops that support the President's delivery—spatial design and modern technology are combined to maximize the visual impact of his speeches. Considerable time and effort goes into the visual production: After White House strategists determine the themes that Bush will communicate in a speech, staff professionals plan how the event should look, and then others implement the plan so that the event pictured is produced.[23]

A person who has had primary responsibility for developing President Bush's speech backdrops, as well as other aspects of spatial design, is Scott Sforza, Deputy Communications Director for Production. In an interview with presidential scholar Martha Joynt Kumer, Sforza said:

> I sort of use the rule of thumb, if the sound were turned down on the television when you are just passing by, you should be able to look at the TV and tell what the president's message is; if you are

> passing by a storefront and see a TV in the window, or if you are at a newspaper stand and you are walking by, you should be able to get the president's messages in snapshot in most cases.[24]

For example, when President Bush, on October 7, 2001, addressed the nation to announce military strikes against al Qaeda and the Taliban in Afghanistan, he used a site no previous president had selected for a speech. He delivered his address in the Treaty Room of the White House, "a location where the picture itself communicated a basic message." And the message? It was a subtle, nonverbal one: Bush delivered the speech at 1:00 in the afternoon, when TV viewers could see through a window behind him traffic in the distance moving along Constitution Avenue. "We wanted that [visible traffic];" Sforza told Kumer, "we'll send a message to the world that, we're still in business here."[25]

President Bush intended the place itself to convey a message that he wanted to get across to the nation and the world. So, at one point in his address, he observed, "I'm speaking to you today from the Treaty Room of the White House, a place where American Presidents have worked for peace. In the face of today's new threat, the only way to pursue peace is to pursue those who threaten it."[26] Bush's words suggested that he thought of how President William McKinley signed the treaty ending the Spanish-American War in the Treaty Room.[27] He thus communicated that his ultimate goal in fighting terrorists was peace.

The symbolism is not always as subtle as it was in the place where Bush gave his address on military action in Afghanistan; often it is very direct. When President Bush spoke in Kansas City in June 2002, for instance, Sforza developed a backdrop for him that included the words "**Protecting the Homeland**" in large print, with the picture of a firefighter that appeared on a wallpaper-like background.[28] The words and image reinforced the theme of homeland security, the restructure of which he promoted in his speech.

In September 2004, Bush spoke at Valley Forge Convention Center in Pennsylvania on several issues, including social security and education; there was a big banner stretched behind him that declared: **STRENGTHENING EDUCATION**, which the television camera could not miss. He emphasized the importance of his policies in the future for people's children and grandchildren, and would turn to look at a number of children seated behind him, as he did so. This proved effective since the children appeared enthusiastic.[29]

The White House itself offers a variety of impressive backdrops, with historic rooms that display the dignity and splendor of the U.S. presidency. The technology of fiber optics enables President Bush to go live on TV within a matter of minutes from four locations in the White House and four sites on the White House grounds. The fact that George W. can address the nation from the White House quickly, without elaborate preparations for the use of cumbersome equipment and technology—such as a satellite truck for a broadcast—likely helps him to be more relaxed and natural in the delivery of a speech. As Sforza informed Kumer: "So this way it's a very short cable line. You just plug it in and you're ready to go."[30]

At times, it would appear that the backdrop of the platform where President Bush is speaking is the design of the organization that has invited him to speak. When he addressed the National Guard Association of the U.S. Conference in Las Vegas on September 14, 2004, the National Guard flags of the 50 states stood in close formation behind him, obviously the work of the organization. Bush's staff could not have created a better backdrop for him to state: "19 Presidents have served in the Guard and I'm proud to be one of them." (Applause.)[31] The firmness with which he uttered the words "I'm *proud* to be one of them," sounded like a rejoinder to Democrats who have tried unsuccessfully to denigrate his Guard service.

On the last day of the Republican National Convention, President Bush strode briskly along a walkway that led to a special platform, both constructed overnight. The platform, from which he would deliver his 2004 "Acceptance Speech" was situated in the middle of the audience at Madison Square Garden. In design, the platform featured ten concentric tiers, each tier several inches high with a white edge. The entire floor of the top tier, which measured about 12 feet in diameter, displayed a painted replica of the presidential seal. The President stood on this platform, waving at all sides of the crowd for a few minutes; then, part of the floor opened and a lectern (or podium) equipped with a teleprompter slowly rose through the opening—a nice bit of technology. Once it was in place, the President began his address. Before he opened his mouth, however, he had already communicated nonverbally: (1) His record and future agenda were based on the testing and experience of the presidency—the seal on which he stood, reminded everyone that he spoke as President of the United States. (2) He saw himself as one of the people, not above them, but with them, which the placement of the platform symbolized. The platform designers had done more than create a unique platform, they created drama, excitement, and anticipation to prepare listeners for the delivery of an important message.

Any political leaders who present speeches to the American people and to the world, deliver more than facts and opinions, they deliver information about themselves. Through nonverbal communication, as well as by their words, they tell much about their character, personality, abilities, and attitudes toward others. What they intrinsically are as persons, speaks louder than their words. This truth is not lost on President George W. Bush's Leftist opponents and critics, who have translated it into a tactic of character assassination, in the hope that it will reduce his power and stature as a person and a leader. They have resorted to lies, insults, false charges, and forged documents.

George W., the man and leader, has risen above such personal attacks and has concentrated on the attacks of 9/11 against our country. Through his speeches—content and delivery—he has shown himself to be a man who has credibility you can count on, intelligence that makes him a match for the challenges of our time, style that mixes humanity with eloquence, humor that entertains as well as instructs, and core values and beliefs that keep him centered on his vision of a more peaceful world, devoid of death-dealing terrorists—all of which infuse the content and delivery of his speeches. Speech theorists, Douglas Ehninger and Wayne Brockriede, advise all those who would become persuasive public speakers: "For attractiveness of presentation demands more than a flexible voice and animated bodily action. It also requires that the speaker reveal himself as the sort of person men admire and want to know better."[32] This describes how many of us who have seen and heard George W. Bush speak feel about him.

NOTES

1. "Remarks by the President to the 2004 National Urban League Conference," July 23, 2004.
2. Podhoretz, *Bush Country*, 9.
3. Hughes, *Ten Minutes from Normal*, 91.
4. Ibid.
5. Carl Cannon, "Standing His Ground," *Reader's Digest*, August 2004, p. 74.
6. Ibid.
7. Ibid., p. 77
8. *Republican National Convention*, Fox News, President's "Acceptance Speech," September 2, 2004.
9. "Assessments of the Experts," *USA TODAY*, October 1, 2004, p.4A.
10. Peggy Noonan, *When Character Was King: A Story of Ronald Reagan* (New York: Penguin Books, 2001), 301.
11. Ibid.
12. *Republican National Convention*, Fox News, President's "Acceptance Speech," September 2, 2004.
13. President's Speech, Bush/Cheney Campaign Rally, Poplar Bluff, Missouri, C-SPAN, September 6, 2004.
14. Alexis Simendinger, "No Bully in the Pulpit," *National Journal*, July 13, 2002, p. 2095.
15. Ibid. See "Remarks by the President on Corporate Responsibility," Regent Wall Street Hotel, New York, New York, July 9, 2002, www.whitehouse.gov.
16. *Republican National Convention*, Fox News, President's "Acceptance Speech," September 2, 2004.
17. Noonan, "Foreword" in Bush, *We Will Prevail*, xv.
18. *Republican National Convention*, Fox News, President's "Acceptance Speech," September 2, 2004.
19. John W. Mashek, "On Campaign Trail with the President," *U.S. News & World Report*, October 1, 1984, p. 28.
20. Ibid.
21. Kumar, "The Contemporary Presidency," p. 385.
22. Ibid., pp. 386-387.
23. Ibid., p. 385.
24. Ibid., p. 386.
25. Ibid., p. 385.
26. Bush, *We Will Prevail*, 34.
27. Kumar, "The Contemporary Presidency," p. 385.
28. Ibid. "Remarks by the President at the Opening of Oak Park High School," June 11, 2002.
29. President's Speech, Bush/Cheney Campaign Rally, Valley Forge, Pennsylvania, Fox News, September 22, 2004.

30. Kumar, "The Contemporary Presidency," p. 386.
31. President's Speech to the National Guard Association of the U.S. Conference, Las Vegas, Nevada, C-SPAN, September 14, 2004.
32. Ehninger and Brockreide, *Decision by Debate*, 294.

Chapter 10
Last Words: Leadership in a New Reality

Only he who keeps his eye fixed on the far horizon will find his right road.
— Dag Hammerskjold, *Markings*

President Bush's hard-fought victory at the polls on November 2nd, has left the cultural-political Left reeling in confusion. After all, they had used multiple high-tech weaponry in their attacks on George W. Bush's character and leadership. The Left's arsenal supplied dozens of Bush-bashing books, internet conspiracy theories, propaganda films, slanted newspaper headlines and editorials, anti-Bush news networks, and Democratic fear-based rhetoric. And the Democrats, aided by most of the media, Hollywood, academia, and unions, pursued a campaign that called every Bush success a failure, every Bush decision a blunder, and every Bush action ignoble. Yet, on judgment day, November 2nd, they lost.

Historians will record that Bush and Cheney achieved a decisive victory over Kerry and Edwards in 2004. Bush secured reelection with 286 electoral votes, and garnered 62 million votes; 10 million more than in 2000—a 51 percent to 48 percent margin, a higher percentage than John Kennedy, Jimmy Carter, or Bill Clinton earned in gaining the presidency. As a matter of fact, Bush won the greatest number of popular votes of any presidential candidate in history. Moreover, not since 1936 has a president picked up seats in two consecutive elections. Republicans increased their control of the Senate from 51 seats to 55. The biggest upset in the congressional elections occurred in South Dakota with Republican John Thune's win over Senate Minority Leader Thomas Daschle, an 18-year Senate veteran and the first Senate leader to be ousted by voters in 52 years.

When one considers the various forces arrayed against President Bush, one might ask, which one created the most trouble for him, while he campaigned for a second term? Certainly, several contenders stand out as deserving of this dubious distinction, since they continue even now to inject the poison of insinuations and false assumptions into the body politic. The answer? The facts point to the elite media (or Old Media).

This contention is bolstered by scientific analysis. According to a Project for Excellence in Journalism analysis of 817 broadcast and print stories presented between October 1 and October 14, the press "battered" George W. Bush in its pre-election coverage. Released on October 27, the study found that President Bush "suffered strikingly more negative press coverage than challenger John Kerry." In fact, "Overall, 59 percent of Bush-dominated stories were clearly negative in nature," whereas "just 25 percent of Kerry stories were decidedly negative." The study concluded, "The tendency toward negative tone stands out because it suggests the press is prone to act as an enabler, accomplice, or conduit for negative campaigning."[1]

Just a short time before the presidential election, *Newsweek*'s veteran journalist, Evan Thomas, spoke plainly about the expected effect that the pro-Kerry media would have on voting. He claimed that the media could give the Senator a 15-point bump, which he later revised downward to five points.[2] Probably, the influence of the media did increase the vote percentage Senator Kerry received; likely, their daily disparagement of President Bush convinced some people—fortunately, most were too savvy to fall for it—to fear him and thus turn to Kerry in their anxiety and desperation.

The reporters of the elite media, in keeping with their secular views, found themselves, almost immediately, at odds with the man from Texas who, in his speeches, spoke of faith and compassion and responsibility and accountability. "They are scornful of the president's 'simple' worldview—where Americans are good and terrorists are evil, where nations are with us or against us—and suspicious of his motives."[3] Of course, a worldview that inspired a whole new grand strategy for foreign policy, is far from "simple." And that fact may explain much of the hostility that journalists on the Left have shown toward President Bush. They fear the definiteness and purposefulness with which he conceptualizes issues and defines problems; they would feel more comfortable with a leader whose thought processes involved more ambiguities and relativity in perceiving right and wrong; they fear the certainty with which he stands behind his final decisions; they would prefer a leader who voiced second thoughts and sought to satisfy the wishes of the U.N. and other nations, even concerning our national security—hence their attraction to Kerry and Edwards.

The media elite often looked to the 1960s in discussing and interpreting the 2004 presidential campaign. Liberal journalists took Kerry's lead and devoted considerable space to his Vietnam service, sometimes comparing it to George W. Bush's service in the Texas Air National Guard. Again, taking Kerry's lead, they gave little emphasis to his more recent service in the U.S. Senate. Neither Kerry nor his apologists in the press did a good job explaining why his Vietnam service more than three decades ago was relevant to presidential leadership in the 21st century. Doubtless, many in the electorate wondered, too, why the press periodically fixated on George W.'s Guard service in the 1970s. Shortly before the election, Dan Rather, CBS anchor, told his audience that documents surfaced suggesting that George W. had been given preferential consideration that enabled him to avoid service in Vietnam and, instead, serve in the Guard. Soon after airing the story, however, various experts pronounced the documents forgeries, something that CBS was warned prior to the broadcast.[4] Rather also seemed unwilling to give the young Bush credit for volunteering to fly in Vietnam, a fact mentioned in an earlier chapter.

Many of the well-known print and broadcast journalists share a common cultural-political philosophy with Democrats, rooted, it seems, in the cultural revolution and the Vietnam War protest of the 1960s. The things that Kerry and Edwards talked about in the presidential campaign, what the Democratic platform stressed at the 2004 national convention, the words and behavior of Democratic celebrities, and how leading Democrats in Congress vote reveal 1960's morals, attitudes, priorities, and objectives. In his insightful article in *The Wall Street Journal*, Daniel Henninger wrote, "The color-coding of the 2004 election [—red states and blue states—] began around 1965 in the politics of the Vietnam era. The Democratic Party today is the product of a generational shift that began in those years." He pointed out that the Party came under the control of people who formed their view of America and its politics as opponents of the Vietnam War. In time, they transformed the Party's worldview on cultural issues and foreign policy, creating a new ethos within the Party that was "aggressively secular."[5] In the same vein, Cal Thomas, writing in *The Washington Times* following President Bush's reelection victory, stated, "The left has lost. The '60s are over. A majority of the public is tired of being forced to accept every ideology, sexual depravity and secular idea the left wishes to shove down their throats. The election showed they have pushed back."[6]

The American public "pushed back" when they voted to retain George W. Bush in the Oval Office. The people chose the candidate who had demonstrated a fearless grasp of the new reality of the post-9/11 world, with the threats it presents to our lives and livelihood. The polls consistently showed that the people perceived Bush as a stronger leader than Kerry when it came to fighting the war against terrorists. And perhaps, as importantly was their conviction that Bush believed, first, in America's ability to defeat the scourge of terrorism and, second, in his own ability to lead America in the fight. He often emphasized the latter in his speeches. At a Victory Rally in Orlando, Florida, on October 30, George W., identifying with other strong presidents, asserted, "As Presidents from Lincoln to Roosevelt, to Reagan so clearly demonstrated, a President must not shift in the wind; a President has to make tough decisions and stand by them." (Applause.) Then, undoubtedly referring to his opponent, he added, "The American President must not follow the path of the latest polls. The role of the President is to lead based on principle and conviction and conscience. (Applause.) Especially in time of war, mixed signals only confuse our friends and embolden our enemies." (Applause.)[7]

By contrast, Kerry made public statements in speeches, interviews, and debates that gave voters reasons to doubt his ability to lead the nation in the war against terrorists. He reversed himself on various issues—several times on Iraq—which made him appear inconsistent, uncertain, or expedient, or all of the above. His voting record in the Senate and his remarks on the stump did not always match. For instance, despite his assertion in the October 8 presidential debate that he opposed partial-birth abortion, Kerry voted at least six times against the banning of the horrific procedure. Moreover, Kerry periodically made remarks that showed his thinking had not advanced to the new reality of the post-9/11 world. His remarks often gave Bush material for his campaign speeches. When Matt Bai interviewed Kerry for an article in *The New York Times Magazine* (October 10), he asked him "how Sept. 11 had changed him, either personally or politically," and Kerry answered, "I mean, it didn't change me much at all."[8]

Following the article's publication, President Bush quoted Kerry's statement in a number of his speeches. On November 1, in his speech at the RNC Victory Rally in Dallas, Texas, Bush stated,

> We have a different understanding about this war on terror. My opponent says September the 11th didn't change him much at all. (Booo!) Well, September the 11th changed me, and it changed my outlook about how to protect you, about how to do my duty to protect the American people . . . . (Applause.)[9]

In his article based on the Kerry interview, Bai wrote, "In his rhetoric, Bush suggests that terrorism for this generation of Americans is and should be an overwhelming and frightening reality." Bai noted that Kerry "displayed a much less apocalyptic worldview" when he asked him "what it would take for Americans to feel safe again . . ." Kerry's response to the question revealed a very different attitude toward, and understanding of, global terrorism from that of Bush, when he declared:

> We have to get back to the place we were, where terrorists are not the focus of our lives, but they're a nuisance," Kerry said. "As a former law-enforcement person, I know we're never going to end prostitution. We're never going to end illegal gambling. But we're going to reduce it, organized crime, to a level where it isn't

> on the rise. It isn't threatening people's lives every day, and fundamentally, it's something that you continue to fight, but it's not threatening the fabric of your life.[10]

Once more, a statement by Kerry suggested a different position on terrorism that confused people, and, like other statements, had to be explained later. His position that terrorists were merely a "nuisance" that could be treated as a law-enforcement issue, like prostitution or illegal gambling, opened him to the rebuttal that the previous administration had tried that approach unsuccessfully, which the deaths of 3,000 people tragically demonstrated. And, that the loss of 17 sailors and the injury of many on the *U.S.S. Cole* at the hands of terrorists, was not just a nuisance to their families. Bush did not exploit Kerry's statement to the extent that he might have, but he did refer to it in his speeches to show the dangers of going back to a pre-9/11 mindset in leadership. For example, speaking to a large crowd at a Bush/Cheney Rally in Marlton, New Jersey on October 18, President Bush warned,

> Most Americans felt terrorism was something distant and something that would not strike on a large scale in America. That is the time that my opponent wants to go back to. (Booo!) A time when danger was real and growing, but we didn't know it. A time when some thought terrorism was only a *nuisance*. But, that very attitude is what blinded America to the war being waged against us.[11]

Americans reelected President Bush not only because they considered him a strong leader intent on protecting the nation, they reelected him also because they considered him a man of high moral character with a deep personal faith, a faith that gave him guiding principles to live by. The people could reason that such a leader would keep his word to uphold and advance the values that had made this country great. In his speech before election day, at the RNC Victory Rally in Dallas, Texas, George W. told a large audience: "Over the next four years, I'll continue to stand for the values that are important to our nation. I stand for marriage and family, which are the foundations of our society. (Applause.) I stand for a culture of life in which every person matters and every person counts." (Applause.)[12]

John F. Kerry also spoke of faith and values. In his "Acceptance Speech" at the Democratic National Convention in Boston on July 29, he said, "I don't wear my own faith on my sleeve. But faith has given me values and hope to live by, from Vietnam to this day, from Sunday to Sunday."[13] And, during the debates, it was not Bush who cited Scripture, it was Kerry. And in one debate, he remarked, "My faith affects everything that I do, in truth." Yet, for many people of faith, his words did not measure up to his actions.

For instance, some people probably doubted his sincerity in that he refused to condemn his Hollywood friends' attacks on the President, when they used crude and profane language; in fact, on one occasion when their attacks became particularly nasty, he referred to them as "the heart and soul of America." Then, a statement Kerry made in January 2004, suggested that he did not see that abortion was a matter of faith or value, even though he said he "always believed life begins at conception." He had voted many times in the Senate to use taxpayer dollars for abortions in the U.S.[14]

The exit polls on November 2nd surprised a lot of people—especially journalists and Democrats—when they revealed how important moral values were to many voters. The polls asked voters to select the most important question facing America from the options: taxes, education, Iraq, terrorism, economy/jobs, moral values, and healthcare, and most voters—22 percent—chose moral values; terrorism and the economy were close behind. Crucial to the outcome of the election, President Bush took 79 percent of "moral-value" voters, while Senator Kerry only 18 percent.[15]

After the voters listened to each candidate speak persuasively on key issues—particularly terrorism and the economy—in various televised events and observed their actions during the campaign, they voted for George W. Bush. They voted for *leadership* in an uncertain age; they voted for *security* in a time of war; and they voted for *character*, *values*, and *faith* in a period of cultural upheaval. The majority of the electorate ultimately cast their ballots on the basis of trust in the man they had come to know through his rhetorical presidency—a presidency that provided clarity and consistency of purpose, specific and substantive goals, and a vision of a better future for Americans and the world. As John Podhoretz, columnist and former speechwriter for Ronald Reagan, observed, "The power of Bush's formal presidential addresses represents the final demonstration of his standing as a true visionary. He has delivered at least six that will be studied by those who want to understand how a president can successfully talk to the American people and the world." Podhoretz further noted, "He has used the bully pulpit to guide the American people through the new reality, in which new presidential policies and a new presidential attitude are required to preserve, protect, and defend the Constitution of the United States."[16]

Prepared to protect and defend our way of life and the Constitution it upholds, President George W. Bush, in a second term, will devote himself to guiding the nation during a critical time in our history. His leadership and demonstrated abilities will be tested in meeting a fourfold challenge: (1) To work with world leaders, agencies, and institutions to oppose global terrorism and WMD proliferation; (2) to bring Republicans and Democrats in Congress together to further advance his domestic agenda; (3) to promote moral and social values for the reclamation of American culture, degraded for decades by secularism; and (4) to increase freedom, health, and prosperity around the world so as to improve people's lives and encourage peace. To meet such a challenge, the President will need the support and cooperation of the American people, not simply for the success of George W. Bush, but for the survival of the United States of America.

NOTES

1. Jennifer Harper, "Bush 'Battered' by Critical Press, Kerry Fares Better, Study Shows," *Washington Times* National Weekly Edition, November 1-7, 2004, p. 4.
2. Stephen F. Hayes, "The Other Losers Tuesday Night," *Weekly Standard*, November 15, 2004, p. 16.
3. Ibid., p. 15.
4. Ibid., p. 16.
5. Daniel Henninger, Blue Democrats Lost Red America Back in 1965," *Wall Street Journal*, November 5, 2004, p. A12.
6. Cal Thomas, "Loser Lamentations," *Washington Times* National Weekly Edition, November 15-21, 2004, p. 31.

7. "Remarks by the President at Victory 2004 Rally," Tinker Field, Orlando, Florida, October 30, 2004, www.whitehouse.gov.
8. Matt Bai, "Kerry's Undeclared War," *New York Times Magazine*, October 10, 2004, p. 44.
9. "Remarks by the President and Mrs. Bush at RNC Victory 2004 Rally," Moody Coliseum, Southern Methodist University, Dallas, Texas, November 1, 2004, www.whitehouse.gov.
10. Bai, "Kerry's Undeclared War," p. 45.
11. President's Speech, Bush/Cheney Campaign Rally, Marlton, New Jersey, Fox News, October 18, 2004.
12. "Remarks by the President and Mrs. Bush at RNC Victory 2004 Rally," November 1, 2004.
13. John F. Kerry, "The Hope Is There," *Vital Speeches of the Day*, August 1, 2004, p. 615.
14. "The Right Values," *Washington Times* National Weekly Edition, October 18-24, 2004, p. 36.
15. "A Question of Values," *Washington Times* National Weekly Edition, November 8-14, 2004, p. 36.
16. Podhoretz, *Bush Country*, 242.

Appendix A
The Story of the "New South Speech" and the Man Who Delivered It – Henry W. Grady

An Essay
by
LeRoy L. Lane

How well speakers can persuade their audiences is a measurement of their public-speaking ability. But one basic rhetorical principle is bedrock: speakers must make their messages relevant to the particular audiences they address.

One Civil War speech that exemplifies this principle was delivered 21 years after the Civil War. The story of this speech shows the power of public speaking and the great influence that one speaker had on our country's history. Entitled "The New South," it was delivered by Henry W. Grady on December 22, 1886. The occasion was an evening banquet at Delmonico's Café in New York City to celebrate the 81st anniversary of the New England Society. The audience assembled by the Society was comprised of 360 distinguished guests, including members of the Northern industrial elite, such as J. P. Morgan, and Civil War veterans who had fought the Confederacy.[1]

When the New England Society invited Grady to speak, he was editor of the Atlanta *Constitution* and a man respected in Southern politics. He accepted the Society's invitation, knowing that he would be the first Southern speaker in its long history. He also knew that he would address an audience of successful and powerful men, older and more experienced than himself, who might share a latent bitterness toward the South and suspicions about him. He realized that some former Union officers present would see him as a representative of a rebellious, enemy state. Moreover, he understood that the press had given a lot of attention to the subject of his speech—the positive changes in the South—without arousing much interest. As Harold Davis, professor emeritus of Georgia State University, wrote, "Dangers and apprehensions attended the address."[2] In planning to speak, Grady knew the challenge was great. "He thought of a thousand things, but if he said five hundred of them, he would be murdered at the banquet table, and if he said the other five hundred, he would be slaughtered at home."[3]

When the day finally came for Grady to address the banquet audience, he discovered that he would be third of three speakers. Dr. T. DeWitt Talmage, nationally-known clergyman, spoke first. The high point in his speech was a description of the triumphant return of the Northern army to Washington. He sat down to cheers.[4] Speaking next was the famous Union general William T. Sherman who, during the Civil War, burned Atlanta. In the course of his remarks, he referred to Georgia in uncomplimentary terms: "Georgia . . . has been standing fast while the great Northeast has been progressing . . . the old State of Georgia has been resting where she was."[5] As Sherman finished his speech, the Seventh Regiment band in the balcony struck up *Marching through Georgia*.

When Grady stood up at the head table to speak, he must have realized that the mood set by previous speakers was not helpful to his purpose. On the table in front of him was only the back of the dinner menu on which he had scribbled some notes to supplement the points he had committed to memory—a few were responses to Talmage and Sherman. From the audience's perspective, Grady seemed younger than his 36 years of age. He was clean shaven and boyish in appearance. Looking pale, but determined, he leaned forward and, speaking slowly and distinctly, in a high-pitched voice, said, "There was a South of slavery and secession—

that South is dead. There is a South of union and freedom—that South, thank God, is living, breathing, growing every hour."[6] The audience showed its appreciation of Grady's opening statement—we know this, because a press stenographer took down the speech and noted how the audience responded and at what points in the speech.

Grady probably surprised the audience when he did not immediately develop his opening statement—his "text" as he called it—but, instead, lightened the mood with self-depreciating humor and funny stories, which drew from his listeners hearty laughter. For instance: "Of the soldier returning home after defeat and roasting some corn on the roadside, who made the remark to his comrades: You may leave the South if you want to, but I'm going to Sandersville, kiss my wife, and raise a crop, and if the Yangees fool with me any more I'll whip 'em again."[7]

Then building on one of Talmage's points, he paid tribute to Abraham Lincoln, whom he saw as embodying "all the strength and gentleness, all the majesty and grace of this Republic."[8] This declaration elicited loud and continuous applause. He then held Lincoln up as a model of one who honored all types of people—the audience likely caught the indirect reference to the South—this time the audience cheered.

Humorously acknowledging he was slow getting back to his text, Grady once again referred to Talmage's speech, so as to contrast his description of the return of the victorious Northern army with that of the defeated Southern army. Rather than compare one army's homecoming with another, he focused on one typical Confederate soldier, whom he personalized by describing his condition at war's end. In the process, he undoubtedly created a strong emotional appeal to sympathy and empathy. He said, "Let me picture to you the footsore Confederate soldier, as, buttoning up in his faded gray jacket . . ., he turned his face southward . . ." Grady asked his listeners, "Think of him as ragged, half-starved, heavy-hearted, enfeebled by want and wounds; having fought to exhaustion, he . . . begins the slow and painful journey."[9]

Grady then returned to his text, finding his transition to it in a reference to Sherman: "I want to say to General Sherman—who is considered an able man in our parts, though some people think he is kind of careless about fire—that from the ashes he left us in 1864 we have raised a brave and beautiful city . . ."[10] He went on to assure the audience that Southerners held no grudges against the North—the New South had "new ideas and aspirations." He said, that they had "put business above politics." Grady set forth, in brief form, a series of economic facts that argued the wisdom of investing money in the South. He also stressed that they had put the "latch-string out" to the "Northern immigrant." His wit interspersed facts with humor, which brought laughter and applause. Perhaps the loudest applause came when Grady said, "Above all, we know that we have achieved in these 'piping times of peace' a fuller independence for the South than that which our fathers sought to win in the forum by their eloquence or compel on the field by their swords."[11]

Every line of Grady's 325-word conclusion was applied to the audience with strong emotional appeal. The cumulative effect of the positive feedback he had received during his speech—he was interrupted 30 times by audience laughter, cheers, and applause (often "loud and continuous")—was given an outlet in the conclusion by asking listeners questions that he could presume would bring the desired response. He began his conclusion by asking, "Now, what answer has New England to this message?"[12] In asking the question in this way, Grady showed that he not only sought a positive response to his "message" from the immediate audience, but on behalf of "the new South," he sought such a response from the North. He then raised a series of questions that suggested the desired answer, the first of which was: "Will she [the North] permit the prejudices of war to remain in the hearts of the conquerors, when it has died in the hearts of the conquered?"[13] The audience shouted, "No! No!" Following these questions, Grady said that if the answer is that she will not, the South will accept that answer with "good-will and friendship," and Daniel Webster's prophecy, he said, will be verified: "Standing hand to hand and clasping hands, we should remain united . . ." His speech received "prolonged applause" from an enthusiastic audience.[14]

At the close of Grady's speech, audience members rushed to where he stood and, surrounding him, showered him with compliments and congratulations. Eventually, southerners present had to escort him out of the crowd of admirers.[15] Newspapers around the country carried Grady's speech and echoed his audience's resounding approval of it. *The Macon Telegraph* expressed amazement that the message of the South's progress had finally been heard. *The New York Evening Post* editorialized that Grady had said what the South should have communicated long before, and the North needed to hear.[16] In his speech to the nation, "Grady presented the South as a born-again region that was economically and socially progressive, investment-friendly, and a potential industrial power."[17] His speech inspired many other editors and speakers in the South to advocate his New South vision.[18]

When people accomplish something through ability and effort, very often the results benefit only themselves and those close to them, and not, in any specific sense, the society in which they live. However, effective public speakers can prove the exception. Their personal success may lead to the success of others also, when they communicate a vision of a better future that receivers perceive is in their own best interest and, therefore, act to realize it. Henry Grady stands as an example of a public speaker with that kind of vision. With regard to the effects of his vision, *The New York Times* reported that "Grady was 'the creator of the spirit' which animated the New South . . . .—a term which had come to imply both economic regeneration and national reconciliation."[19]

One way of estimating the effectiveness of public speakers in communicating their message to an audience is to match the level of their success with the degree of resistance they faced. In the case of Grady, he confronted an audience that was potentially hostile, or, at best, indifferent. Probably, members of the audience expected certain remarks from Grady that would confirm their prejudices against the South, which 21 years of negative feelings had reinforced. General Sherman's speech and the band's selection served to take the audience back to the strife of the Civil War.

In Grady's own words, "When I found myself on my feet, every nerve in my body was strung as tight as a fiddle-string, and all tingling. I knew then I had a message for that assemblage, and as soon as I opened my mouth it came rushing out."[20] His opening statement or "text" implied that in the South "freedom" had replaced "slavery" and "union" had replaced "secession," with the subtle suggestion that this was the right outcome and that it had produced a more vital South. Then, without extending his text further, Grady proceeded to alter the mood to one of greater receptivity of the message he would ultimately bring. He did this by entertaining the audience with humor, appealing to listeners' emotions with illustrations, and acknowledging Lincoln as a great leader and a martyred hero. His references to the preceding speakers gave the impression that he was speaking mostly spontaneously in response to the situation. Certainly, in devoting about half of his speech to his introduction, focusing on his text in a brief substantive body, and ending with a standard-length conclusion, Grady was adapting his speech to the audience and occasion. While his adaptation opened minds and hearts, his sincerity, optimism, and skill filled both with a new understanding of the South and a new purpose for the North.

NOTES

1. Mike Butler, "Grady, Henry Woodfin," in David S. Heidler and Jeanne T. Heidler, eds., *Encyclopedia of the American Civil War*, vol. 2 (Santa Barbara, CA: ABC-CLIO), 2000), 858.
2. Harold E. Davis, *Henry Grady's New South* (Tuscaloosa University of Alabama Press, 1990), 175.
3. Raymond B. Nixon, *Henry W. Grady: Spokesman of the New South* (New York: Alfred A. Knopf, 1943), 241.
4. Davis, *Henry Grady's New South*, 176.
5. Ibid.
6. Ibid.; Nixon, *Henry W. Grady*, 8.
7. Mayo W. Hazeltine et al., eds., *Masterpieces of Eloquence*, vol. 25 (New York: P. F. Collier & Son, 1905), 10729.
8. Ibid., 10727.
9. Ibid., 10728.
10. Ibid., 10729.
11. Ibid., 10730.
12. Ibid., 10735.
13. Ibid.
14. Ibid.
15. Davis, *Henry Grady's New South*, 178.
16. Ibid.
17. Butler, "Grady, Henry Woodfin," 858.
18. Ibid.
19. Nixon, *Henry W. Grady*, 332.
20. Ibid., 244.

Appendix B
United by a Common Hatred

A Commentary
by
Tony Blankley

Mr. Blankley's commentary was published in The Washington Times *National Weekly Edition, August 2-8, 2004, p. 30. It is reprinted here with Mr. Blankley's permission.*

BOSTON.

There was a story told by arch-Nazi villain Reinhard Heydrich—the evil genius who designed the bureaucracy and methods for the Holocaust—that once there was a son whose mother was kind and loving, but whose father was brutal and tormenting. When the mother died, the son could find no tears at her graveside. But when the hated father died, the son collapsed in paroxysms of grief and committed suicide.

It was an ironic cautionary tale by Heydrich that perhaps after the Nazis destroy the Jews—the object of their all consuming hatred—they will have nothing left to live for (after telling the tale, he rejected its moral and went on to start the terrible genocide machine).

That old story from a dark past came to mind here in Boston, as the Democratic Party activists assembled to consummate four years of carefully nurtured Bush hatred with the crowning of a previously inconsequential senator as the Democratic candidate for president. All during the primary campaign, media exit polls identified electability as the primary reason Democratic voters supported Sen. John Kerry. And here in Boston, that reality continued to reflect itself in the mood and chatter of the assembled Democratic foot soldiers. They hate Bush and will do anything to destroy his presidency—even pretend, briefly, that they don't hate him.

There are different kinds of hate. There is the wild, out-of-control hate that sometimes leads to sudden barroom or bedroom homicides. And then there is the cold-blooded, premeditated strain, more typical of tribal or other forms of group hate. Such is the Democratic Party's self-induced hatred of George Bush. And, curiously, this great hatred has induced in the usually rambunctious and cantankerous Democratic Party a perverted joy, rapture and inner tranquility.

I have been going to Democratic Party conventions, episodically, since the 1960 convention in Los Angeles, in which the Democrats chose their young prince John Kennedy. (I was a politically precocious boy at the time, let the record reflect.) While that was not one of their nastier conventions, nonetheless, Lyndon Johnson was contending for the nomination by passing around rumors of Kennedy's degenerative disease. In 1968, of course, blood spilled outside their convention while invectives flew furiously inside. 1980 saw Ted Kennedy coyly keeping out Jimmy Carter's eager embrace on the stage of the convention's Thursday night finale. And throughout the history of the Democratic Party, passionate battles over platform planks have never, until here in Boston, failed to give evidence to the intellectual ferment of the world's oldest political party.

What is one to make of a political party in which, according to the Boston Globe, more than 90 percent of the delegates oppose the Iraq war—the defining issue of this election—while the candidate and the platform support it. And there isn't even a murmur of complaint? The easy answer is that it's just about power. The Democrats will do anything to get back into power, so it is said. But that is not it. Of course, both the Democratic and Republican parties can't stand being out of power and yearn to regain the power, the patronage and the sheer pleasure of being in office. But until now, neither party has been willing to go against its most heartfelt convictions to gain power.

No, I think the clever boys and girls in the backroom of the Democratic Party have created a monster in this carefully manufactured Bush-hatred. Let's remember where this hatred started—in Florida. From Al Gore, through the Democratic National Committee and into the mouths of rank-and-file Democratic congressmen and senators, the word went out that the Democratic Party would not respect the election results. They methodically asserted that Mr. Bush was illegitimately in office because Mr. Gore actually got more votes in Florida. Even after the major liberal media outlets did their own recount and found Mr. Bush won Florida fair and square, the knowingly false charge was slammed into the brains of Democratic Party true believers. Mr. Bush was "selected, not elected" became the slogan.

They carefully nurtured this resentment into a small hatred. Then they compounded it by ridiculing the president's intelligence—even though Mr. Bush got better grades at Yale than Al Gore, while still enjoying a vigorous frat life. They repeated endlessly their contempt for Mr. Bush's Christian faith—which apparently induces contempt and hatred among the Democratic Party faithful.

And all of this was before Iraq. This carefully cultivated little hatred was elevated to industrial strength with the accusations that Mr. Bush lied his way into war. While disproven by bipartisan findings, the charges persist. Mr. Gore accused Mr. Bush of "betraying" the country. Mr. Kerry used the word lie just enough to keep his lunatic pack happy.

The result is a hatred of Mr. Bush by the party activists that has consumed their policy passions and convictions. They hate Mr. Bush more than they hate the Iraq war. Their great intellectual battle of the 2000s—whether they should stay in the Clinton center or go back to their liberal convictions—has been subsumed temporarily by their common hatred of Mr. Bush. Should the American voters succumb to poor judgment and elect Mr. Kerry, a united Democratic Party may face the plight of the son in the Nazi story of hate and meaning. Bush hate is the glue that holds the party together. If he leaves the scene, the party may quickly fall apart.

INDEX

C

D

E

ABOUT THE AUTHOR

LeRoy Lane is the author of *By All Means Communicate*, 2/e (Prentice Hall). He wrote the pioneering article on biological rhythms and communicative behavior. He headed communication departments at Columbia Basin Community College, George Fox University, and Northwest Christian College, where he is professor emeritus of communication and management. He earned his M.A. in speech education at Willamette University, where he received the Phi Delta Kappa award as "Outstanding Student in Teacher Education." He holds a Ph.D. in communication and rhetoric from the University of Oregon; while there, he was selected to present a paper to the Doctoral Honors Seminar in Communication Theory at Michigan State University. At the University of Washington, he studied history, journalism, linguistics, and classical rhetoric. He has taught persuasion, public speaking, nonverbal communication, interpersonal communication, organizational communication, argumentation, and logic. Dr. Lane is listed in *Who's Who Among America's Teachers*.